Llewellyn's 2025

Sabbats

ALMANAC

Samhain 2024
to
Mabon 2025

Rituals • Crafts • Recipes • Folklore • Spells

Llewellyn's 2025 Sabbats Almanac
Samhain 2024 to Mabon 2025

Cover art © Carolyn Vibbert
Editing by Hanna Grimson
Interior Art © Carolyn Vibbert, except on pages 13, 38, 71, 74, 77, 78, 110, 113, 148, 185, 187, 224, 226, 230, 264, 267, 271–272, 305, 307, which are by the Llewellyn Art Department

You can order annuals and books from *New Worlds*, Llewellyn's catalog. To request a free copy, call 1-877-NEW WRLD toll-free or order online by visiting our website at http://subscriptions.llewellyn.com.

ISBN: 978-0-7387-7198-4

Published by Llewellyn Worldwide Ltd.
2143 Wooddale Drive
Woodbury, MN 55125-2989
www.llewellyn.com

Printed in China

2024

JANUARY
S	M	T	W	T	F	S
	1	2	3	4	5	6
7	8	9	10	11	12	13
14	15	16	17	18	19	20
21	22	23	24	25	26	27
28	29	30	31			

FEBRUARY
S	M	T	W	T	F	S
				1	2	3
4	5	6	7	8	9	10
11	12	13	14	15	16	17
18	19	20	21	22	23	24
25	26	27	28	29		

MARCH
S	M	T	W	T	F	S
					1	2
3	4	5	6	7	8	9
10	11	12	13	14	15	16
17	18	19	20	21	22	23
24	25	26	27	28	29	30
31						

APRIL
S	M	T	W	T	F	S
	1	2	3	4	5	6
7	8	9	10	11	12	13
14	15	16	17	18	19	20
21	22	23	24	25	26	27
28	29	30				

MAY
S	M	T	W	T	F	S
			1	2	3	4
5	6	7	8	9	10	11
12	13	14	15	16	17	18
19	20	21	22	23	24	25
26	27	28	29	30	31	

JUNE
S	M	T	W	T	F	S
						1
2	3	4	5	6	7	8
9	10	11	12	13	14	15
16	17	18	19	20	21	22
23	24	25	26	27	28	29
30						

JULY
S	M	T	W	T	F	S
	1	2	3	4	5	6
7	8	9	10	11	12	13
14	15	16	17	18	19	20
21	22	23	24	25	26	27
28	29	30	31			

AUGUST
S	M	T	W	T	F	S
				1	2	3
4	5	6	7	8	9	10
11	12	13	14	15	16	17
18	19	20	21	22	23	24
25	26	27	28	29	30	31

SEPTEMBER
S	M	T	W	T	F	S
1	2	3	4	5	6	7
8	9	10	11	12	13	14
15	16	17	18	19	20	21
22	23	24	25	26	27	28
29	30					

OCTOBER
S	M	T	W	T	F	S
		1	2	3	4	5
6	7	8	9	10	11	12
13	14	15	16	17	18	19
20	21	22	23	24	25	26
27	28	29	30	31		

NOVEMBER
S	M	T	W	T	F	S
					1	2
3	4	5	6	7	8	9
10	11	12	13	14	15	16
17	18	19	20	21	22	23
24	25	26	27	28	29	30

DECEMBER
S	M	T	W	T	F	S
1	2	3	4	5	6	7
8	9	10	11	12	13	14
15	16	17	18	19	20	21
22	23	24	25	26	27	28
29	30	31				

2025

JANUARY
S	M	T	W	T	F	S
			1	2	3	4
5	6	7	8	9	10	11
12	13	14	15	16	17	18
19	20	21	22	23	24	25
26	27	28	29	30	31	

FEBRUARY
S	M	T	W	T	F	S
						1
2	3	4	5	6	7	8
9	10	11	12	13	14	15
16	17	18	19	20	21	22
23	24	25	26	27	28	

MARCH
S	M	T	W	T	F	S
						1
2	3	4	5	6	7	8
9	10	11	12	13	14	15
16	17	18	19	20	21	22
23	24	25	26	27	28	29
30	31					

APRIL
S	M	T	W	T	F	S
		1	2	3	4	5
6	7	8	9	10	11	12
13	14	15	16	17	18	19
20	21	22	23	24	25	26
27	28	29	30			

MAY
S	M	T	W	T	F	S
				1	2	3
4	5	6	7	8	9	10
11	12	13	14	15	16	17
18	19	20	21	22	23	24
25	26	27	28	29	30	31

JUNE
S	M	T	W	T	F	S
1	2	3	4	5	6	7
8	9	10	11	12	13	14
15	16	17	18	19	20	21
22	23	24	25	26	27	28
29	30					

JULY
S	M	T	W	T	F	S
		1	2	3	4	5
6	7	8	9	10	11	12
13	14	15	16	17	18	19
20	21	22	23	24	25	26
27	28	29	30	31		

AUGUST
S	M	T	W	T	F	S
					1	2
3	4	5	6	7	8	9
10	11	12	13	14	15	16
17	18	19	20	21	22	23
24	25	26	27	28	29	30
31						

SEPTEMBER
S	M	T	W	T	F	S
	1	2	3	4	5	6
7	8	9	10	11	12	13
14	15	16	17	18	19	20
21	22	23	24	25	26	27
28	29	30				

OCTOBER
S	M	T	W	T	F	S
			1	2	3	4
5	6	7	8	9	10	11
12	13	14	15	16	17	18
19	20	21	22	23	24	25
26	27	28	29	30	31	

NOVEMBER
S	M	T	W	T	F	S
						1
2	3	4	5	6	7	8
9	10	11	12	13	14	15
16	17	18	19	20	21	22
23	24	25	26	27	28	29
30						

DECEMBER
S	M	T	W	T	F	S
	1	2	3	4	5	6
7	8	9	10	11	12	13
14	15	16	17	18	19	20
21	22	23	24	25	26	27
28	29	30	31			

Contents

Ostara

Beltane

Litha

Lammas

Mabon

Introduction

NEARLY EVERYONE HAS A favorite sabbat. There are numerous ways to observe any tradition. The 2025 edition of the *Sabbats Almanac* provides a wealth of lore, celebrations, creative projects, and recipes to enhance your holiday.

For this edition, a mix of writers—Ariana Serpentine, Enfys J. Book, Irene Glasse, Nathan M. Hall, Ian Chambers, and more—share their ideas and wisdom. These include a variety of paths as well as the authors' personal approaches to each sabbat. Each chapter closes with an extended ritual, which may be adapted for both solitary practitioners and covens.

In addition to these insights and rituals, specialists in astrology, cooking, crafts, and more impart their expertise throughout.

Michael Herkes gives an overview of planetary influences most relevant for each sabbat season and provides details about the New and Full Moons, retrograde motion, planetary positions, and more. (Times and dates follow Eastern Standard Time and Eastern Daylight Time.)

Lupa explores flora and fauna and how these beings and their lives connect to each sabbat.

Dallas Jennifer Cobb conjures up a feast for each festival that features seasonal appetizers, entrées, and desserts.

Elizabeth Barrette offers instructions on DIY crafts that will help you tap into each sabbat's energy and fill your home with magic and fun.

Charlie Rainbow Wolf provides divination systems to celebrate and utilize the unique forces in each season.

About the Authors

Sheri Barker has been a solitary practitioner for nearly forty years. Her relationships with magic, elemental energies, spirits, and her ancestors are the foundation of her daily life. They enrich her work as a witch, writer, homesteader, and human being. She is a columnist at *The Wild Hunt* (https://wildhunt.org) and also publishes perspective essays on her blog at https://www.onthebearpath.com. Sheri lives in an ancient river valley in the Appalachian Mountains of North Carolina, immersed in nature, spirits, and realms beyond this one. Oh, and books…there are always books, words, and creative activities to be explored!

Elizabeth Barrette has been involved with the Pagan community for more than thirty-four years. She served as managing editor of *PanGaia* for eight years and dean of studies at the Grey School of Wizardry for four years. She has written columns on beginning and intermediate Pagan practice, Pagan culture, and Pagan leadership. Her book *Composing Magic: How to Create Magical Spells, Rituals, Blessings, Chants, and Prayers* explains how to combine writing and spirituality. She lives in central Illinois, where she has done much networking with Pagans in her area, such as coffeehouse meetings and open sabbats. Her other public activities feature Pagan picnics and science fiction conventions. She enjoys magical crafts, historic religions, and gardening for wildlife. Her other writing fields include speculative fiction, gender studies, social and environmental issues. Visit her blog, *The Wordsmith's Forge* (https://ysabetwordsmith .dreamwidth.org/), or website PenUltimate Productions (http:// penultimateproductions.weebly.com). Her coven site with extensive Pagan materials is Greenhaven Tradition (http://greenhaventradition .weebly.com/).

Enfys J. Book (they/them) is the author of the Gold COVR award-winning *Queer Qabala* (Llewellyn, 2022) and coauthor (with Ivo Dominguez Jr.) of *Sagittarius Witch* (Llewellyn, 2024). They are a nonbinary, bisexual clergy member within the Assembly of the Sacred Wheel, and the high priest of the Fellowship of the Ancient White Stag coven near Washington, DC. Enfys has been teaching in-person and online classes on magickal practice since 2015, including presenting at the Sacred Space Conference, Paganicon, the Goddess Conference, ConVocation, and several local events in the Washington, DC area. They are also the creator of Major Arqueerna, a website devoted to queer magickal practice, and they host a podcast called "4 Quick Q's: Book Talk with Enfys," where they interview Pagan authors using questions determined by a roll of the dice. Visit them at majorarqueerna.com.

Ian Chambers is a long-time practitioner of traditional forms of witchcraft and folk sorcery through the fields of magic, mysticism, philosophy, and history. Ian has studied both solitary and with a few craft groups, taking a broad purview of the subject as a practitioner scholar. A selection of Ian's writings has appeared in various magazines, including *The Cauldron*, *White Dragon*, and *The Hedgewytch*, as well as more recent essays in *The Enquiring Eye* and *Coire Ansic*. Ian's first book, *The Witch Compass: Working with the Winds in Traditional Witchcraft*, was published by Llewellyn in 2022.

Dallas Jennifer Cobb lives in a magickal village on Lake Ontario. A Pagan, mother, feminist, outdoorswoman, and animal lover, she enjoys a sustainable lifestyle with a balance of time and money. Widely published, she writes about what she knows: brain injury, magick, herbs, astrology, healing, recovery, and vibrant sustainability. When she isn't adventuring with her golden retriever, she likes to correspond with like-minded beings. Reach her at dallasjennifer.cobb @outlook.com.

Irene Glasse is a Heathen witch based in Western Maryland. She is a longtime teacher of witchcraft, meditation, and magic in the mid-Atlantic. She is the coauthor of *Blackfeather Mystery School: The Magpie Training* (Dragon Alchemy, 2022), a contributing writer for *Gemini Witch: Unlock the Magic of Your Sun Sign* and *Llewellyn's 2024 Sabbats Almanac* (Llewellyn, 2023), and a blogger and columnist. Irene has performed, taught workshops, and led rituals at many festivals and conferences over the years. She is the main organizer of the Frederick Covenant of Unitarian Universalist Pagans (Frederick CUUPS), offering events, rituals, classes, and workshops to a large, vibrant community.

Nathan M. Hall is an animist and witch who lives in South Florida. His book, *Path of the Moonlit Hedge*, is available wherever books are sold. Find him online at moonlithedge.com.

Michael Herkes (aka The Glam Witch) makes magic across the windy city of Chicago as a genderqueer author, astrologer, intuitive stylist, tarot reader, and glamour witch. After practicing privately for two decades, Michael stepped out of the broom closet and into the role of teacher—dedicating their energy to uplifting and mentoring others on using witchcraft for self-empowerment. Since then, they have authored numerous books, written a variety of digital content, and presented workshops across the United States as a speaker on modern witchcraft. Focusing primarily on glamour magic, Michael's practice centers on magical aesthetics and adornment, using fashion and makeup to cultivate inner and outer makeovers—inspiring others to tap into their personal power and creativity to manifest positive change in their lives and the world around them. For more information visit www.theglamwitch.com.

Lupa is an author, artist, and naturalist in the Pacific Northwest. She is the author of several books on nature-based Paganism, as well as the creator of the Tarot of Bones and Pocket Osteomancy divination sets. More information about Lupa and her works may be found at http://www.thegreenwolf.com.

Dodie Graham McKay is a writer, Green Witch, Gardnerian priestess, and filmmaker. She is inspired to document and share stories that capture the beauty of nature and the visible and invisible realms of magic and witchcraft. She is the author of the books *Earth Magic: Elements of Witchcraft* (Llewellyn, 2021), *A Witch's Ally: Building a Magical Relationship with Animal Familiars & Companions* (Llewellyn, 2024), and her documentary films include *The WinniPagans* and *Starry Nights* (featuring Kerr Cuhulain). Dodie spends her spare time walking her dogs and facilitating a busy coven. She lives in Treaty One Territory, Homeland of the Métis Nation, Winnipeg, Manitoba, Canada. Visit her at www.dodiegrahammckay.com.

Tomás Prower is the award-winning Latinx author of books on multicultural magic and mysticism, including *Queer Magic* and *Morbid Magic*. Fluent in English, French, and Spanish, he previously served as the cultural liaison between France, the United States, and various nations of South America, which allowed him to live and work all over the Western Hemisphere, including Buenos Aires, Santiago de Chile, Tijuana, Reno, Las Vegas, and the Amazon jungle. Tomás is also a licensed mortuary professional and former External Relations Director of the American Red Cross. He currently lives in the desert oasis of Palm Springs, California. Visit him at TomasPrower.com.

Ariana Serpentine is a multi-traditional witch, polytheist, and animist. She is transgender and queer and has worked in political trans activism, raising awareness for the needs of her community within Pagan and other circles.

Charlie Rainbow Wolf is an old hippie who's been studying the weird ways of the world for over fifty years. She's happiest when she's got her hands in mud, either making pottery in the "artbox" or tending to things in the yarden (yard + garden = yarden). Astrology, tarot, and herbs are her greatest interests, but she's dabbled in most metaphysical topics in the last five decades because life always has something new to offer. She enjoys cooking WFPB recipes and knitting traditional cables and patterns, and she makes a wicked batch of fudge. Charlie lives in central Illinois with her very patient husband and her beloved Great Danes.

Samhain

Samhain Grave Tending

Irene Glasse

MODERN WESTERN CULTURE ENCOURAGES a separation from death. Our friends and family, for the most part, transition out of this life in hospitals and hospices, and the post-death tending of their bodies is performed out of sight. The entertainment industry largely depicts the dead as harmful or dangerous in the rare times they are depicted at all. The cacophonous advertising of yet another ghost show promising chills is pervasive across media platforms. Religions whose mythologies include rigid separation from the dead are dominant. This barrier of culture, media, and prevailing belief systems can cut us off from a profound, impactful, and nourishing connection.

Ancestral Veneration

Our ancestors, our beloved dead, can be our best allies. Although many Pagans serve gods of varying persuasions, deities do not have the same understanding of human problems that other humans do. Raising kids, managing annoying coworkers, finding ways to make the household budget work, and other mundane yet vital aspects of our lives fall outside the realm of deity experience. Our ancestors, on the other hand, know these struggles all too well.

We are also the legacy of our ancestors alive in the world. We are living, breathing proof of all they fought for, loved, and survived. Our ancestors have a stake in our success. I sometimes joke that the gods love us the way we love our pets—we adore them, but know their lives are finite and scale our attachment accordingly. Our ancestors love us because we are their family. It's a very different kind of bond. Even if we do not know their names, our ancestors know ours and want us to succeed.

One question that comes up frequently when I talk about ancestral practice is "What if my ancestors were terrible?" It's a great, relevant question. Out of every family line, there were some wonderful people, some horrible people, and a lot of folks who did their best to get by within the confines of their time and culture. If your most recent ancestors were awful to you, go back a few hundred years when seeking an ancestral ally. You have thousands of ancestors. If they were all terrible, you simply wouldn't be here. The children of the line would not have survived.

We can honor different types of ancestors as well. Ancestors of blood are our direct relatives—those we share DNA with. Ancestors of milk and honey are ancestors who are not blood relatives but are definitely family. These are ancestors who took us or our relatives in as though they were kin. My own line includes an adoption a few generations ago. The line that adopted my great-grandfather is no less my family without a blood bond. Indeed, chosen family can be much stronger than family connected through birth. This category is also where I place dearly loved friends who are no longer with us: the family of my heart.

Ancestors of the order are the dead who are unrelated to us through blood but whose lives follow the same pattern that ours do. Jimi Hendrix is an ancestor of the order for musicians. Marie Curie is an ancestor of the order for scientists. Marie Laveau is an ancestor of the order for magical practitioners. When you are exploring ancestral work, consider the dead who shared your own passions, values, and priorities. This type of ancestor can be connected with through offerings, prayer, and work undertaken in their name.

Ancestral veneration links us to an incredible source of support, empathy, and wisdom. By approaching our ancestral practice with a wider understanding of who our ancestors are, the possibilities for connection are endless.

Graves and Grave Tending

In older times, travel was challenging and time-consuming. As a result, most people spent the better part of their lives in one small region. For our ancestors, the land where they lived was a very real part of them. Our ancestors ate the food that grew close by, built their homes out of materials sourced from the local environment, and when they died, they were buried close to where they lived. A grave is not just a final signature on the document of life: it is a memory of place and a monument to a life lived in a specific environment with all that land's blessings and challenges.

Graves are the last physical holdings of our ancestors. Tending these sacred places is a beautiful way to connect with and honor our ancestors. Unfortunately, the separation from death and the dead within Western culture means that we do not always know where our dead are buried. Too often, after a family member is interred, the gravesite is left to the graveyard's caretakers to look after. The good news is that websites like Find A Grave and Ancestry offer us ways to repair this break in family knowledge.

One other option is the use of a symbolic representation or proxy headstone when we do not have access to our ancestors' graves. By consecrating a stone to act as the headstone for an ancestor, we can still perform grave cleaning as an offering. Memorial gardens often serve to honor our beloved dead when we do not have access to their burial site. Creating a proxy headstone takes the idea behind a memorial garden a little further. Indeed, if you decide to add a memorial garden to your home, it's a wonderful place for proxy headstones and other statuary or stone remembrances.

Every year, my spouse and I spend two days around Samhain tending graves. We visit the graves of our loved ones, clean and tidy them, make offerings, and spend time in communion with our beloved dead. Although I would not describe two days of mourning and ancestral veneration as easy, I would describe it as deeply nourishing on a spiritual level. It is good to connect to the memory and spirit of those we love. It is good to see their names, tell their stories, and talk to our ancestors about what has been happening in our lives. It is good to open the well of grief and allow the tears to flow. It is good to maintain the final worldly holding of our dead and to show in a real, physical way that they are loved and remembered.

Our last stop each year is Arlington National Cemetery (ANC) near Washington, DC. ANC is one of the oldest national cemeteries in the United States and comprises some 639 acres. It is the final resting place of over 400,000 veterans of the United States military. My grandparents, who both served in the navy, are buried in Arlington, and we always start with their graves. However, one tradition that we began many years ago expands our visit: I keep a file of all graves marked with pentacles (for those of Pagan belief) and Thor's hammers (for those of Heathen belief). We visit each Pagan and Heathen grave and make offerings to the veterans interred there as well. As a Pagan veteran, I keenly feel how much of a minority we are in the faith path. These dead are my family as well—my siblings in arms through military service. I am proud and grateful to visit them at Samhain every year.

How to Safely Clean a Grave

Although grave offerings and light tidying (clearing up leaves, twigs, and spent flowers) can be performed for the dead we do not know, please remember that full grave cleaning should only be performed for members of your family. There have been cases in the United States of well-intentioned people cleaning graves they are not connected to through bloodline and causing distress to the family (or damage to the grave).

For most grave cleaning, you will need:

- 3–5 gallons of water. If you are lucky enough to be able to run a hose to the gravesite, that's the best option. Otherwise, plan to bring a good deal of water with you.
- A spray bottle of water
- 1–2 buckets
- Scissors if you live in a region where grass is a common groundcover in cemeteries.
- Waterproof cleaning gloves. I prefer the kind that cover my forearms as well as my hands.
- One natural sponge like a sea sponge. Avoid sponges that have been dyed—the color can transfer to headstones.
- Brushes and scrapers. Lichen can be carefully removed with a wooden scraper like a craft stick or spatula. You will need at least 1 toothbrush and 1 larger soft-bristled brush.
- An abundance of old towels and rags or a few rolls of paper towels.
- A trash bag

Do not bring or use:

- Metal or hard plastic brushes and scrapers
- Soap, detergent, or spray cleaners of any kind
- Scouring sponges or steel wool pads

Additional supplies:

- Tissues. Cleaning a grave can bring up a lot of emotions.
- Your divinatory tool of choice
- Offerings. Biodegradable offerings like fresh flowers, herbs, baked goods like soul cakes or bread, beverages, and fruit are all good options. Avoid anything that includes a plastic wrapper. If you are leaving a type of candy your loved one adored, unwrap it and take the wrapper with you. Some traditions encourage the use of coins (Mercury head dimes are particularly potent in ancestral work), seashells, or small stones, but

be aware that nonbiodegradable offerings will have to be disposed of at some point. One type of popular nonperishable item permitted at some cemeteries are solar-powered lights that glow after the sun sets. If you bring incense, stay until it has fully burned down and extinguished itself or snuff it out yourself. Never leave a burning offering unattended. Be sure to look up the policies of the cemetery before you select your offerings. Some cemeteries prohibit food or nonperishable offerings but welcome flowers.

Before setting off to clean a grave, make note of the temperature. Avoid days that are very hot and sunny as well as days that are very cold. Both of those weather conditions can compromise a headstone through surface temperature issues.

When you arrive at the grave, begin by greeting your loved one and talking for a while. Explain to them what you are going to do so they understand what's happening to their grave. If you are concerned about whether your loved one would welcome grave cleaning, use your divinatory tool to find out. A simple, "Aunt Agatha, may I clean your grave?" followed by a single card, rune, or sigil draw is generally enough to get a good yes or no answer.

Begin grave cleaning by evaluating the headstone and grave. If the headstone is chipped, cracked, or flaking, do not clean it (or at least do not clean those parts of the headstone). The act of cleaning can further damage an already-compromised headstone.

Start by removing twigs, leaves, spent offerings, and any other debris that has gathered on or near the grave. If grass or other plants immediately around the headstone are tall, use scissors to trim the greenery back. If the grave you are tending has a damaged headstone, this is where you stop. If the headstone is still in good shape, you can safely continue cleaning.

Using your natural sponge, or by pouring water from your container, thoroughly soak the surface of the headstone. The entire time you clean, the surface should be wet—if it dries out, add more water. This is where the spray bottle of water can come in handy.

Starting at the bottom of the headstone, use your natural sponge to wipe the stone using circular motions. Rinse the headstone frequently as accumulated dirt releases from it. Slowly and reverently work your way up the headstone. I often talk to my loved one while I'm cleaning their headstone.

After your first pass with the natural sponge, thoroughly rinse the headstone. Notice if there are areas where lichen, moss, or algae are growing. Carefully use your wooden scraping tools to remove these growths, rinsing and wiping with the sponge as you remove them. For parts of the headstone with more accumulated dirt or environmental deposits, use your soft bristled-brushes to clean them. Toothbrushes are great for getting into the narrow grooves of lettering and cleaning decorative carvings.

Rinse the headstone regularly as you work. Once you've finished, use the old towels or paper towels to dry the headstone and soak up any lingering water. Clear away your cleaning supplies, or at least gather them up and set them to the side.

Spend some time in communion with your beloved dead. Make any offerings of flowers, food, or other objects you brought with you. This can be a good time for divination if you are seeking further guidance from your loved one.

Grave tending is a wonderful way to cultivate a stronger connection with your ancestors, make an offering, and celebrate the Samhain season. It can be performed on its own or as part of a full ritual.

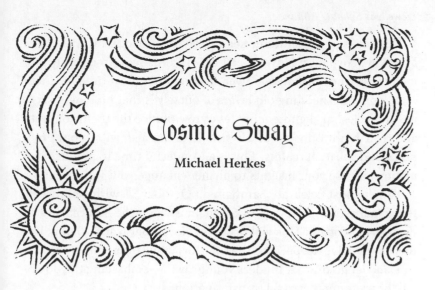

Cosmic Sway

Michael Herkes

NOW IS A TIME when death and decay fill the air. As the veil between the worlds thins and darkness envelops the autumn nights, Samhain celebrations begin on October 31. This ancient Celtic festival, which has evolved into modern-day Halloween, holds deep significance for those who honor nature's cycles and embrace their magical essence. For witches, Samhain is a time to connect with ancestors and spirits. It is a moment to honor those who have passed on before us, seeking their guidance and wisdom. Embrace this season as a time to honor life's cyclical nature while embracing your own journey of death, rebirth, and transformation.

Celebrating Samhain

One way to celebrate Samhain is by creating an altar adorned with photographs or mementos of loved ones who have crossed over. Lighting candles in their memory can serve as a beacon for their spirits to find their way back to this realm. It is also an opportune time to visit the cemetery and leave offerings to the dead, or leave a white candle lit in your window to help guide spirits. To add a bit of flair to the festivities, you can also dress up as someone you admire for Halloween.

The energy of Samhain seamlessly transitions into the New Moon in Scorpio on November 1 at 8:47 a.m. Scorpio is known for its intense transformative power, making it an ideal time for inner reflection and shedding old layers of ourselves that no longer serve us. This celestial alignment invites us to embrace the theme of death and rebirth not only in our physical lives but also within our emotional and spiritual realms. This is a wonderful time to practice divination and use your insights to further enhance your introspection.

While most celebrate Samhain on October 31 with Halloween, the actual astrological date of Samhain is when the Sun reaches 15 degrees in Scorpio. This will occur on November 6 at 5:20 p.m. Use this day to delve deeper into the transformative influence of the season, and let go of what hinders your growth—embracing the potential for profound personal transformation.

Full Moon in Taurus

On November 15 at 4:28 p.m., we are graced by a Full Moon in Taurus, which is classically ruled by the planet Venus, making this a wonderful time for you to practice self-care rituals. Taurus is a sign that fully indulges in beauty and the senses. Celebrate this Moon by doing rituals that invigorate what and how you see, feel, hear, taste, and smell. Light pink or green candles, eat a decadent delicacy, bathe in richly scented oils and flower petals, dance to a playlist of sensual tracks, and maybe even treat yourself to a massage. Move slowly now to fully experience each aspect of your senses with devotion and love.

November's End

The Sun shifts from Scorpio and welcomes Sagittarius season on November 21, welcoming the centaur archer into the energetic fold. Sagittarius themes include adventure and travel as well as intellectual and philosophical pursuits. Get out of your routine and explore uncharted territory near your home. Visit the library and indulge in intellectual curiosity. Work color magic into your wardrobe to celebrate the Sag season with shades of purples, oranges, yellows, browns, and blues that resemble burning embers, which align with this fiery sign.

At 9:42 p.m. on November 25, the final Mercury retrograde of 2024 comes into full swing and will remain here until December 15. It joins Jupiter and Uranus who are also in retrograde, adding additional astrological tension. It is important to remember that retrogrades are all about taking pause and reassessing. When Mercury retrograde strikes, it is typically a time when communication of all kinds goes a bit haywire—especially with technology. This has the potential to add unnecessary holiday stress over communication mishaps with Thanksgiving on November 28, and can also cause delays in travel. If traveling, be sure to carry angelite or unakite crystals on you to help assist in safe travel and ease tensions in the event of delays.

Plant a Seed for Action

December is welcomed with a New Moon on December 1 at 1:21 a.m. Use this time to plant a seed of inspiration. Burn orange candles with cinnamon or balsam incenses to conjure the essence of Sagittarius and to call upon the energy of action to set goals in motion. This will be very important as Mars joins Mercury, Jupiter, and Uranus in retrograde on December 6 at 6:33 p.m. until February 23, 2025.

Because Mars rules action, aggression, ambition, and passion, when it is in retrograde, it is common to feel tired and slow down. Being that Mars is currently in the fire sign of Leo, this will no doubt have an effect on your drive. Leo loves being the center of attention, so be gentle with yourself if you are experiencing a low drive of ambition or creativity now. Take a much-needed pause to rest and recharge the flame within. Pull inward and lean into the coming winter season as a time of reflection on your goals so that once Mars moves direct again, you know what direction to take in achieving your desires.

Conjure Better Communication

On December 15 at 4:02 a.m., the Full Moon in Gemini rebounds to spice up communication. With this being the last day for Mercury retrograde, use this Moon to reflect on lessons you have learned over the past weeks when it comes to expressing your emotions and personal truth. Craft spells or rituals that focus on clear and open communication in all areas of your life. Meditate on how far you have come and release what is no longer working. Burn blue candles and diffuse essential oils of mint or lavender to help facilitate this.

Tales and Traditions

Lupa

OUR NEW YEAR CELEBRATIONS welcome in the dark time of the year, but this is far from a terrible time! Life still thrives even as it prepares for the challenges of winter, and there is much to appreciate in the nature around us. It is often a time of abundance for cultures around the world as berries and other fruit, fat fish and game, and other foods are collected in the final harvest. And the seeds are sown for next year's new life too.

Chum Salmon (*Oncorhynchus keta*)

All of the species of Pacific salmons along the North American coastline are anadromous, and that includes the chum salmon. They are born in quiet areas of cold-water streams and rivers, often deep in the interior of the continent. Once they are large enough to leave the safety of the nursery, they then allow the water's flow to carry them from tributary to river to the great ocean itself, where they spend the next few years dodging predators and growing large on the bounties of the sea.

Once they are mature, salmon "run," or return to their birthplace to spawn; this journey upstream may be well over a thousand miles long, wrought with dangers. Those that successfully make it back home will spawn, and other than exceptions like the coast steelhead (*Oncorhynchus mykiss irideus*), they die soon thereafter. While different species and populations of salmon may run in spring or summer, the biggest chum salmon runs are in the fall.

Samhain sees my local chum salmon running up local streams. One of my favorite rituals is to make the hike through an old-growth cedar forest to watch these mighty fish as they spawn. Even as the forest around me prepares for the sleep of winter, the salmon ensure that their next generation will be there to greet the following spring.

In spite of their impending deaths, these fish are an important source of life. Their fertilized eggs produce the next generation of salmon. And they bring the great wealth of the ocean to the forest, nutrients that this terrestrial ecosystem would otherwise not have access to. As the salmons' bodies decay or are processed through the digestion of those who eat them, these nutrients disseminate further and further into the forest. Without the salmon, the great forests of the West Coast would not be so healthy or magnificent.

Shore Pine (*Pinus contorta* var. *contorta*)

You may have heard of the lodgepole pine, so straight and tall that Indigenous people and settlers alike used it to build their homes. Yet, come out to my home on the Washington coastline and you'll see why these trees' scientific name means "contorted pine"! The constant winds off of the ocean put enough pressure on the trees that they grow into twisted, stunted shapes, and it's not until you get several hundred yards inland that the pines take on their more characteristic straight and tall shape. Even so, all of the pines in this area are known as shore pines.

In order to survive the hazards of winter, people living close to the land must be inventive and adaptable. Even when you have deep, intergenerational knowledge of food sources in your area, there's no guarantee that every year will be as abundant as the last. A cold snap in spring might freeze off the flowers that would have become fall's fruit, or disease might wipe out many of the deer. Farmers may find that their crops fail due to drought or insects. So other food sources must be relied upon instead.

Shore pines are a reminder to be willing to twist and change according to how the winds blow. A tree that can only grow straight up will be snapped in two in a gale. The tall, straight lodgepoles further back from the ocean commonly break or are toppled entirely in winter's storms. Yet the shore pines closest to the water, lacking in shelter, grow low to the ground and let their limbs turn such that they are less vulnerable to breakage. They might be more humble in appearance, but their strength is in their adaptability.

Fly Agaric (*Amanita muscaria*)

Fly agaric is the classic toadstool, seen everywhere from Victorian fairy illustrations to Nintendo's *Super Mario Bros.* game series. This fungus produces a large, conspicuous mushroom with a broad red cap covered in white spots and with white gills underneath, balanced on a straight white stem. Largely considered to be inedible, the mushroom contains toxins that might cause hallucinations—but are more likely to make the hapless consumer throw up for many hours.

In certain Indigenous settings, such as the reindeer-herding Evenk of Siberia, these hallucinogenic substances (and their side effects) are harnessed within the crucible of long-standing cultural traditions. This may or may not have inspired the red and white garb of Santa Claus and his "flying" reindeer. Yet here in North America, you're more likely to see the mushrooms themselves pop up around Samhain, not Yule, where they could be seen as bridges between worlds as the veils thin.

No need to risk your health by eating these toxic fungi, though. It is enough to meditate upon how—like the salmon—the fly agaric spreads its spores to promote the growth of its offspring once conditions improve in the far-off spring. The mushroom pops up out of the ground for a period of a few days, and then once its job is done, it melts away as though it was never there.

Meanwhile, the rest of the fungus lives as mycelium buried safe and sound in the soil, where throughout the year it breaks down and feeds upon dead, decaying matter. Some of the nutrients it frees up are shared with pines, cedars, and spruces with which it has a mycorrhizal relationship. The mysteries of Samhain may pass as ephemerally as a mushroom, but the day-to-day business of survival through cooperation continues throughout the year.

Feasts and Treats

Dallas Jennifer Cobb

KITCHEN WITCH OR NOT, every one of us creates magic in the kitchen. Some days, especially those spent with small children, it is not just magic, but miracles that we perform in the kitchen.

Sabbat feasts are an opportunity to make magic and miracles to share with our family, friends, neighbours, and sacred circle.

With each of these sabbat meals, the recipes offered for Feasts and Treats are those that have graced my kitchen, hearth, and heart over the years. I offer them with the magical wish that they nourish your heart, bless your kin, please your kids, and make your home a fragrant, nourishing, and nurturing place. I envision the recipes listed at each sabbat served together, forming a one-meal, fabulous sabbat feast.

I offer these recipes in the spirit of community and sabbat celebration that they may help you mark the turning of the Wheel of the Year and make each of the astronomical points on the wheel easy to celebrate and remember because of the delectable feast foods prepared. I have tried to offer vegan alternatives and gluten-free options for those who choose them.

The end of the year for Pagans, Samhain is a bittersweet time. Traditionally a time of endings and new beginnings, Samhain sees the Wheel of the Year turning to the halfway point between Mabon (autumn equinox) and Yule (winter solstice). Translating to "summer's end," Samhain celebrates the dead and dying, and is also the third of the three harvest festivals.

Traditionally associated with Samhain are the crops being harvested at this time of the year: pumpkins, squash, parsnips, tomatoes, carrots, and potatoes, as well as cranberry, apples, pomegranates, and nuts. Our Samhain feast will include Savoury Walnut Meatballs, Roasted Parmigiano Broccoli, and Heirloom Tomato Sauce over Rice Pasta.

Savoury Walnut Meatballs

I spent many years as a vegetarian before becoming an omnivore. Many of my recipes have their roots in the old days, pre-meat. Some of my older recipes have been changed or added to with the inclusion of animal products, but this one remains unchanged.

I love the meaty texture of the walnuts. Not only do they provide something to chew on, but because of the delicious savoury sauce, many people are not even aware that this is a vegetarian recipe.

Prep time: 5 minutes

Chilling time: 15 minutes

Cooking time: 25 minutes

Servings: 8

1 15-ounce can white cannellini beans, rinsed and drained

¾ cup walnuts, chopped

¼ cup red onion, finely chopped

¼ cup Parmesan cheese, for vegans substitute vegan cheese

⅓ cup oat flour (instead of traditional bread crumbs, because oats are gluten free)

½ teaspoon dried basil

½ teaspoon dried oregano

½ teaspoon dried parsley

2 cloves garlic, finely diced

¾ teaspoon smoked paprika
1 egg, for vegans substitute with flax egg
½ teaspoon sea salt

Preheat oven to 400°F.

In a food processor, pulse the beans, walnuts, and onion until finely chopped. Add cheese, oat flour, herbs and spices, and egg, and pulse until completely mixed.

Chill the mix for 15 minutes to make it easier to shape. Then shape the mixture into medium-sized balls and place them on a lightly greased baking sheet. Drizzle olive oil on your hands and gently pat the balls so they have a light coating of oil.

Bake for 15 minutes on one side, flip the balls, and bake for 10 minutes on the other side.

Boil the rice pasta while meatballs are cooking. Then remove the meatballs from the oven and let sit while you drain, rinse, and plate the pasta. Add meatballs on top and generously pour Heirloom Tomato Sauce to cover. Dust with a pinch of Parmesan cheese.

Heirloom Tomato Sauce over Rice Pasta

Heirloom tomatoes are those which have been grown without crossbreeding for over forty years. Usually suited to the soil and climate of a specific area, heirlooms produce seeds and are great for seed saving. This means you can regrow your favorite varieties from year to year. I prefer to use heirloom tomatoes because they are not genetically altered, are specific to my climate and geographic area, and they contribute to my food security over time because I can harvest the seeds to save and replant in years to come.

Prep time: 5 minutes
Cooking time: 45 minutes
Servings: 8

3 pounds ripe heirloom tomatoes
⅓ cup olive oil
5 cloves garlic, peeled and finely diced

A small bunch of fresh basil, leaves picked off the stems, and diced.
(If you don't grow basil, you can always use 1½ teaspoons of
dried basil.)

1 teaspoon sea salt to taste

Ground black pepper to taste

1 teaspoon balsamic vinegar

1 box store-bought rice pasta (I like the size and shape of fusilli.)

Put the heirloom tomatoes in a food processor and pulse until
coarsely chopped. Then heat a large pot with a heavy bottom or a
big cast-iron frying pan on medium-high heat. Add olive oil and
garlic.

Sauté for about 30 seconds to 1 minute until the garlic is translucent. Add all the tomatoes and bring everything to a boil.

Reduce the heat to medium-low and simmer uncovered for 40
minutes to 1 hour to evaporate some of the juice, thickening your
sauce. Then add basil, salt, pepper, and balsamic vinegar (which
magically deepens the flavour). Simmer for 3–4 minutes until the
basil wilts, stirring continuously. Remove from heat and set aside
until you are ready to plate the meal.

For the rice pasta, bring a medium pot of water to a boil. Add
a dribble of olive oil to keep the pasta from sticking, and throw in
a pinch of salt. When the water reaches a rolling boil, add the rice
pasta. Follow the package instructions and stir so nothing sticks to
the bottom. You'll want the pasta to be al dente for this dish. That
means cooked yet firm.

Drain the pasta when it's ready, and rinse with warm water to
reduce its starch content. Then drain again. If you aren't serving it
right away, toss it with a little bit of butter (or olive oil for a vegan
version) so it doesn't clump together, cover, and keep it warm until
you are ready to plate.

Roasted Parmesan Broccoli

For most of my life, I only ever ate broccoli steamed or boiled. But
when it is boiled, broccoli becomes soggy and tasteless. When it is

steamed, broccoli cooks quickly and can retain more crunch and flavour. But by far my favorite way to cook broccoli has recently become roasting it. Done in the oven, the process warms the house and produces a crunchy, textured broccoli with lots of flavour.

Prep time: 3 minutes
Cooking time: 10 minutes
Servings: 8

1 large head of broccoli, cut into bite-sized pieces
Olive oil
Salt and pepper
⅓ cup grated Parmesan cheese (While ready-ground Parmesan is widely available, the flavour of the hard cheese, which you have to grate before serving, is delicious and worth the added effort to grate. Even the process of grating the cheese is magical. We create little snowflakes that fall as we grate.)

Prepare the broccoli while pasta is cooking. Preheat the oven to 400°F. (You can bake the Savoury Walnut Meatballs and the broccoli at the same time.) On a lined cooking sheet, toss broccoli in a drizzle of olive oil, salt, and pepper. Then spread the broccoli in a single, even layer on the cooking sheet.

Roast in the oven for 10 minutes, flipping broccoli halfway through. (Add the broccoli when the walnut meatballs have been in for 5 minutes, then flip both broccoli and meatballs at the same time.)

After flipping broccoli, sprinkle with grated Parmesan cheese. Return the cooking sheet to oven and roast for 8–10 minutes more, until the broccoli is tender. Done this way, the broccoli and meatballs will finish baking around the same time.

Plate the pasta, meatballs, and broccoli, cover with Heirloom Tomato Sauce, and sprinkle everything with grated Parmesan cheese and enjoy.

Crafty Crafts

Elizabeth Barrette

As the world turns toward the dark side of the year, holidays such as Samhain remind us of the richness of harvest and the weight of mortality. Just now, it is becoming noticeable that the days are shorter than the nights and the weather is growing colder with winter's approach. These aspects of the season influence the traditions around its holidays and also the macabre decorations that we choose to display for them.

Posable Spiders

Spiders appear across many traditions and holidays at this time of year. They spin their shimmering webs between the dry stems to trap the last insects aloft before winter's cold arrives. They symbolize life, death, knowledge, and spirit. While it's easy to find spiders in the stores, they are often simple plastic ones that don't lend themselves well to ritual decorations. These posable spiders are much more versatile and magical.

Materials
Large beads (at least two sizes)
Medium beads (like pony beads)
Pipe cleaners/chenilles

Adhesive
Optional: craft paint, googly eyes, craft spiderwebs
   Cost: $5–$15
   Time spent: 5–10 minutes per spider

Design Concepts

Beads come in many materials; for this project, wood or plastic work best. Wood is easier to glue and more natural. Plastic is lighter and comes in larger sizes. In nature, spiders come in various sizes and colors. For most purposes, black or brown beads at least 1 inch wide will work well. For homes with small children, use beads at least 2 inches wide with painted eyes, and display finished spiders well out of reach from little hands.

Pipe cleaners or chenilles are available in a wide range of colors, sometimes even multicolored. They may be thick, thin, or a combination of both. Thick-and-thin ones are especially nice for spider legs with beaded joints. How many you need depends partly on spider size, but they're cheap so get plenty.

Below the shoulder, spiders typically have three or four major joints in their legs, but the amount of articulation varies somewhat. Two or three pony beads make good joints in the middle of the leg, and if you bend a "foot" at the end, it doesn't need a bead unless you want a contrast color. Some spiders, such as pink-kneed tarantulas, have brightly colored legs, knees, or feet that stand out against a darker body. This feature makes for eye-popping Samhain decorations if you enjoy a realistic touch. For a less detailed approach, look at species like wolf spiders that are a more uniform gray or brown color.

Craft glue will bind a variety of materials. Hot glue requires more tools and care to use but creates a very secure bond. Make sure your chosen adhesive will work with the craft materials you have.

Eyes can be attached with adhesive or painted on. Googly eyes are more animated. Painted eyes are more secure. Craft paint such as quick-drying acrylic can also be used to paint plain beads a uniform color or to add details such as stripes. Most natural spiders are black or brown, but some are brighter. You can make spiders in your chosen ritual colors, even if you're working with things like purple and orange.

Assembly

Spider bodies have two main sections: a head and thorax fused into the cephalothorax (the front bead) and an abdomen (the back bead). In many species, the cephalothorax is smaller than the abdomen, but some are similar sizes. They can be round, oval, or almost cylindrical. Round beads are the easiest to work with for this project, but if you wish to mimic a specific type of spider with a different shape, you can use longer beads.

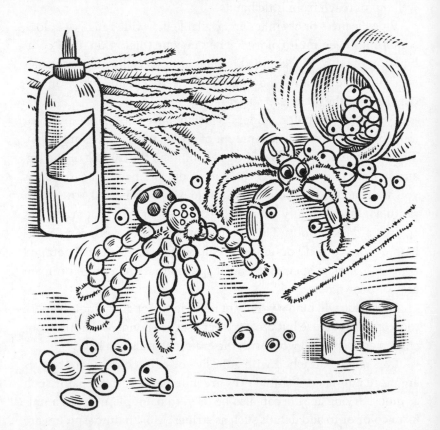

Start by choosing your two beads. If they are already the right color, move to the next step. If you want to change the color or add details like stripes, then paint the beads and let them dry before moving on.

Attach googly eyes or paint eyes on the front bead. Spiders typically have eight eyes, but many species have either two or four eyes larger than the rest, so not as many have eight visible eyes. Either looks fine on a craft spider. If you want to mimic a certain species, look at a picture of its "face" or a diagram of its eyes in relationship to each other.

Spiders have eight legs. Choose pipe cleaners for the legs. If you're making rather large spiders, each pipe cleaner will make one pair of legs. For small spiders, you'll need to trim the pipe cleaners so they will be proportional to your beads; often, cutting each in half works well. In any case, you need four lengths to make the eight legs.

There are two ways to attach the legs, depending on the size and shape of the beads. If the front bead has a big enough hole, you can thread all four pipe cleaners through there, then dab adhesive on both sides of the hole to secure them. If the holes are smaller, you may divide the legs to put two in the front bead and two in the back bead. If the pipe cleaners won't go through at all, you can attach the legs to the bottom of the bead(s) where they look good, using craft glue or hot glue.

Slide two or three pony beads onto each pipe cleaner to create the "knees" for the spider, bending the pipe cleaner just above or below each bead. Spider legs tend to arch up above the body and back down on the same side, holding the body suspended between them. In many species, the four middle legs provide most of the support, while the front legs extend as feelers, and the back legs trail behind for stability. Using similar positions for your posable spiders will make them stand better.

Attach the front and back beads together with craft glue or hot glue. Some species of spiders have the cephalothorax and abdomen level, while in others the abdomen sticks up at an angle. Do what looks good and will stay stable with the beads you have.

Once complete, spiders can be posed in many ways. The pipe cleaner legs will bend to stand on or cling to many different objects. You can put them on decorative cobwebs, which come in many styles such as white floss that you stretch out or more distinct webs of string or rubber. You could even make your own from yarn. Spiders could be hung from string or thread, attached to a besom, scattered on an altar table, and so on. They also make fun gifts for your coven members to take home.

Samhain and Osteomancy

Charlie Rainbow Wolf

SAMHAIN IS THE FESTIVAL of the ancestors, when the dead are celebrated and remembered. It's not by accident that many of the Samhain festivals—and even modern pop-culture Halloween films and displays—are centered around graveyards and themes of death and dying. Holding mass in a cemetery is a long-standing Catholic tradition. In Europe, Samhain is often a three-day event: the dead are honored on All Hallows' Eve, the saints are revered on All Saints' Day, and everyone else is remembered on All Souls' Day.

Another reason Samhain is associated with the dead is because it's believed the veil between our living world and that of the dead is thinnest at this time of year. In order to make a connection between the living and the dead easier to establish, the resting places of the dead are visited. Offerings are frequently left on graves of loved ones in order to strengthen the connection between the giver and the spirit of the recipient.

I like to see this as a liminal time. It's the sabbat between the autumnal equinox and midwinter. It's that transitional time of year between the balance of light and day and the longest night of the year. Graveyards, boneyards, and final resting places might also be interpreted as a liminal space, the bones representing the threshold between what lived and what has passed on.

Personally, I think it's a great time of year to work with osteomancy—reading the bones. I think the best oracles are those that are made by the person using them, and osteomancy lends itself to this nicely. It's not as complicated as it might sound; there are even osteomancy kits (resin "bones" and a casting cloth) available for purchase through New Age shops and online retailers.

Making an Osteomancy Set

There are two ways to make an osteomancy set. The first is to use bones from an animal that's been eaten. Chickens are good because they're readily available, inexpensive, and provide many different bones in several shapes and lengths. Wash the bones in warm soapy water, then set aside. In a small bowl, mix water and peroxide at a ratio of 10 parts water to 1 part peroxide (hairdressing cream peroxide is recommended). Soak the bones in the solution for 5–10 minutes. Old bones that have been found and bleached by the weather won't take as much soaking as newer bones that still have animal fat clinging to them. Usually the smaller the bone, the less time it will need to soak. Wearing protective gloves, work the bones gently with a toothbrush to ensure all residue is removed and the bones are clean, then set them on a paper towel to dry. Smaller bones will take less time to dry than the larger ones.

I mentioned older sun-bleached bones not taking as long in the peroxide bath, and this is the second method of getting bones. Be alert as you're walking through the countryside to see what can be respectfully scavenged. (When scavenging from old skeletons, please ensure that the carcasses and the area are not protected by law. It might be prudent to wear vinyl gloves.) Because every animal represents a different energy, this is a wonderful way of creating a diverse set of osteomancy bones. A coyote tooth for adaptability, intelligence, and perhaps insecurity or arrogance. A bit of deer antler for sensitivity, vigilance, and perhaps a lack of confidence or a bit of fearfulness. A badger claw for determination and endurance, and perhaps for aggression or a quick temper.

The bones used in osteomancy usually resonate strongly with the person using them. Perhaps they hunted the animal for food and used the bones for casting. Maybe they found them in a sacred space and collected the bones to use in their work. Every bone tells a story—whether it is a bone you have found or one you have "made" using a chicken carcass. The only way to really understand osteomancy is to understand the spiritual, the healing, and the magical energy of each animal represented.

What the Bones Mean

Of course, if you are using bones from one animal—like the chicken mentioned previously—then it's possible to assign whatever meanings you want to each bone. Here, consistency is the key. To me, longer bones could represent something that is farther away or that will take a longer time to come to pass, while shorter bones could mean something is closer or will happen quickly. Small round bones may be given the meanings that something is a given, or a fact; short thick bones might indicate confusion, something not clear, or something that has stability and substance. These are just suggestions, though; what do the bones say to *you*?

The Casting Cloth

Another important part of casting the bones is a cloth on which to cast them. Even if you don't want to embellish the cloth (and I recommend you do), you'll want a way of protecting and carrying your bones when they're not in use, and you'll want something to protect them from the ground or floor or table when you are casting them. An idea for the casting cloth might be to divide it into eight sections representing the Wheel of the Year, or twelve sections to represent either the twelve zodiac signs or the twelve months. There's no right or wrong way to do this. Even if you choose not to use one that is embellished, a casting cloth will still protect your bones as you store and use them. One way of using a plain cloth is to drop the bones onto the cloth from a height of about 6 inches and then interpret them in the same way as detailed below. Bones closer to the center of the cloth have the most importance; bones near the edges may not be as pressing or may be distant in their timing.

My casting cloth has fifteen segments on it. It accompanied one of my first divination tools (not counting my astrology tools) back in the late 1980s. I have used it for stones, runes, ogham…it's a good starter cloth. The segments start at the top with health and go clockwise to activity, danger, money, career, communication and the arts, self, blocks, service, partnership, love, family and friends, opposition, hidden resources, and spirituality. Your cloth could have the same divisions, or you could make your own areas.

Posing the Question

Most people consult an oracle because they are seeking more insight about some area of their lives. The best way to formulate any question for any oracle is to quiet your mind, open your heart, and prepare to listen and be objective. Let the oracle coach you into seeing the best way forward. Try to ask open-ended questions, such as ones that begin with "How do I…" or "What are my best options…"

Reading the Bones

When you are ready to cast the bones, hold them in the palm of your hand, close your eyes, then let the bones fall. Generally the bones that fall closest to the center of the cloth are the more immediate issues, while those that fall toward the outside are less important. If the bones fall off the cloth, you can decide if they are calling attention to themselves or if they are of no consequence for this reading and should be disregarded. Pay attention to bones that touch; these are forced working together. Are they bringing challenges, canceling each other out, or working in your favor? Like any pursuit, the more you consult the bones, the more they will speak to you with clarity.

Samhain Ritual

Irene Glasse

THIS SAMHAIN RITUAL CELEBRATES and honors an ancestor with grave cleaning, either using their real grave or a symbolic representation of it. Through the act of cleaning a grave, we increase our connection to our beloved dead. Grave cleaning can be deeply moving and is a way service, offering, and ritual come together in one beautiful experience.

A Grave Cleaning Ritual

In this Samhain ritual, we will connect to a beloved ancestor through offerings, invocation, a shared meal, and the sacred act of grave cleaning. This ritual should be performed during the day on or near Samhain.

For this ritual, you will need

Access to an ancestor's grave or a stone to use as a representation or proxy of your ancestor's headstone.

Grave cleaning supplies: 3–5 gallons of water, a spray bottle of water, 1–2 buckets, scissors, cleaning gloves, a natural sponge, wooden scrapers, 1 small and 1 medium soft-bristled brush, paper towels or rags, and a trash bag.

Offerings for your ancestor. Fresh flowers, Florida water, sweet liquor, and incense all work well.

A small stone, jewelry item, figurine, or other object to consecrate as a symbol of connection to your ancestor.

Cakes and ale: preferably something your ancestor enjoyed, and any plates or cups needed.

Any additional ritual tools or supplies you prefer to use.

Tissues. Grave cleaning and ancestral work are often quite emotional.

Prepare for the ritual by bathing and dressing for it in the way most suited to your practice. Remember that grave cleaning can be a little messy, so comfortable clothing that is easy to wash is a great idea. I like to wear dark colors and include some jewelry I inherited from my ancestors (not rings or bracelets—you will be using your hands). If you have pre-ritual purification practices that you prefer, perform those as well.

Gather your supplies and set them up so that they are easily accessible wherever you are performing this ritual. If you are using a stone as a symbol or proxy for your ancestor's headstone, feel free to work by a sink or other source of clean water.

Take a few centering breaths and concentrate on your connection to your ancestor. If you have memories of them, allow those memories to surface and linger.

Cast sacred, protected space in the way best suited to your spiritual practice. Be sure to include the entire area where you will be working.

Holding the memory or thought of your ancestor in mind, make your first offering to them. Using the following words or your own, invoke your ancestor:

Hail to [your ancestor's name], I call to you here.
The veil is grown thin at the close of the year.
Offerings and love, grave work and time
I give to you now at your own sacred shrine.

[Your ancestor's name], I call. Awaken, arise.
Join me here now under Samhain skies.
A gift has been given, your name has been called.
Come to me now from death's sacred hall.
[Your ancestor's name], hail and welcome!

Feel the presence of your ancestor growing strong. Talk to them and explain that you are going to make an offering to them by cleaning their grave. If you are using a stone in place of their headstone, you can enchant it using these words or similar:

Stone calls to stone, the connection runs deep.
Bones of the earth, a vigil do keep.
This one is now also the headstone and shrine
On the grave of [your ancestor's name], ancestor mine.
From this moment to the close of the rite,
Two sacred stones for this ritual unite.

Mindfully and carefully clean the grave of your ancestor. You may feel moved to talk to them while doing so, or simply hold reverent silence. Listen for any messages, memories, or feelings that arise. Pause as needed to reflect, rest, or grieve. When you have cleaned the grave and headstone to your satisfaction, set your cleaning supplies to the side.

Place the object you have chosen to consecrate to your ancestor on the headstone or proxy stone. Take a few centering breaths and feel the connection between you and your ancestor.

In the name of [your ancestor's name], I now dedicate
This [object name] to the bond we create.
Beloved one, fill it with your energy,
Forming a link between you and me.
When I [hold it or wear it], I will feel the love that we share,
And know that wherever I am, you are there.

Allow the consecrated item to continue gathering energy on the headstone or proxy stone and lay out your cakes and ale. Offer a small quantity of both to your ancestor first, then sit down and share food and drink with them. Feel free to talk to your ancestor as you eat and listen for any responses. When you are finished, clean up the remains of the meal. Small food offerings can remain at the ancestor's grave or be thrown away depending on the rules of the cemetery. If you are using a proxy stone and working at home, offerings can be placed outside after the ritual or simply thrown away.

To close the ritual, put on the consecrated item or place it in your pocket or bag. Make one last offering to your ancestor, feeling deep gratitude and love as you do so. Using the following words or your own, bid them farewell:

> *With intention, offerings, and unending affection,*
> *And deep gratitude for our growing connection,*
> *I bid you farewell. May our bond be a light.*
> *Hail to [your ancestor's name] for this Samhain rite!*
> *Hail and farewell.*

Release sacred space in the way that best suits your practice. Take a moment to ground, breathe deeply, and connect to the physical world. Clean up your space, remembering to take your supplies and trash away with you if you performed this ritual in a cemetery.

Journal or otherwise record any messages or moments you wish to remember. Keep a journal or notepad by your bed for a few nights after the ritual—the dead often communicate in dreams. When you wish to speak to your ancestor, or simply feel their presence, wear or hold the item you consecrated to them.

Notes

Notes

Yule

Keep Your Courage

Tomás Prower

YULE HAS ALWAYS BEEN an interesting time of year. So close to the winter solstice, the darkness and coldness of life start ascending toward their annual apex. In some regions of the world, going outside without the proper preparation can literally kill you via Mother Nature's indifferent iciness. More so than most others, this is an unusual spoke on the Wheel of the Year when the earth we love and upon which we live seems so hostile toward us. Even if not actively producing conditions that can destroy us and our mortal frailty, the elements are at least dispassionate toward us and withhold from us many of the basic necessities of survival.

It's not a coincidence that many spiritual traditions across the globe and throughout time have imagined paradise—our many versions of heaven—to be a place of warm, verdant summertime where the sun is always shining and food is in easy abundance—the opposite of how the world around us is during Yule.

Still, we humans are a resilient bunch, and throughout our history on this planet, our optimism has often won out over our pessimism. Among cultures all over the world, the global celebrations akin to Yule are synonymous with the very opposite realities of winter: light, warmth, and abundance. This is because amid the darkness, coldness, and lack that epitomize this season, we know all those external conditions are only temporary, and the light, warmth, and abundance will come again. Just because they are not present right now doesn't mean we won't ever experience them again. All we have to do is keep our courage and hold on until that inevitability.

And so, in our modern times, Yule is studded with multicolored lights on all edifices, holiday get-togethers surrounded by people we love and who love us, and lots and lots of food. We are safe inside the warmth of a home, which brings internal warmth to our spirit and soul. We focus on the good times to come and count our blessings for the goodness here and now, despite being entrenched in the lower depths of winter. *Now* does not dictate *forever*.

Yet still…this joyous holiday season is also the most difficult time of the year for so, so many of us. Having worked as a licensed mortuary professional for quite some time, I know the dismal secret that Yule is our "busy season" in the funeral industry. The harsher weather conditions and spread of diseases from those indoor get-togethers are partly the cause for this, yes, but Yule is also when we see our annual spike in suicides.

Those going through grief and experiencing the first holiday season without their loved one can sometimes find it too difficult. The warmth and light of get-togethers can be ostracizing and send those who have neither the family nor friends with whom to share that warmth into the abysmal pits of loneliness. They are left alone to agonizingly look into others' bright, happy homes from their cold isolation outside. And the multicolored lights and jolly music that inundate the season just come off as garish and mocking to those whose sadness and depression have made their inner world a musicless gray.

Depending on your current circumstances, Yule is either the most wonderful time of the year or the most arduously difficult, wherein just waking up, going to work, and existing are all little victories in and of themselves. And for those of us with an aptitude and interest in magic and manipulating the natural forces of the universe toward our will, the challenge that Yule presents is to just maintain that will and keep its candle of hope lit and protected when the coldness and darkness are at their strongest and most punishing.

Depression and dark nights of the soul are things we all face. We each have our own personal battles in our own private lives. Still, there is something more seemingly hopeless about it when it occurs during Yule. I know because I have been there. A more piercing sense of abandon is felt, as if having been betrayed by the gods. Where are they in this time of need? Why have they allowed me to even get this despairingly low? Haven't I been good? Or if we have been in this abyss before, the question is always, why again?

And like many, I instinctively turned outward in such times to renew my connection with the gods, the Universe, some being out there who would come and save me from all this. Because that is what faith is all about, right? It's easy to have faith when all is going well, but the true test of faith is to have it and maintain it when all is going to hell.

Still, this battle simply exhausted me further. I was trying to be worthy enough, pass this test of faith, show the Universe that I could overcome what may and what currently is. But I was already fighting a battle just to exist every day and to just feel something, which was made more difficult by the sense of "I *should* be happy because it's the holiday season." Having to prove myself in this extra way when society said I should be jolly, thankful, and bright was just too much. I couldn't jump from sadness to joy in a single, grand leap.

What I could do, however, and what ultimately saved me from myself and my own mind, was deciding that I didn't have to prove anything to anyone else or even internally make it all the way to joy. I just had to prove it to *me* and get myself a little closer to joy, however negligible the distance. I didn't need the grand blaze of a phoenix rising in some glorious comeback story or to find the "holiday spirit" and be merry like everyone else. This didn't have to be a Hallmark Christmas movie. I just needed to keep my little candle of hope lit and make it through till better days. If that candle could grow just a little bit brighter, then at least a little bit more of the darkness would be overcome. I didn't have to illuminate the whole room or the whole path toward joy; I just had to keep my light bright enough to see the next step and carry forward. And for some, this next step forward might even be seeking professional help, and there is no shame in that.

After all, there is a great difference between being happy and not being sad, and in that difference is all the difference. The external yoke-like pressures of Yule to "be happy" were shrugged off, and instead, the idea of "I don't *have* to be happy" brought a bit of relief. I didn't need to be the epitome of Yule's iconic brightness amid the darkness of winter; I just had to keep a small, flickering flame alive.

Taking time to go inward may be the most healing, productive, magical thing you can do this Yule, even though others will call it selfish and "not in the spirit of the season." Yet, I argue that keeping your own courage, your own inner flame, alive, no matter how small or flickering, is indeed at the heart of the spirit of Yule. And do know, though, that it does take work. Physics shows us that, if left to their own devices, things naturally fall apart and that coldness and darkness are the natural way of things. The vacuum of space away from the sun or other stars is cold and dark, and when you enter a room, there is never any "dark switch." All you have to do for the darkness to come is turn off the light. Light and heat take constant energy and fuel, including your inner small candle of light. But even a small candle of light is oh so bright and stands out amid the deepest darkness…so long as it can remain lit.

Going through a tunnel of darkness during Yule was difficult, but it did make it easier knowing that I just had to keep my little candle lit and feel a little better, thus bringing me a little closer to joy than I was before. Whether it be a dark tunnel or even hell itself, when you're in the middle of it all, the other side is just as far forward as the entrance is as far back, so you might as well keep on going forward.

And rather than pray to some outside source for sudden salvation and escape from all that you're feeling, denying the darkness all around you, focus your intentions and inner magic on being there for yourself and being your own source of light. You don't need the sun if you can provide your own light. And when lost in those tunnels of darkness, sadness, and emptiness, where the sun's warmth and rays cannot reach, you can still bring light to that tunnel if *you* are that light. And remember, you don't have to have the biggest, largest fire that illuminates the whole tunnel. You don't have to see the exit or know how you're going to get out. You just need a light bright enough to see where to take the next step. Like driving anywhere at night, your headlights don't need to shine all the way to your destination; they just have to show you a little more of the road ahead, and that's all the light you need to get you anywhere in the darkness of night.

And it doesn't matter if other people are burning brighter right now or are more in tune with the holiday spirit; that's fine and good for them. It also doesn't matter if *you* burned brighter last year. You are where you are right now. Yule is about light and warmth amid the coldest, darkest time of the year. It's not about the intensity of the light or radiant degree of the warmth. You are deserving of your own magic and of your own light. All you have to do is keep moving forward step-by-step and keep that light burning despite everything going on and all you're going through. Keep your courage.

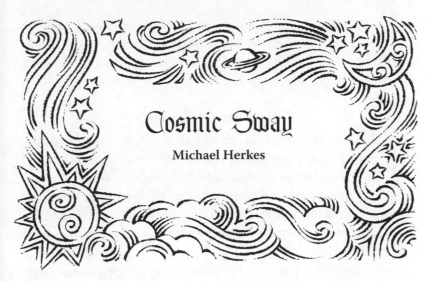

Cosmic Sway

Michael Herkes

As WE ENTER THE enchanting time of Yule and the beginning of Capricorn season, there is a unique opportunity to harness the energies of both celebrations for magical and ritual work. The convergence of these two energies can create a powerful synergy, amplifying intentions and manifesting desires.

Celebrating Yule

Yule marks the winter solstice on December 21 and is a time to focus on the rebirth of light in the natural world. Creating a sacred space adorned with evergreen branches, candles, and symbols of renewal is one way to celebrate this festival. Lighting a Yule log or white candle is a traditional celebration and represents the return of warmth and light during this darkest time of the year. Reflect on personal growth, letting go of what no longer serves you and setting intentions for the coming year.

Capricorn season coincides with Yule, further enhancing its energy with determination, discipline, and ambition. This earth sign encourages us to set practical goals and work diligently toward their achievement. Incorporating this Capricorn energy into your rituals can bring an added sense of stability and grounding. Now is a great time to meditate on your aspirations for personal growth while visualizing them taking root in fertile ground. Create vision boards or write down your goals to solidify your intentions and burn the list to celebrate the return of the Sun.

Full Moon in Cancer

The Full Moon in Cancer on January 13 at 5:27 p.m. marks a time when emotions are heightened, and we are encouraged to connect with our inner selves to nurture our emotional well-being. This is a great time to engage in self-care activities that promote emotional healing, such as taking a relaxing bath infused with soothing herbs, or essential oils can help release any emotional tension and provide a sense of comfort.

Since Cancer is ruled by the Moon, this is a prominent time. Journaling is also highly recommended during this time. Use this opportunity to write down your thoughts, feelings, and intentions for the coming lunar cycle. The Full Moon in Cancer offers an ideal moment for introspection and gaining clarity on your emotional needs. Additionally, gathering with loved ones or participating in group activities centered on nurturing emotions can enhance the celebratory experience. Sharing stories, expressing gratitude, or engaging in heart-centered conversations can deepen connections and create a supportive atmosphere.

Saturn-Venus Conjunction

On January 18 at 8:26 p.m., Venus and Saturn form a conjunction. This is a time when the energies of the two planets combine, offering an opportunity to blend the energy of love with structure and discipline since Venus rules over love, beauty, and harmony, and Saturn rules over structure, discipline, and manifestation. The energy of a Venus-Saturn conjunction is characterized by a balance between passion and practicality. It encourages individuals to take a grounded approach to matters of the heart and relationships while also fostering a deep sense of commitment and loyalty. This alignment can help witches in matters related to love spells, attracting healthy relationships, or even strengthening existing partnerships. It would also be an opportune time to work magic that is aligned with self-love, commitment, stability, or manifesting abundance. You may wish to create a crystal grid utilizing rose quartz and black tourmaline to amplify the energy of grounded love during this conjunction.

The influence of Saturn adds an element of discipline and perseverance to this energy. Witches can utilize this aspect by focusing on long-term goals or working toward personal growth and self-improvement. The Venus-Saturn conjunction supports efforts to build solid foundations for success in various aspects of life.

Aquarius Season

Aquarius season kicks off on January 19; along with a New Moon in Aquarius at 7:36 a.m. on January 29, this is a powerful time to tap into the unique energy of this innovative and forward-thinking zodiac sign. As we plant the seed of intention during this celestial event, there are several meaningful ways to celebrate and align with the Aquarius energy. To celebrate the New Moon in Aquarius, one powerful way is to "plant the seed" of your intentions. This involves reflecting on your goals and aspirations, then writing them down or creating a vision board to manifest them into reality. The forward-thinking nature of Aquarius encourages us to think outside the box and embrace unconventional approaches.

Another way to honor the New Moon in Aquarius is to engage in rituals that reflect the sign's progressive nature. Since Aquarius is associated with innovation and originality, you can take this opportunity to brainstorm fresh ideas or embark on a creative project that pushes boundaries. Embrace your inner rebel and think outside the box as you set intentions for personal growth and positive change.

It is also appropriate to engage in community-oriented activities at this time. As an air sign, Aquarius values collaboration and social connections. Consider organizing a gathering or joining a group that shares common interests or causes. This can be a powerful way to harness collective energy and manifest intentions that benefit not only yourself but also those around you.

Additionally, incorporating technology into your rituals can be fitting for celebrating the New Moon in Aquarius. Whether it's using digital tools for journaling, creating vision boards online, or participating in virtual gatherings with like-minded individuals, embracing technological advancements can amplify your connection with this tech-savvy sign.

Tales and Traditions

Lupa

IN THIS TIME OF shortest days and longest nights, it may sometimes feel as though the sun will never rise high in the sky again. How can we even remember summer's heat and late-evening light when cold winds blast us and the darkness shows up not long after it left?

Now is not the time to despair, though. If other beings can persist in spite of the cold and gloom, then so can we. Some have the luxury of sleeping through the worst of it, but others continue their waking lives despite snow, cold, and short, gray days. Know that you are not alone in these trying times, and be heartened that life persists yet.

Snowshoe Hare (*Lepus americanus*)

It doesn't always take a big, tough animal to defy winter's harshness. A snowshoe hare may not even break four pounds, and yet it's one of the most beautifully adapted animals this time of year. Their coats turn white in winter to give them effective camouflage. And their big, furry hind feet spread wide to keep them from sinking into snowdrifts, allowing them to skim across the snow's surface where larger animals may break through.

These hares are also able to make use of a wide variety of plants throughout the year. When summer's abundance gives way to winter's scarcity, they may eat twigs and stems of any plants within reach, and even the tips of conifer needles and the bark of various trees. Like many herbivores, they will resort to eating meat now and then to get necessary nutrients, and in desperate times may even resort to cannibalism.

Full-time carnivores and savvy omnivores are more of a threat, though. The Canadian lynx, for example, is so dependent on snowshoe hares for food that hare populations directly affect lynx numbers from year to year. Other animals like wolves, coyotes, and owls also rely on the hares for winter sustenance; without the hares, they would likely starve.

Because snowshoe hares feed so many animals, they must breed quickly and abundantly. Mating season begins around Yule and will last until the middle of summer. It's not uncommon for a female hare to have four litters in a year, each with three to five young. So even though many other species may not have mating on their minds just yet, snowshoe hares must get an early start now if they're to stay ahead of the many dangers they face.

Sitka Spruce (*Picea sitchensis*)

If the snowshoe hare is an animal in search of any food it can eke calories out of, then the Sitka spruce tree is one of its saviors. Growing along the West Coast of North America from Northern California to Alaska, this stately conifer provides crisp needles that will at least hold off starvation. For some species, like the blue grouse, spruce needles comprise the bulk of their cold winter diet. The broad, dense branches, especially of younger, shorter trees, create much-needed shelters against the wind and snow. Taller, older trees may even block enough snow to create pockets where the ground is only lightly covered.

Like almost all other conifers, Sitka spruce retains its needles throughout the year. While it may shed older, worn ones in smaller amounts, it doesn't have to expend energy growing a whole batch of new ones every year. Instead, each sprig of needles produces a few inches of new growth each spring. In the meantime, though, the existing needles continue to photosynthesize through the winter, albeit more slowly than in summer's long days.

Evergreen trees have long been a symbol of Yuletide festivities. Their constant greenery is a reminder to us that winter will not last forever and that life persists in spite of hard times. But the Sitka's adaptation to difficult environments isn't just limited to winter's conditions. This hardy, adaptable tree is a pioneer species throughout its range. It's capable of growing on disturbed land, helping to restore forest ecosystems damaged by natural or human-caused disasters.

Here on the coastline, it can even become one of the venerable old trees in ancient forests. Massive trees over five hundred years old and well over two hundred feet tall may still be found in small patches that avoided logging. With time, persistence, and a little luck, the Sitka spruce shows that just about anything is possible if we can just find ways to weather the hard months.

Yellowfoot (*Craterellus tubaeformis*)

Mushroom foragers are usually hard-pressed to find much of anything in winter. Fall's rainy abundance has long since died back, and spring's first flushes are still months away. Yet a few intrepid species insist on continuing to grow until Yule and beyond. One of these is the yellowfoot, a trumpet-shaped mushroom that was once categorized as a type of chanterelle, but was unique enough to be given a whole new genus. With its bright yellow stem holding up a brown-to-gray cap, this mushroom is a welcome sight for winter foragers.

While it has mycorrhizal relationships with conifers like hemlock trees and Douglas firs, the yellowfoot fungus can produce mushrooms even while these trees are relatively dormant this time of year. It's also one of the few fungi that can grow either in soil or on very rotten wood, making it especially adept at finding good places to live. This means that old growth and other mature mixed conifer forests are excellent habitat, with an abundance of both live trees to partner with and dead, decaying wood to colonize.

Because the yellowfoot is smaller than its chanterelle cousins, it's often overlooked, both by human foragers and by animals able to eat wild mushrooms. It's a reminder that sometimes the most important gifts we can get in hard times are seemingly small ones. Once Yule's bright celebrations are done, we're left with long, gray months of winter. At times like this, it may be the little joys and comforts that help us get through to spring's promise. The yellowfoot's bright, sunny tint is even a nice reminder of the changes to come, a pleasing color against brown and gray forest floors during this season.

Feasts and Treats

Dallas Jennifer Cobb

ON THE SHORTEST DAY of the year, it is traditional to cook foods that warm the hearth, heart, and home. Cook what you love, what warms your heart, and what pleases you. And offer that love, joy, and pleasure to others through the feast foods. Yule invites us to honour this by making foods that warm us and stick to the ribs.

Our feast meal will include Warming Curry with White Rice and Cardamom Cashew Snowballs. I always make the Cardamom Cashew Snowballs in advance. On the day of the feast, I choose to prepare the rice first, and while it simmers, I cook the curry. Both are relatively quick dishes to prepare and come together around the same time. I like food to be hot when served, especially at Yule, when we all need to be warmed.

Homemade Indian Curry Powder

I make my own curry powder and use this recipe with dry ingredients. Make it and store in a jar for ready use. Alternately, you can seek out fresh turmeric root, ginger, peppers, and chilies if you want to make it fresh. These fresh ingredients are more readily available in the summer and in large grocery stores in urban areas.

You can multiply this recipe, make lots, and keep it on hand for warming meals throughout the winter. You can also make up smaller Mason jars, label and decorate them, and give them away as Yule blessings. I love giving the magical gift of warmth to people.

Prep time: 1 minute

Servings: About 4 pots of curry, which can each serve 4 people. When making the Warming Curry recipe, use about half of the pre-made powdered curry powder.

2 tablespoons ground coriander

2 tablespoons ground cumin

1½ tablespoons ground turmeric

2 teaspoons ground ginger

½ teaspoon ground black pepper

1 teaspoon ground cinnamon

½ teaspoon ground cardamom

½ teaspoon cayenne pepper or ground chilies

1 teaspoon sea salt

Optional: Many people add dried mustard to their curries, but I don't like the flavour. If you do, try 1 teaspoon added to this recipe.

In a large bowl, combine all ingredients. Stir gently until mixed. Transfer to a jar, label with the name and date, and seal. When making a medium-sized pot of curry, use about 2–2½ tablespoons of the mixture, adding more, to taste, if wanted. For the Warming Curry recipe below, use 4 tablespoons and adjust to taste.

Warming Curry with White Rice

I grew up eating brown rice. The hippie in me thought it was superior because it retained its hull and had more fibre. However, I have since dropped brown rice in favour of white and experience fewer inflammatory effects in my body because of the lesser amounts of lectin—a substance that creates inflammation, especially for me.

I love the scent of rice cooking and delight in this quick-to-cook version. When I dish it up on the plate, I make fluffy, snow-white drifts or use a rounded ice cream scoop to make "snowballs."

This is an omnivore curry recipe with tons of veggies and some chicken. If you are vegetarian or vegan, skip the chicken. If you are feasting with a mixed omnivore or vegetarian group, prepare the chicken separately, rewarm it, and add it to the omnivores' plates. The curry is called "warming" because many of the ingredients in it contribute to increased metabolism and a feeling of warmth.

Prep time: 15 minutes
Cooking time: 20 minutes
Servings: 8

Curry

2 tablespoons coconut oil
1 tablespoon grated ginger
2 cloves of garlic, finely diced
1 medium onion diced
2 chicken breasts, deboned and cubed
4 tablespoons Homemade Indian Curry Powder (add more to taste)
1 can coconut milk
2 carrots, sliced in rounds
2 cups cauliflower
2 cups broccoli
Water as needed

Rice

2 cups long grain white rice (I love basmati and jasmine, but almost any long grain rice will do.)
3 cups water
1 teaspoon butter, or a drizzle of olive oil to make it vegan
1 teaspoon sea salt

Rice can be started before you cook your curry. Use a medium-size stainless steel pot with lid for the rice. Rinse your rice to remove excess starch and then drain. Add water, butter, and salt.

Bring the rice to a boil, then turn down to simmer, and put the lid on. Cook for 15 minutes covered, and do not stir. Turn off the stove, and do not open the pot. Remove the pot from burner, and let it sit covered for 10 minutes. Steam contained inside the pot finishes the cooking so that what remains is fluffy white rice.

While the rice is cooking, warm a large skillet over medium heat. I use a deep cast-iron skillet and like the constancy of heat that cast iron provides. Add coconut oil and watch it melt. Then add ginger, garlic, and onion, simmering them until translucent. Add diced chicken, searing on all sides.

Note: If you are preparing chicken separately so the curry is vegetarian friendly, set the chicken aside now. It can be quickly warmed later and added individually to omnivores' plates. Carefully clean out the skillet and begin the recipe again, without the chicken, to make a strictly vegetarian dish.

When chicken is mostly cooked, add curry powder and coconut milk to make a sauce. When sauce bubbles, add carrots and cauliflower. Stir to cover all veggies with sauce, adding water if needed. Add broccoli last so it doesn't go soggy. Two minutes before plating food, stir the broccoli in. Simmer until veggies are tender.

When the rice and the curry are ready, scoop a half-cup snowball or an ice-cream scoop snowball of rice onto each plate. If you separated the chicken earlier, now is the time to quickly rewarm it and add it to the omnivores' plates. Add a huge scoop of curry on the chicken and either on or next to the rice.

Cardamom Cashew Snowballs

The original recipe for this dish came from the 1976 edition of *The New Laurel's Kitchen*. I make these for Yule because they are delicious, nutritious, and look like snowballs, and they contain many ingredients traditional to Yule consumption. Dates and nuts are

Yule favourites. They store well and are readily available through the winter.

While I love Laurel's original recipe, I often add a teaspoon of vanilla extract to the date mixture for an extra-flowery scent and flavour. You can add or omit, or even consider adding a teaspoon of Amaretto for a slightly different flavour.

Prep time: 15 minutes

Servings: 18 balls

1 cup cashews, chopped into small pieces
½ cup dried coconut
½ teaspoon ground cardamom, or more to taste
1 cup pitted dates
1 orange peel, very finely shredded
1 teaspoon vanilla extract

Toast the cashew pieces in a skillet over medium heat until they smell good, then set aside. Next, toast the dried coconut in a skillet over medium heat until it smells good. Then pulse it in a food processor until powdered. Set aside.

Place everything but the coconut in a food processor and pulse until everything is well mixed and forms a consistent texture. It is fine to see bits of nut or peel. Roll this goo into 1-inch balls. Coat each ball in powdered, toasted coconut.

References

"Curry Powder: Are There Health Benefits?" WebMD. Internet Brands. Reviewed March 15, 2023. https://www.webmd.com/diet/health-benefits-curry-powder#:~:text=One%20study%20found%20that%20people%20who%20eat%20more%20curry%20powder,makes%20heart%20disease%20less%20likely.

Robertson, Laurel, Carol Flinders, and Brian Ruppenthal. "Cashew Cardamom Balls." In *The New Laurel's Kitchen: A Handbook for Vegetarian Cookery & Nutrition*. Berkeley, CA: Ten Speed Press, 1976.

Crafty Crafts

Elizabeth Barrette

WINTER DEEPENS, AND THE world approaches the longest night of the year. Days are short and cold. Trees are dormant and so are many animals, leaving the world still and quiet. Snow drifts down from the sky and piles up in sparkling mounds on the ground. Yule and other midwinter holidays create a sense of light and cheer against the cold, dark background of the season. Some decorations are all about that contrast, like hanging holiday lights to shine at night. Others celebrate winter motifs such as snow, ice, evergreens, and winter-active animals like deer and birds.

Snowscape Ornaments

Ornaments appear on Yule trees, Christmas trees, and many other places. You can find plenty of styles in stores. However, they don't always match Pagan ideals precisely. Inside the clear shell, you can create your own winter scene using whatever embellishments you like.

Materials
Clear ornament shells (glass or plastic)
Craft snow (faux snow, white confetti, cotton balls, etc.)
Scenic figures (pine trees, deer, etc.)

Tweezers or long craft pliers
Craft glue or hot glue
 Cost: $10–$15
 Time spent: 5–10 minutes per ornament

Design Concepts

Clear ornament shells are easily found in glass or plastic. Some open along the equator, ideal for this project. Others have a permanent opening, and some just have a small hole at the top. Choose based on what you want to put inside. A fully sealable version is best unless all the contents will be glued down.

Your "snow" can be almost anything fluffy and white. Faux snow for crafts is great if you want it to move inside a sealed ball; glitter, white confetti, or kosher salt also work. For more solid "snow" in an open ornament, try cotton balls or cobweb floss.

Scenic figures let you create a tiny diorama. Choose from plants (pine trees, spruce trees, holly, poinsettia, etc.), animals (deer, snowshoe hares, cardinals, etc.), buildings (rustic cabins, cute cottages, candy stores, etc.), and other items. You may find wintery god or goddess figurines such as Father Frost or the Snow Queen.

Assembly

If your ornament comes apart, start by opening it. Otherwise you'll need to work through whatever hole it has. For manipulating small items inside tight spaces, tweezers or long craft pliers help.

Decide which figures to place inside each ornament. For most ornaments, one to three will fit well. Larger ornaments may have room for more. Place taller figures such as trees or buildings toward the back. Put medium figures like deer or people in the middle. Place small figures like birds or snowshoe hares toward the front. Fasten them in place with craft glue or hot glue.

Add fake snow to your ornament up to the desired depth, making sure not to cover your figures. Then close the globe and seal it thoroughly with glue, so the snow can't escape to make a mess.

Hang the finished snowscape ornament from your Yule tree or in a window to admire it.

Snow Pillows

Snow pillows are easy to make, with sewing or no-sew options. You can make them in whatever colors you like for celebrating Yule. They make great sit-upons for seated rituals or meditation. Unlike holiday-specific decor, these work well all winter long. They also make popular gifts.

Materials

Pillow form or stuffing
Backing fabric (like cotton or muslin)

Contrast snowflake fabric (like cotton, felt, or lamé)
Scissors
Attachment equipment (sewing machine, needle and thread, heat-bonding film, or fabric glue)
Optional: paper
    Cost: $15–$20
    Time spent: 45–60 minutes per pillow

Design Concepts

Plain throw pillow forms are available to use as insides with a variety of sizes and shapes. Solid furniture-foam blocks can be cut as desired. You can also get fiberfill or foam-chunk stuffing to fit any pillow parameters.

Backing fabric can be thinner (like muslin) or thicker (like denim) but should be plain and solid rather than fancy. Quilting fabric and canvas are good, sturdy options for a throw pillow. Blue jean legs make excellent bolsters. You can choose a dark background like black or indigo to go with white snowflakes, or a pale background like white or silver to go with dark snowflakes. Red and green are also popular seasonal colors.

Snowflake fabric should contrast with the background. Avoid knits that unravel. Felt and quilting fabric are good. Lamé or holographic fabric is spectacular, but can fray and won't stand up to high heat, so they require careful handling. Iron-on patch material comes in denim blue and dark red, so with that you don't need separate fabric and attachment. Choose one large or several smaller snowflakes per pillow; you can use multiple colors and sizes of snowflake to create a snowy sky.

You can sew pillows by hand or on machine. Appliqué makes a very nice quilted pillow that will last a long time, especially if you anchor it with a strong and decorative stitch like blanket stitch. Heat-bonding film or fabric will fasten two layers together when you iron over it, so for this method, choose natural fiber like cotton. Fabric glue should say on the bottle what it works with.

Assembly

Start by cutting two squares of background fabric. Many throw pillows are 18 inches square, occasionally round, but you can make whatever you want.

Cut out your snowflakes. If you've ever made paper snowflakes by folding paper into sixths and snipping the folded edges, you can do the same with thin fabric like cotton or lamé. For thick fabric like felt, first snip a pattern from folded paper, then pin it to the snowflake fabric to cut out. It is easier to attach a snowflake that is chunky with just a few holes and branches than one which is very fancy with lots of details.

Attach snowflakes to the background with a sewing machine, hand sewing, bonding film, or fabric glue. Felt is very user-friendly,

but some other fabrics need more care to cover all edges so they don't fray.

Place the backing squares face-to-face. Start to sew or glue the seam around the edges. If you're using a pillow form, turn the cover right side out, put the form inside, and close the last edge. For loose stuffing, close everything but a hand-sized gap. Then turn the cover right side out, stuff it, and close the gap.

Tug gently to make sure everything is securely fastened and won't come loose easily, since a throw pillow is a craft that people will actually use. If necessary, tack any loose bits.

Yule and Card Divination

Charlie Rainbow Wolf

PICK A CARD, ANY card. Tarot? Lenormand? Poker cards? Something else? Whatever type of cartomancy you favor, there's an oracle and a spread for that.

It's human nature to want to know what is coming up after the New Year, and this is one reason why I like to use my oracles over Yule. They give a glimpse into the future, and let's be fair: once the holidays are over, things can get dull and uninspiring rather quickly! What better way to perk things up than to have a chat with a favored set of tarot or other cards?

You're probably familiar with tarot cards and may even have a deck (or in my case, a few dozen). The Lenormand deck is kind of a cross between playing cards and oracle cards. Maybe your great-grandma read playing cards. Perhaps you favor something different, like one of the other popular card oracles such as angel cards, fairy cards, or those that share positive affirmations. There are literally *hundreds* from which to choose.

Yule Spreads

I've listed some of my go-to spreads below, but in reality there are as many different ways to read the cards as there are card readers. No method is better than another one. These are just suggestions that reflect the midwinter energy.

The Yule Tree Spread

A "Yule tree" spread lends itself to this time of year, and, you've guessed it: the cards form a tree as they are laid out.

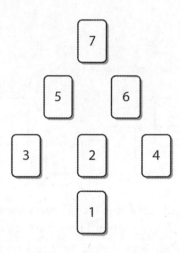

- Card 1 is the immediate heart of the matter. What is the foundation of the current issue?
- Card 2 is what is influencing matters right here, right now.
- Card 3 reveals things from the past that helped to create the current situation.
- Card 4 indicates what might be coming to resolve things.
- Card 5 reveals challenges working against the issue.
- Card 6 reveals things that are working in favor of a solution.
- Card 7 reveals the potential final outcome.

The Wheel Spread

Another layout I use at any time of the year but especially around New Year is the Wheel of the Year spread. It appeals to the astrologer in me and looks something like this:

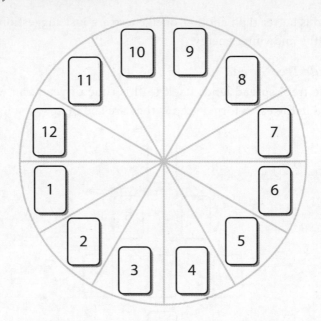

There are several ways this layout can be interpreted. I like to use the astrological houses when I read the cards in this manner.

- Card 1 indicates the self, potential, and what is impacting things on a very personal level.
- Card 2 reveals information about income, self-worth, and possessions, and what is influencing the immediate surroundings.
- Card 3 points to communication, short-term travel, basic education, local community, and what is affecting the neighborhood environment.
- Card 4 hints at customs, traditions, ancestors, and what might have a bearing on home and family.
- Card 5 refers to creativity, children, entertainment, games and hobbies, potential romances, and what is in store on a social level.
- Card 6 alludes to information regarding day-to-day environment, including things like pets, housework, work environ-

ment, and what is impacting day-to-day activities, even if they're mundane.

• Card 7 mirrors card 1, which was all about the self; now the focus is on partnerships of all kinds, including marriage, business partners, and even those people with whom you might not have a good relationship.

• Card 8 expands the energy of card 2; there the focus was on self worth; now it is on relating to others through sex, death, rebirth, big business, institutions, and what is influencing regeneration and renewal regarding current situations.

• Card 9 reflects card 3, and now the attention goes to higher education, long-distance travel, and philosophical matters.

• Card 10 echoes card 4 and places the attention on career and vocation and what might be affecting social standing, either through challenges or positive circumstances.

• Card 11 is all about friends and hobbies and reflects the creativity of card 5, focusing on adding meaning and substance to social circles and the people in them.

• Card 12 reveals what is hidden—how's that for a contradiction! Where card 6 was all about what's out in the open in day-to-day life, card 12 reveals dreams and nightmares, hidden enemies, and what may be in store on a spiritual level.

It's possible to use this layout to time events, and again, there is more than one way of doing this. Card 1 could represent January, card 2 February, and so on. Astrologers might like to have card 1 represent the time frame of the Sun sign of Aries, card 2 represent Taurus, through to card 12 representing Pisces. This layout could even represent weeks or days or hours; there's no limit to how it can be used.

Using Other Tools

If you like this idea of the wheel spread, look into exploring astrological houses. There are entire books written on the topic, far more information than I could hope to cover here! And if you like the concept of the wheel but don't want to get into all the astrology, use the layout cloth that I described in the Samhain section, and let each one of the fifteen cards represent one of the areas on the casting cloth.

Before jumping into doing a complicated reading, though, I must stress that it is important to know your oracle. Handle it, and get a good exchange of energy going. It's not necessary to memorize the meanings that come with the cards or other divination set, but a thorough understanding of the meanings of the cards (even if they're what they mean to you, rather than what the author suggested) will go a long way to enabling you to provide a great reading—not just for Yule, but for any other occasion, too!

Different Ideas

At time of writing there are two authors creating something quite exciting. Juliet Diaz and Lorriane Anderson have so far published Seasons of the Witch oracle cards for the sabbats of Yule, Beltane, Mabon, Imbolc, and Samhain, and it looks like they are going to cover all the sabbats eventually. They're easy-to-use oracles that carry a profound message and are worth looking into for celebrating the Wheel of the Year in divination.

The author Kristoffer Hughes has also created a beautiful *Yuletide Tarot* (Llewellyn, 2023). It's based on the Rider-Waite tarot, and the atmospheric images remind me of Georgian-era Christmas cards. The cards come with a guidebook and five spreads to assist with layouts and interpretations.

Yule Ritual

Tomás Prower

DARKNESS IS ONE OF the most powerful detriments to our advancement in life. However, whether it be the darkness outside on a moonless night, darkness in a room that has no windows, or even our own darkness that we carry within us, darkness does not actually harm us. It has no actual power. Darkness just enables and encourages us to harm ourselves with our own thoughts and mind. Fear creeps in and manipulates us to believe that what awaits and lingers in that unseen darkness are all things we consider "bad," but why is it that, when in the midst of darkness, we automatically assume that what lies in the unseen are bad things? Why don't we assume that in that unknown lie unseen joy, friends, and treasures waiting to be known? Darkness is just darkness, and the unknown is, by nature, not known. It's us who morph the unknown into monsters.

We have all the power. As we have known from experience since childhood, if we are scared in a dark room, all we have to do is turn on the light, and all the self-conjured fears sitting in that darkness disappear. And once we see that all the monsters that "hid" in that dark unknown were all in our mind, we chuckle to ourselves in embarrassment and wonder why we got ourselves so scared over nothing. All we have to do is keep that light, even a dim nightlight, alit within. With this inner light, wherever we go, our fears of an uncertain future will dissipate along with the darkness with every step forward that we take.

The Fire Inside

This fire inside is our most important asset in hard times. It is why light and the warmth it radiates are so important. Light is part and parcel of winter holiday celebrations around the world, including (and especially) Yule. It allows us to see the next step on our pathway no matter how dark the tunnel or terrain through which we traverse, all the while keeping us warm and safe. Fires outside of us can fall prey to winds and rain in nature and to fellow humans intent on snuffing out our light.

Yet still, the fire inside needs work to help it stay alight and grow in size. This ritual is a working to help keep that light strong regardless of the darkness, coldness, and seeming emptiness that surround you. You will turn your breath into holy bellows, whose insufflation will add energy and potency to your inner light so that you can keep moving forward, keep the faith, and keep your courage wherever and everywhere you go, whether with others or alone. Remember, no magic can make the darkness disappear, and no amount of darkness can put out the light. Pump the bellows into your own inner light and watch how the world around you lights up as a result and shows you the next step on the path.

Meditation

Go into your meditational space (however your tradition, practice, or self prefers). For me, my meditational space is my heart space, or the heart chakra area of my spirit. To get there, I sit quietly and focus on the steady rhythm of my heartbeat, using it as an internal metronome. Once its rhythm becomes familiar, I count down from ten to zero with each beat and imagine my center of consciousness descending from my head down to my heart as if in an internal elevator. Upon zero, I see the elevator door opening and enter my heart space, wherein I can be in touch with my true spirit now that my "mind" and my "feelings" are in the same space.

In your mind's eye, see a light source, however dim or strong, emanating from your solar plexus. The light source can be whatever you prefer it to be so long as it has a flame, such as a candle, a torch, a lighter, etc. Grab hold of that light source in your mind while also miming the actions with your physical body, and bring it up to the level of your head, a foot or two away from your face.

Take a deep, slow breath inward in your mind's eye and with your physical body, inhaling as much air into your lungs as you can, all the while sensing the energy that is collecting within you. Once you reach maximum capacity, hold the air within you as long as you comfortably can. Feel the energy vibrate, bounce, and ricochet within you as its frenetic vigor crescendos faster and faster the longer you hold your breath.

Unleash the energy in your mind's eye and physically by blowing it slowly and steadily outward onto your light source, and see the fire of your light source grow as if you compressed bellows onto it. Your lungs are your magical bellows. You are the energy source of your own light. As long as you can breathe, you can keep your flame alight. Repeat this breath work in a rhythmic, steady pattern, seeing your fire grow and grow each time.

Once your light is as big and bright as you can make it right now, in your mind's eye and mimicking with your hand, move it around you and see how the darkness retreats from you, revealing no monsters or obstacles to where you want to go. Do not feel forced to create a blazingly bright flame that lights up the room. If all you can muster at the moment is a singular sigh that keeps the flame of a tiny candle alive, then that is enough. Have that tiny flame dissipate just enough of the unknown for you to see your next step, and continue forward with your head down if you have to. Step-by-step, you'll get there.

Once you feel safe (or at least less unsafe) at the sight that there is nothing around you at this moment that is near to harm you, take the light source and place it, with its bigger flame than before, back into your solar plexus.

Come out of your meditational space. If you followed my entrance into the meditation ritual by visualizing an elevator-like descent that brought your consciousness down into your heart space to the rhythm of your heartbeat, all you have to do now is reverse that process. Visualize your consciousness in your heart space and refind the rhythm of your heartbeat. Once you've got that rhythm again, count upward from zero to ten, slowly moving your consciousness up toward your head space like a steady elevator ascent. Once you reach ten and feel your consciousness around eye level, open your eyes and move your body around to get your physical bearings back.

Conclusion

Whenever you feel scared or surrounded by too much darkness and too many unknowns, simply clutch at your solar plexus, grab that light from within, and blow onto it, imagining the bellows pumping up that inner fire and warmth from within. Do this physically, and keep breathing slow and steady bellows breaths onto that light source until you feel less immobilized by worry and fear. If you do this often enough and make it a habit, just the physical motion of clutching your solar plexus will act as a calming trigger, subconsciously reminding you of your own inner light and safety.

Keep this ritual handy and know that wherever you go, your protective, revealing, warmth-giving light will always be there too. Remember, Yule is not about ignoring or denying the darkness of the season. It is about creating our own light and celebrating anyway in spite of the darkness. It doesn't make the darkness go away; rather, it is the hopeful reminder to ourselves that the darkness doesn't last forever, and it will diminish of its own accord in time without needing to be rushed by us. And until that time comes, we can make and be our own light.

Notes

Imbolc

A Time of New Beginnings

Ariana Serpentine

SOME OF MY EARLY associations with Imbolc were air so cold it hurt my face; wind that carried the scent of snow and ice, the smell that only comes from a complete lack of moisture because all water has been frozen out of the air; ice beneath my feet, sometimes with a thin layer of snow that helped my boots keep a grip while I walked; warm company around a candlelit table, a tiny flame against the hellish cold outside.

I began my life as a practicing Pagan teenager in Western New York, and the time of year that Imbolc happens (late winter to early spring—February 1, specifically) was a time of utter cold. While it had been snowing for months, February brought on a special level of freezing weather. It sucked the moisture out of the air and your skin, it drained the warmth and energy from your limbs no matter how thick your coat, and it made it seem like the long winter would never go away.

Yet for us (myself and the groups that I practiced with), Imbolc was a time to hold up that tiny candle of warmth against the cold and darkness. It was a time to be thankful that we were still alive despite the razor-sharp, howling wind. It was a time to remember that, despite the fact that your feet had been cold for six months, there would again be a time when you'd be able to walk outside without your coat (or even your shoes!). In short, to me, Imbolc represented hope—hope that things were going to get better, that the days would get longer, and that the chill gales would become warm breezes, when the scent of water and wet earth, the scent of life, would fill the air again.

Over time, as I studied the background of Imbolc and the goddess (and saint) associated with it, Brighid, I came to realize how appropriate that sense of hope was for this festival.

The name *Imbolc* has been translated in a few different ways: "ewe's milk" and "in the belly" have both been proposed for the meaning of the name of the festival. The festival marks the timing of the agricultural year in Ireland and Scotland. This is the time when lambs (and often human children) would be born, the end of the long winter when life was beginning to peek out from under the cold ground. It is a time of new beginnings as the lambs were being born and the world was beginning to stir. It is a time of fire and warmth and light, of hope and creation, a time of healing and blessings. It is the time of the goddess (and saint) Brighid.

The Goddess Brighid

Imbolc (as it is celebrated today in Ireland and Scotland) is associated with Saint Brighid, who is undoubtedly a surviving expression of the Celtic goddess Brigid (also spelled Brigit, Brig, Bride in Scotland, and Ffraid in Welsh), whose name means "exalted one." Brighid was described as a triple goddess, not in the modern Maiden-Mother-Crone sense, but either as a goddess with three aspects or three goddesses by the same name with different specialities: Brighid of the healers, Brighid of the smiths, and Brighid of the poets. In Irish lore she is the daughter of the Dagda, a deity associated with wisdom, magic, and the hearth and hospitality. We see a connection between her and her father in the associations with the hearth and its fires, hospitality, and poetry, which was seen as a form of magic in ancient Ireland. Brighid and similarly named goddesses were revered throughout Ireland, Scotland, England, and Wales, as well as parts of the European continent. She may very well have served as a great goddess-type deity for the many Celtic peoples of those regions.

Brighid is connected to fire through her associations with the forge and with the fires of inspiration, and Imbolc is observed as one of the four fire festivals. She is also associated with agriculture, having been said to have "kings" of various animals: two kings of oxen, a boar, and a ram, making the time when the sheep begin birthing an especially appropriate time to have a festival in her honor. While nowadays the celebration of Imbolc and Brigid's Day is focused on the Catholic saint, many Pagans and polytheists view her as an extension and survival of the goddess Brighid and are comfortable engaging in the folk customs associated with Brigid's Day as a way of honoring and connecting to her. We don't have a lot of information about how it was practiced in pre-Christian times, but it is likely that many of the practices involved in Brigid's Day are descended from Pagan practices.

Given the origins of the holiday, I can't imagine practicing Imbolc as a Pagan without incorporating Brighid, as she is central to its existence and history. Whether you view her as a goddess, a saint, or both, she is the warm fire in the cold season, the heat of the forge smithing new life, the healer of the pains brought on by the cold, the source of the sacred and blessed words that bring light to the hearts tired from a long winter. She is, as they say, the "reason for the season."

Imbolc Practices, Both Modern and Ancient

In Brighid's many attributes and stories, one can find inspiration for a deep understanding of the holiday as well as ways to practice it. In Scottish tales, Bride was trapped under the ice during the winter, and in the version of the story I originally heard, it was the warming light of the sun on Imbolc that gave her the heat she needed to break free from her frozen prison. In this we can see Imbolc as a time of beginnings, a time of hope for the future, and a reminder that the sun will come again and what was lost to the cold and the long nights will be renewed. As a smith, she can be seen as a creatrix, helping in the forging of the new things that will come to pass for the year. As a healer, she can be seen as a protector of health and well-being in the times to come. As a poet, she can be seen as a magician and a weaver of fate, one who knows the spells and words to bring blessings for the future and fortify you against the still-clinging darkness of the old year. All of these things can be incorporated into an Imbolc celebration: asking for blessings on new ventures, healing of illness and a reinforcement of wellness, a source of inspiration, and of course a light against the darkness and a fire against the cold nights.

There are many folk customs associated with Brigid's Day, and thus quite a bit to draw inspiration from for Pagan practice. The making of Brighid's crosses out of reeds is a popular one. There's a trick to creating them, but once begun, the process can be quite meditative (and there are many how-to videos online if you are interested in making them yourself). Brighid's crosses come in a few different forms, both four- and three-pointed. The three-pointed ones could be associated with the triple Brighid in her three aspects of smith, healer, and poet. While reeds are traditional, I've seen them made from many different kinds of flexible materials, including pipe cleaners. I love making Brighid's crosses and at one point built up a collection of them.

I've had a lot of different Imbolc practices over the years. I usually incorporate some kind of meal or feast with offerings for the ancestors, the land, and Brighid (and sometimes other deities that seem appropriate). I will at the very least light a candle for Brighid and offer some devotion or meditation to her.

Another popular custom is the creation of a doll of Brighid, called the *Brideog*, and inviting her into the house to bless it on Imbolc eve. The Brideog itself would usually be created from agricultural materials such as straw or wheat, and sometimes with a turnip for the head. It would be clothed in a white dress and decorated with shells or crystals. A small wand of white wood (the *slat Bhride*) would be left beside the bed, and a cloth, or Brighid's mantle (the *brat Bhride*), would be left out for her to bless.

Sometimes children would come to the front door bearing the Brideog, which would be invited into the home, all while asking Brighid for blessings on the home and family in the upcoming year. This would also be accompanied by a feast for Brigid's Day. An alternate practice with the Brideog would be for children to take it door-to-door, asking for donations for Brighid. They would be given food or money. This was sometimes done by "Biddy Boys" but also by girls. In some cases some of the girls would dress up as Brighid and play her part when going door to door asking for food and conveying her blessings.

The Brighid's mantle was left out on the evening of Imbolc. Prayers for healing were made over it, asking Brighid to bless it as she visited. The brat Brighid would be placed on those who were ill or otherwise afflicted in hopes that the goddess's blessings would help to alleviate the sickness of those who suffered.

Simple forms of divination would often be performed on Imbolc. Sometimes this involved reading the ashes of the hearth fire or observing the way candles lit on Imbolc would burn. Those without access to a hearth and who use other tools for divination can use those instead. Given the origins of the holiday, it might be the perfect time to learn and practice divination by Ogham, an ancient Irish writing system. Brigid's Day is a time of new beginnings, and as such, it serves as an excellent time to ask about how things will go during the upcoming year.

Brigid's Day is also a time for feasting! Given her agricultural associations, it's a good time to make bread. After all, in a way, the oven is a forge for the bread, and the heat of the cooking fire is a source of life for everyone who partakes of the meal. Imbolc is also associated with milk, as sheep were a major source of milk in Ireland; dairy products such as milk, cream, and cheese—and foods cooked with them—are perfect for an Imbolc feast. A feast is a celebration of life and fertility and a good beginning to the coming year.

Imbolc is also a good time for spring cleaning. After a long winter in a cold climate, a house tends to accumulate dust and detritus. The energy and air get stagnant, and things often feel heavy and tired. A good way to help ensure prosperity and good fortune over the coming year is to prepare your house properly, so doing a thorough cleaning on the days leading up to Imbolc is a good way to set intentions and make room in your life for new, good things to grow. In addition, if you're welcoming Brighid into your house and asking for blessings, it's only appropriate that your home be as clean as you can manage; it's not every day that you have a goddess as a guest of honor.

For the first time in 2022, Imbolc, or Saint Brigid's Day, was celebrated as a national government, or bank, holiday in Ireland. Many cultural events were held, centering the role of women in the building and history of the country. Museums and other cultural institutions prepared presentations and exhibits speaking to Ireland's history of and commitment to gender equality while tapping into the rich heritage of the holiday.

Celebrate Brighid and This Sacred Time

I've only been able to give a few brief examples of ways that this festival is and can be practiced. I encourage people who celebrate Imbolc to look into how it is done by the living peoples of the cultures that it originated from. Giving those cultures due respect by learning from them can only deepen your understanding and appreciation of it, as well as the blessings you receive by participating in this beautiful holiday.

However you choose to celebrate, Imbolc is a time of fertility, new beginnings, and hope for the future. Cleaning your house and yourself of the things that have accumulated is a good way to prepare yourself to receive new blessings and show that you appreciate the ones that you already have. Inviting Brighid into your home and your life calls the divine in to bring warmth, light, creativity, fertility, healing, and all sorts of good things to replace what has been washed away. Divining on the future can help you prepare for it, whether the omens are good or ill. It is the best time to prepare yourself, your household, and your community for the coming year and the return of light and life.

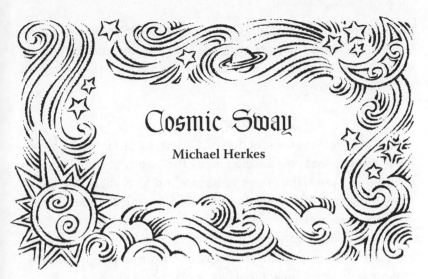

Cosmic Sway

Michael Herkes

IMBOLC, ALSO KNOWN AS Candlemas, is a sacred holiday that marks the halfway point between the winter solstice and the spring equinox. It is a time of transition and renewal, symbolizing the awakening of nature after the long winter months. Celebrated on February 1 or 2, Imbolc holds deep historical and cultural significance. The energy of Imbolc is one of hopefulness and new beginnings. As we emerge from winter's hibernation, we can tap into this energy by setting intentions for personal growth or embarking on creative projects. It is a time to reflect on what we wish to nurture in our lives as we move forward into brighter days.

Celebrating Imbolc

When it comes to celebrating Imbolc, there are numerous ways to honor this special day. One popular tradition is lighting candles to symbolize the growing strength of the Sun and its power to bring warmth and growth back into our lives. Another way to celebrate Imbolc is by preparing a feast using seasonal ingredients such as dairy products, grains, and winter vegetables. This not only connects us with nature but also serves as a reminder of abundance and fertility. Imbolc is also an ideal time for cleansing rituals and purification ceremonies. As we bid farewell to winter, we can release any negative energy or stagnant emotions that may be holding us back. This allows us to embrace the fresh energy of spring with open hearts and minds.

A Magical Makeover

The Venus-Neptune conjunction on February 1 at 11:33 a.m. brings forth a unique and enchanting energy that captivates the imagination. When Venus, the planet of beauty and love, aligns with Neptune, the planet of dreams and illusions, a magical atmosphere is created. This celestial event offers an opportunity to explore the realms of glamour magic and indulge in a transformative experience. Embrace your inner creativity and express yourself in ways that are both beautiful and enchanting. One option here is to have a magical makeover and pamper yourself. Take the chance to enhance your physical appearance or try out new styles that make you feel confident and glamorous. Allow yourself to be swept away by the allure of this conjunction as you embrace self-care rituals that nourish both your body and soul.

Ignite the Flame of Passion

The Full Moon in Leo on February 12 at 8:53 a.m. brings forth a powerful surge of energy that is sure to ignite the passions within us. As Leo rules the heart, this celestial event encourages us to embrace our inner desires and explore the depths of our emotions. One way to celebrate this Full Moon is to ignite the flame of passion through solo sex magic for pleasure and self-love. By embracing our own sensuality and connecting with our bodies, we can tap into a profound sense of empowerment and self-acceptance. This practice allows us to honor ourselves fully and cultivate a deep love for who we are.

This energy from the Full Moon in Leo can be carried into Valentine's Day on February 14, providing an opportunity to extend this theme of self-love and passion into our relationships with others. Take time to express gratitude for the love in your life, whether it be romantic partners, friends, or family. Show appreciation for their presence and let them know how much they mean to you.

Communication, Discipline, and Dreams

Following the fiery energy of the Full Moon in Leo, we welcome the beginning of Pisces season on February 18 bringing about a time of emotional adaptability. The Mercury-Saturn conjunction on February 25 at 7:02 a.m. signifies a merging of communication, intellect, structure, and discipline. It can bring about a heightened sense of focus, clarity, and determination in our thoughts and actions, encouraging us to be more methodical in our approach to problem-solving and decision-making. Create an action plan now before entering the dreamy territory with the New Moon in Pisces on February 27 at 7:45 p.m.

This Moon shifts us to connect with our inner selves, listen to our intuition, and explore the depths of our emotions. Pay attention to your dreams, as they may hold valuable insights or messages from your higher self or the universe. Trust your intuition when setting intentions or making decisions. Allow yourself to be guided by your inner wisdom rather than external influences. Additionally, engaging in creative activities such as painting, writing poetry, or playing music can be highly beneficial during this period. These activities allow you to express yourself authentically and tap into the artistic flow that Pisces energy often brings.

Venus and Mercury Retrogrades

A Venus retrograde begins on March 1 at 7:36 p.m. and will be in effect until April 12. This time is known to bring forth introspection and reflection on matters of the heart, in addition to affecting aesthetic appearance and money. It urges us to reevaluate our relationships, values, desires, self-expression, and finances. It can uncover hidden issues or unresolved conflicts within partnerships and prompt us to reassess our approach to love and self-worth. It is highly recommended to avoid getting married or starting a new relationship, doing any sort of drastic change to your appearance, or making any big purchases during this time.

On March 2 at 11:22 a.m., Mercury, the planet of communication and rational thinking, joins forces with Neptune, the planet of dreams, imagination, and spirituality. This brings forth an energy that transcends logical boundaries and taps into the realm of intuition and higher consciousness. During this conjunction, you may find yourself experiencing heightened creativity, enhanced psychic abilities, and a deep sense of empathy. Communication takes on a poetic quality as words become infused with emotion and symbolism. Ideas flow effortlessly as the mind becomes attuned to the subtle nuances of the unseen world.

Then, on March 11 at 6:55 p.m., Venus and Mercury form a conjunction that combines a blend of energy focusing on how we communicate with others—particularly, expressing our needs. This is only intensified more and more in the lead-up to Mercury joining Venus in a retrograde journey on March 15 at 2:46 a.m. The simultaneous occurrence of these two retrogrades amplifies their effects on our lives, creating significant shifts in communication dynamics and interpersonal connections. It is a time when miscommunications may be more prevalent, resulting in misunderstandings or conflicts in relationships. Speak from your heart now.

Full Moon in Virgo Lunar Eclipse

On March 14 at 2:55 a.m., a Full Moon in Virgo lunar eclipse will occur. To celebrate, engage in rituals that focus on grounding, purification, and organization. This is an ideal time to declutter both physically and energetically, clearing out any stagnant or negative energies that may be holding you back. Additionally, working with earth elements such as herbs like lavender or lemongrass and crystals like peridot or fluorite can enhance your rituals during this eclipse. Incorporate practices like meditation, journaling, or divination to gain clarity on your intentions and goals.

However, it is important to note that eclipses are known for their intensity and unpredictability. It is advisable to approach any spellwork or ritual with caution during this time. Focus on inner work rather than trying to manifest external changes immediately. Take the opportunity to reflect on your spiritual path, set intentions for personal growth, and release any patterns or beliefs that no longer serve you.

Tales and Traditions

Lupa

IT'S THE DEEP OF winter, and for many in the Northern Hemisphere, the promise of spring seems to be impossibly far away. Snow may blanket the ground, and temperatures often dip well below freezing, especially at night. How can anything survive this time of year?

And yet—life continues. It adapts, and even as we light candles against the darkness, many living beings make their way through woods and fields outside. These persistent beings hold the hope that as the days lengthen, better times will be ahead. After all, they carry the energy of the sun in their bodies—and so do we.

Trumpeter Swan (*Cygnus buccinator*)

The trumpeter swan is a conservation success story. In the late 1800s and early 1900s, before the passage of the Migratory Bird Treaty Act of 1918, numerous bird species were decimated by plume hunters, who would kill many birds each day simply for their feathers. Trumpeter swan feathers were prized for their softness, and soon fewer than a hundred remained—or so we thought. In the 1950s, several thousand were found in a remote area of Alaska, and some of these were transplanted to other areas of the species' historic range to help recovery efforts.

Sometimes when things seem worst, we discover untapped resources that help us survive to the future. These may be external supports, like caring people or unexpected windfalls. But we must also have internal resolve if we are to make the most of the small but growing light of hope. If we give up, then we never have the chance to see if things will indeed get better. Imagine the joy that must have been rampant when scientists discovered a seemingly lost pocket of rare swans and how that must have dispelled so much despair!

A singular boost doesn't necessarily mean all hardships will magically disappear. While trumpeter swan numbers have indeed grown in the last few decades, they still face challenges. The loss of most of North America's beavers robbed the swans of many of their nesting sites arranged on beaver dams and lodges. While beaver numbers are on the rise, they have a long way to go to full recovery. And trumpeter swans are especially vulnerable to lead poisoning from lead shotgun pellets they may eat by accident when grazing on grass.

Spring is still weeks away. But it will return, and in the meantime—like the swans—we do the best we can to flourish in spite of setbacks.

Stairstep Moss (*Hylocomium splendens*)

One of the things I love about Pacific Northwest winters is that they're so incredibly green! While some areas do get snow, especially in the mountains, even amid the white blankets there are verdant patches of plant life. Along with the conifers, rhododendrons, and salal, the forest's winter greens include many species of perennial mosses. Among my favorites is the stairstep moss, also sometimes known by the more flashy name *glittering wood-moss*.

Like other bryophytes, stairstep moss never grows especially tall, as it lacks the complex vascular system that can move water and nutrients along the stems and trunks of taller plants. But if it can't grow up, at least it can grow out! The plant's fluffy fronds split into new branches each year, and by counting how many times each one branches, you can estimate how old the moss is. Over time, this allows it to spread across larger areas of ground, as well as climb out from underneath leaves, sticks, and other debris that may have fallen on them.

Not every journey must be a long and arduous one. Nor is every solution to a problem going to be a massive, sudden shift. Sometimes, like the stairstep moss, the best thing to do is break things down into smaller components, work on one at a time, and watch your progress over time. Many of us this time of year are impatient for spring's arrival and just trying to get through each winter day in the meantime. We can't make time go any faster, nor can we bring the sun back at a swifter pace. But we can appreciate how far we've come—halfway through winter's span. And we can look even further back at our progress since earlier times, appreciating how even small steps forward got us to where we are today.

Reindeer Lichen (*Cladonia rangiferina*)

Not everyone is so focused on what's ahead, though. If you're a lichen, chances are that you're tough enough to withstand whatever the season throws at you and thrive in spite of it. Lichens are unique composite beings made of a fungus, a photosynthesizer (usually an alga or a cyanobacteria), and a yeast (itself another sort of fungus). By working together, these partners can live as a colony in conditions that are too harsh for fungi or algae alone.

The reindeer lichen got its common name because it is one of the few things that caribou in the Arctic have to eat during those harsh, cold winters. It is a slow-growing lichen, and overgrazing or habitat damage can mean decades before a colony is able to recover. And yet it does return at its own careful pace, even through summer drought and winter chill.

Not that it asks for much help in growing where it likes. It's a pioneer species that can reappear on burned or otherwise damaged land within just a couple of years. By offering food to other species and even shelter to the tiniest of its neighbors, it's able to jump-start the recovery of the land simply by being itself.

We are who we are regardless of the time of year. External conditions may change, but our strengths remain the same. During Imbolc, it's a good time to assess what constants you have in your life, especially those that enhance or improve it. Some of those may be elements of your environment and the people and other beings you share it with. But take stock of what you yourself bring to the table regardless of day or time, and be generous in your assessment. You may find that, like the reindeer lichen, you are an important part of your own ecosystem.

Feasts and Treats

Dallas Jennifer Cobb

AS THE MIDWAY POINT between solstice and equinox, Imbolc literally translates to "in the belly of the mother." It speaks to how the seeds that lay beneath the soil of the earth are dreaming of their potential, and if we are lucky, our sheep and cows are pregnant with their lambs and calves.

Here in Southern Ontario, Canada, we usually have lots of snow at Imbolc, which invites the dreaming of the coming warmth and the potential of what can grow. This is a time of quietude and introspection, of dreams and looking to the future.

Dairy of all kinds is traditional in the Imbolc feast, as are foods that honour the sun such as oranges, mandarins, and clementines. If you are vegan, consider substituting oat, almond, or coconut milk products for animal-sourced dairy.

Our Imbolc recipes include Quiche for Days, Maple Microgreens Salad, and yummy Warm Vanilla Custard for dessert. Salad is almost instant, so prepare the quiche and custard first, and whip up the salad dressing just before eating.

Quiche for Days

Since I have become an empty nester, I live alone, and that has changed my cooking. My favourite quiche recipe has become known as Quiche for Days, because it literally feeds me for several days of breakfast, lunch, and sometimes dinner.

I love the celebration of Imbolc because I can make Quiche for Days, share it at a feast, and there are no leftovers.

While quiche can be made into almost any flavour with the addition of a variety of vegetables and different cheeses and meats, my favourite is bacon, cheese, and onion. Cheese is a traditional Imbolc food, and bacon makes everything taste better. Traditionally, onions could be kept in a root cellar and be a flavourful addition to deep winter foods. Onions have antibacterial properties and are rich in antioxidants. They may support heart, bone, and gut health, and have anticancer properties.

Not just the usual yellow cooking onions, I also use diced green onions in this quiche. I love how the little bits of green are visible within the creamy white quiche, and they remind me that soon the green grass and growing plants will be visible within the snow.

Prep time: 15 minutes
Cooking time: 1 hour
Servings: 8

6–8 bacon slices, cooked and diced
1 cup shredded cheddar cheese
1 small yellow onion, diced
2 tablespoons olive oil
2 tablespoons green onion, chopped
1 frozen pie crust (You can always make your own, but I love the convenience of frozen.)
5 large eggs
½ cup cream (You can use whole milk or skim, but cream really adds to the flavour and texture of the quiche.)

¾ teaspoon sea salt

¼ teaspoon ground black pepper

Preheat the oven to 375°F.

Partially prebake the frozen pie crust by putting it in the oven for 5 minutes. Experience has taught me that the easiest thing to do is to sit it on a baking sheet. It stays there through the pre-baking, extraction, and filling, and makes it really easy to slide the full pie crust back into the oven after.

After prebaking, remove the pie crust from the oven and use a fork to burst any bubbles formed in the pastry. Return it to the oven and bake until it is golden brown (about 10 more minutes). While the pastry is prebaking, sauté the onion in olive oil until translucent.

Remove the pie crust from oven and turn the temperature down to 350°F.

In a big bowl, whisk together the eggs, cream, salt, and pepper. In the pie pastry, spread the sautéed onions in the bottom, crumble bacon on top, and cover with shredded cheese.

Slowly pour the egg mixture over top, and sprinkle green onions onto it. Transfer it to the oven.

Bake for 45 minutes, until the eggs appear uniformly set. Then remove quiche from the oven and let it rest for 5 minutes. Plate and serve with Maple Microgreens Salad.

Maple Microgreens Salad

Microgreens can be grown quickly and easily at home. I discovered that I like them more than sprouts, and I have found that I like the bigger seeds like speckled peas and sunflowers, because they produce bigger microgreens. The phytonutrients in microgreens are highly nourishing and just what our body needs as we begin to internally prepare for the end of winter. Dense nutrients include rich antioxidants, plus microgreens add color and texture to the salad, providing a nice crunch.

Microgreens are widely available throughout grocery stores in North America, but consider learning how to grow your own.

If you really want to bump up the crunch and nutrition of this salad, you could add chopped walnuts which pair well with the maple flavour.

Prep time: 5 minutes

Servings: 8

1 cup salad greens (per person)

¼ cup microgreens (per person)

3 tablespoons balsamic vinegar

4 tablespoons olive oil

2 tablespoons water

2 tablespoons maple syrup

1 tablespoon grainy mustard

Salt and pepper to taste

Optional: 4 tablespoons chopped walnuts (sprinkled on top of the salad when you plate it)

Put the balsamic vinegar, olive oil, water, maple syrup, grainy mustard, salt, and pepper in a medium-sized jar. Shake well, until emulsified. (You can blend this dressing too, if you are so inclined, but the shaken version works well. And whatever isn't used goes into the fridge in its jar.)

When you are ready to plate the quiche, dress each plate with a handful of washed and dried salad greens and a big pinch of microgreens. Each person can add salad dressing to taste. And sprinkle on some chopped walnuts, also to taste. (Always remember to check for nut allergies!)

Warm Vanilla Custard

Imbolc is traditionally a time when the ewe's milk comes in to feed the lambs. Desserts like custard, made from milk were traditionally enjoyed. You can purchase custard powder, which makes the process of whipping up a custard very quick and easy, but here is the traditional recipe that my British grandmother used to make.

Prep time: 10 minutes
Cooking time: 15 minutes
Servings: 8

1⅔ cups whole milk
½ cup sugar, divided
4 large egg yolks
3 tablespoons cornstarch
2 teaspoons vanilla extract (Always buy the best vanilla you can
    afford.)
2 tablespoons soft, unsalted butter

In a large pot, combine the milk and about half of the sugar. Bring the mix to a boil, stirring constantly so it cannot burn. Once it is bubbling, reduce the heat to medium, simmering the mixture.

In a separate bowl, whisk the egg yolks. And in another bowl, combine the rest of the sugar and cornstarch and mix well.

Add the wet mix (egg yolks) to the dry mix (sugar and cornstarch) and mix it all together. Slowly add the simmering milk mixture to the egg yolk, sugar, and cornstarch mixture, pouring in one cup of the warm milk and mixing, then another, and eventually mixing all of the milk mixture into all of the egg mixture.

Put these back on low heat and stir constantly. It will thicken and make a gooey custard in 3–5 minutes. You can also use a candy thermometer and look for a temperature of 185°F, which sets custard. Remove the pot from the heat and add the butter and vanilla. Stir until completely mixed.

Custard can be eaten warm, cool, or cold, on its own or with fruit, as a sauce over cake or scones, and even as a dip. If you want cool custard, cover it and allow it to slowly cool to room temperature.

Reference

Williams, Jo. "Top 5 Health Benefits of Onions." BBC Good Food. January 10, 2023. https://www.bbcgoodfood.com/howto/guide/ingredient-focus-onions.

Crafty Crafts

Elizabeth Barrette

TOWARD THE BEGINNING OF February, winter is at its deepest cold and the nights are still dark. Yet it holds a spark of hope for spring because the days are visibly beginning to lengthen. Ewes and does give birth, freshening with new milk. Tiny lambs and kids romp around the barn. Though the trees remain bare, sap begins to quicken, and the maple sugar season approaches. Decorations for this holiday capture both aspects, the fading winter and the approaching spring. Candles and fire, sheep and goats are all popular.

Nonflammable Candles

Many rituals call for candles as a focus. However, not everyone lives where they can burn candles, and some people may not want to. Symbolism provides similar effects without live flames. Nonflammable candles may be made in various ways for ritual use.

Materials
Wooden dowels
Craft paints
Craft glue or hot glue
Optional: LED "candle lights," power drill, string or yarn for wicking, yellow and orange fabric for "flames"

Cost: $10–$15

Time spent: 15–20 minutes per candle

Design Concepts

Wooden dowels make the best symbolic candlesticks. They're made of natural material and come in a wide range of styles. They're affordable and easily found at craft or hobby shops. Paint them any color you like. You can drill into the top to hold a "candle light" LED. If a ritual calls for writing or carving on a candle, you can do that too.

Craft paints come in a variety of styles suited for wood. You can use acrylic or oil paints. If you prefer natural choices, egg paint or milk paint can be brought to a waxy sheen with wood wax or finishing oil. Traditional colors for Imbolc include the fire colors of red, orange, and yellow; you can throw in flame-blue for contrast.

LED "candle lights" most often resemble tealights. They come with steady or flickering bulbs.

String and fabric can make a "burning" wick. Glossy or transparent fabrics like silk or lamé make excellent symbolic flames. It's okay if they fray a bit.

Assembly

If using LED "candle lights," then you need to decide whether you want the light sitting on top of the candlestick or sunk inside it. To put it on top, use a dowel the same diameter as the "candle light" and simply glue the base of the "candle light" to the top of the dowel. Then paint the dowel and sides of the "candle light" together. To sink it inside, you need a dowel about ¼ inch wider and a drill bit just slightly wider than the "candle light." Drill a shallow well in the top of the dowel, insert the "candle light," then paint.

For a cloth flame, first glue on a 1-inch wick of string. Paint the dowel and just the base of the wick. Cut several teardrops of hot-colored fabric and glue them around the wick to look like flames.

Fit the base of the "candle" into a suitable candleholder to make it look even more realistic.

Upcycled Sweater Sheep

Imbolc rituals often focus on sheep and their milk. This makes it useful to have craft sheep for decorating the altar. You can easily make a whole flock of sheep by upcycling one old woolen sweater.

Materials

One old sweater (preferably wool or wool blend)

Assorted oval beads (preferably wood, bone, or horn)

Optional: craft paint, googly eyes, craft glue, tapestry needle, and
button thread

Cost: $5–$10

Time spent: 1 hour or more for whole sweater

Design Ideas

This craft starts with an old sweater. Wool or wool blends will hold the crimps best, though if you're allergic, you can choose a different fiber. You need a sweater where the yarn is not felted so that it can unravel. Unlike other yarn crafts, though, you don't need it to come apart in big pieces, so you can use a sweater with side seams—in which case, one or two of those short lengths will make a good sheep. Natural-colored yarn will make realistic sheep, but you can also use dyed yarn to match your ritual colors.

For each sheep you need one short, thick oval bead and four longer, thinner ones. Natural materials will work better with natural fibers, but you can use plastic instead. Sheep can be solid-colored or have head and legs in a contrasting color (like a white sheep with a black face).

You can give your sheep details if you wish. Faces can be painted on. You could also glue on googly eyes.

Assembly

If you want to detail the sheep heads, paint faces or glue googly eyes on the thick oval beads. You can also paint hooves on the long, thin beads. Let these dry while working on the next steps.

Break down the sweater. Remove the neck and cuffs so you have access to the main body. Remove the sleeves. If the sweater has seams, undo them. These may be sewn and need careful cutting or may be knitted together, which you can just unravel. Then unravel the yarn from the main body. It will make a curly mass called "yarn ramen" to use as-is for this craft. If it has multiple colors, you probably want to separate those.

For each sheep, begin by cutting off a slice of sleeve about two fingers wide. Fold that down to a rectangle and wrap some yarn snugly around it to make a firm oval. This will become the core of your sheep.

Next, gather up a good handful of yarn ramen to make the woolly coat. Carefully pack it around the core so it looks fluffy;

don't press it so tight that the crimps flatten out. You can tack it in place with needle and thread or use dabs of glue. Make sure the coat is well attached to the core, so you have a fluffy, oval sheep body.

Press the head bead through the coat to the core and attach it with thread or glue, thus defining the "top front" of the sheep. Press the leg beads to what is now the "underside" of the sheep and attach them the same way. Adjust them so the sheep stands up securely.

Variations: If you want some "lying down" sheep, then you can make those without legs. To make lambs, just use half a sleeve loop, less yarn ramen, and smaller beads for the head and legs; remember that lambs have extra-long legs in proportion to their bodies.

Imbolc and Tasseomancy

Charlie Rainbow Wolf

IMBOLC IS WHEN THE first flowers are starting to break through the still-frosty ground and the signs of spring start to emerge. There's still nothing quite as soothing as a hot cuppa on a cold morning or to share "tea and sympathy" with a friend. This is where my introduction to tea leaf reading started: my life was in shambles, and a neighbor lady read my tea leaves.

Brewing the Tea

There are a few rules that have to be met for tasseomancy to be done properly. First, no tea bags! This has to be done with proper leaf tea so the patterns and images can be left on the teacup. Secondly, no mugs! The straight walls of a mug do not lend themselves to catching tea leaves. Use a cup and saucer.

Brew the tea in a pot, one that has no strainer holes. The leaves must flow from the pot to the cup as the tea is poured so that there is something to read once the tea has been consumed. While the tea is brewing, think of the question or the issue at hand. It is best to use tea leaves that are not so large they will clump and not so small that they will be insignificant. I like to use floral or herbal teas that echo the situation, but I've read with rooibos or even Tetley tea before!

Once the tea has brewed, pour it into the cup without a strainer. This will ensure that there are enough leaves to read once the cup is empty. Drink the tea, but leave just a bit of liquid in the bottom of the cup. This gives something for the leaves to swirl in—besides, it's not pleasant to take a drink of tea and get a mouthful of dregs!

The tea can also be brewed right into the cup. Put a pinch of loose tea in the cup and add boiling water. Let it brew, drink the tea, and leave just a small amount of liquid in the bottom, as above.

Reading the Leaves

Give the teacup with the leaves in the bottom of it a good swirl to get them moving up the side, then invert the cup on the saucer. The liquid and some of the tea leaves will fall from the cup, but the saucer will catch them and it (usually) won't make a mess. Carefully lift the cup from the saucer. Try not to disturb the leaves as they lie on the sides of the cup. These are the leaves to be read.

The handle represents the person being read. Anything close to the handle on the right side of the cup indicates things coming toward the querent. Anything to the left of the handle reveals things moving away from them.

The cup is divided into three sections. Anything close to the rim of the cup is here and now. Anything down the sides of the cup is in the near future. Anything toward the bottom of the cup is a distant future. The closer it is to the handle, the more importance it takes on for the person being read.

The Symbols

- Airplane: Journey, a rise in status
- Anchor: Stability—the closer to the bottom, the more intense it becomes
- Axe: Challenges—the closer to the bottom, the bigger the obstacle

- Ball: Uncertain outcome
- Bell: Spiritual growth
- Bird: Good news
- Broken circle or wheel: Disruption
- Butterfly: Beginnings toward the top, endings if closer to the bottom
- Cat's head: Deception, usually from someone thought to be a friend
- Chain: Engagement or wedding
- Chair: Someone coming, a guest—the closer to the top, the sooner they arrive
- Closed circle or wheel: Completion
- Closed umbrella: Something being hidden
- Cross: Protection, faith
- Crow: Evolution, death, and renewal
- Cup: Ancestors
- Dog: Loyal friend
- Duck: Organization needed
- Egg: Fertility, something new
- Fence: Temporary setbacks
- Fish: Good luck
- Flame: Passion
- Gate: Opportunity
- Gun: Fear or anger
- Hammer: Hard work
- Hat: Improvement
- Handbag: Money—toward the top indicates gain, toward the bottom points to loss
- Heart: Love, trust, not necessarily romance
- Horseshoe: Upright is good luck, downward the luck is running out
- House: Stability
- Kite: Something wished for is coming true
- Knife: Caution needed

- Ladder: Progress—if sideways, progress is stagnant
- Leaf: New beginnings
- Mushroom: Moving to a new home
- Nail: Prejudice
- Octopus: Hazard
- Open umbrella: New information coming
- Palm tree: Achievement
- Pig: Overindulgence
- Question mark: Confusion
- Saw: Conflict
- Scale: If balanced then things are fair, if unbalanced then they are not
- Scissors: Separation
- Shell: Emotional fulfillment
- Ship: Friendly visit
- Shoe: Movement needed
- Snake: Transmutation
- Spider: Wisdom, fate
- Star: Hope, a light at the end of the tunnel
- Straight line: Clear path ahead
- Sun: Brighter days ahead
- Sword: Arguments
- Table: Social functions
- Tent: The truth is being hidden
- Tree: Improvements
- Triangle: Love triangle
- Turtle: Movement is slow but steady
- Wavy line: Uncertain path ahead
- Wing or wings: Messages

Other Ways of Reading Tea Leaves

It's also possible to read coffee grounds! The method is slightly different, but the symbols are the same. A coffee reading requires finely ground coffee, a small metal pan, and an espresso cup and saucer. Fill the pan with water and bring it to a boil. Remove from the heat and add a spoonful of coffee grounds. Return to the heat, and boil again. Watch it carefully, and when it comes back to boiling, remove it from the heat before it boils over. Immediately pour it into the espresso cups.

Drink the coffee slowly, from one side of the cup only. Leave just a sip in the bottom of the cup. Swirl it around and empty it onto the saucer, same as with tea leaves. The main difference is the coffee cup is left inverted on the saucer for at least 5 minutes to give the grounds a chance to slide down the sides of the cup and make their patterns.

There are cups and saucers sold with guidelines on them specifically for the purpose of tasseomancy, available from New Age shops and online retailers. If you like the idea of reading tea leaves but you don't like tea (or coffee), there are card sets that mimic tasseomancy. Take a look at Tea Leaf Fortune Cards by Rae Hepburn (US Games Systems, 2011). This is a boxed set of two hundred cards and an illustrated paperback book. The cards are round like the teacup, and each card has a lovely nostalgic image on it.

Imbolc Ritual

Ariana Serpentine

FOR THIS RITE, YOU are going to be inviting Brighid into your home and life to bring her blessings. You'll want to choose a day near Imbolc, preferably Imbolc eve. Allow yourself some wiggle room for mundane entanglements but also try and stay as close to the actual date as possible.

Brighid's Invitation

The first step is cleaning. Now, a thorough, traditional, floor-to-ceiling spring cleaning would be completely appropriate and even a good thing! But not everyone has the time in their busy schedule, as well as the support needed for a full house cleaning. However, if you live with other people, this might be a good time to coordinate with them to get the house ready. Even if your roommates or family aren't practitioners, they will appreciate the results of this preparation. If you can't get any help with it, at least doing some tidying of common areas and your own room is sufficient. Chase out the dust and shadows, wipe up the old stains, and wash your coffee mugs; even a little bit of work in this direction helps to clean and prepare your home and allows for a better flow of energy and blessings.

After the physical part of the cleansing, you can take a bowl of water and ask Brighid to bless it and make it sacred. You could mix in a few drops of scented oils (rosemary is especially appropriate here) or put fragrant flower petals or herbs in it. Hold it over a candle and say something like,

Holy Brighid, I call on you. Please bless this water and make it holy. Let it banish all harmful energies, entities, and wills.

Then you can take the water and sprinkle it around your house using a small branch of pine, juniper, hawthorn, or another plant that you have a sacred connection to. Alternately, you can put it in a misting bottle and spritz the air with it.

Now that your space has been cleansed and blessed, it's time to collect the materials that you will need for the ritual. The most basic requirements are a cloth and a candle. However, you can expand on this if you have appropriate materials. If you have a doll you can use as a Brideog, you can incorporate that, especially if you have a bed that fits it. If you would like her to bless a Brighid's mantle for you, find a cloth, preferably white, that you can use for that purpose. Undecorated linen napkins are a favorite of mine for ritual purposes and are easily available online. You can also take a small branch of wood and strip the bark off if you want to incorporate the slat Brighid, the Brighid's wand. Collect ritual offerings if you can as well: cream or milk, butter, and honey are all appropriate. Make sure all of the materials have been physically cleaned, and bless and spiritually cleanse them with the sacred water that you made as well.

Light the candle. Say,

Blessings to the land and to the pure and holy spirits of the land. Blessings to the lands from which Brighid comes.

Blessings to the Ancestors, to those who came before. Blessings to the Ancestors who have brought Brighid to us.

I call on Brighid, the Exalted One, in all her names and forms. I call on Brighid of the healers. I call on Brighid of the poets. I call on Brighid of the smiths.

It is Imbolc, your festival, your sacred day. My home has been prepared for you. I ask you to come and visit it.

At this point, take the Brideog and the slat Brighid if you have them, and go to the door of your house or your room if you're in a roommate situation with nonparticipating people. Open the door and say,

I invite you into my home, Brighid, on this, your holy day. Be welcome in my hearth. Be welcome in my home. Be welcome in my life. Come and cleanse me of the old year and the long winter and bring your many blessings to my home for this year.

Close the door, and if you have the Brideog, carry it back to the shrine. At this point, you can place it in the bed with the slat Brighid next to it. If you have brought offerings, you can hold them up to the Brideog or over the candle and say,

Oh, Brighid, I give you this gift of hospitality. Please enjoy this [your offering]. May it please you and bring you joy.

Put the offering back down. Sit down in front of the shrine. Now we're going to begin the meditative portion of the ritual.

It starts with a chant. The chant is from the Morrigan's peace prophecy, an old Irish poem. The Morrigan has a familial connection to Brighid, being the wife of the Dagda in Irish myth (though not necessarily Brighid's mother). This chant can be used to cleanse and bless the area as well and bring a person into a meditative trance. I learned this from the Coru Cathubodua, a polytheist Morrigan priesthood based out of the Bay Area in California. I've used this many times before in ritual to great effect.

The lines are,

Peace up to heaven.
Heaven down to earth.

In Irish it is,

Sith co nem.
Nem co doman.

(Pronounced "seethe coh nev, nev coh doven")

Relax your body, breathing deeply while doing so. Let your body relax part by part from your feet up to your head. Let your eyelids droop, or close them altogether, all while keeping your eyes facing toward the candle flame. Consciously relax your muscles, trying to release tension that you find on your exhale. After a minute or two of deep breathing, begin the chant.

Chant and continue to consciously relax your body as you do so. You can focus on the sound of the chant or the way that it makes you move and the vibrations in your flesh and bones. You may find yourself gently rocking or swaying; this is fine as long as you aren't getting agitated or tensing up. Continue the chant for at least a few minutes, but follow your own inclinations; if you find it peaceful and want to do it longer, it may be helpful.

When the chant ends, let your eyes close completely if they haven't already. Sit in the warm darkness, breathe, and simply be. This may be a time when you find connection or communion with Brighid or an associated spirit. It may also be simply a time to be at rest in the gentle darkness, like a seed beneath the earth preparing to begin its new life.

Continue to sit with your eyes closed and dream. Dream of new things beginning. Dream of the days, months, and year to come. Dream of new things beginning: new ideas, new plans, new creations. Pay attention to the thoughts that come to mind; this is a time for *awen*, for inspiration—inspiration for all the new and good things that you can bring into your life.

After a few minutes, you will reach a natural stopping point. Open your eyes slowly, taking in the candle's light and your surroundings.

Now is the time to ask Brighid for specific blessings over the coming year. Remember, Brighid has her specialties, but people have prayed to her for all sorts of things. At Imbolc, blessings of healing, prosperity, fertility, creativity, abundance, and safety of home, family, pets, and animals are all especially appropriate. Address her while facing the Brideog (if you have one) or the candle, and ask her for what you need over the coming year. If you want something specific or formal to say, you can use this,

Brighid, Exalted One, daughter of the Dagda, Brighid of the healers, Brighid of the poets, Brighid of the smiths, I ask you to bless [myself, my family, my pets, my animals, and my home] over this coming year. Grant us abundance and prosperity, creativity and good opportunities, and keep us safe from danger and harm. Watch over us and this home from now till you visit again. Thank you, Brighid.

If you have a brat Brighid, you can now ask for her blessings on it. Lay out the Brighid's mantle near the Brideog and say,

Brighid, mighty healer, bless this brat Brighid with your power of healing. Let it alleviate illness, sickness, and harm when worn. I leave it out here tonight for you to bless it. Thank you, Brighid.

Now, you are done with the rite. Thank Brighid, the ancestors, and the land, then go about the rest of your evening. The next day, you can place the Brideog somewhere of prominence or on an altar and drape the brat Brighid over its shoulders when it is not in use.

Brighid's blessings on you, and may your coming year be a prosperous, abundant, safe, and healthy one.

References

Gray, Elizabeth A., trans. *Cath Maige Tuired: The Second Battle of Mag Tuired*. CELT. Revised 2009. https://celt.ucc.ie/published /G300010.html.

———. *Cath Maige Tuired: The Second Battle of Mag Tuired*. Sacred Texts. N.d. https://sacred-texts.com/neu/cmt/cmteng.htm.

Notes

Ostara

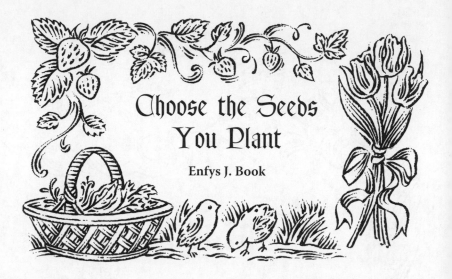

Choose the Seeds You Plant

Enfys J. Book

FOR ALL OF MY adult life, I have wanted a garden. When I was a kid, my family had a big yard with raspberry bushes, a rose garden, a big vegetable garden, apple trees, a strawberry patch, and a flower garden that, as I got older, I was allowed to choose seeds for, plant, and tend.

I remember the fresh, summery smell of the marigolds and daisies I planted and grew. I remember being sent out into the yard with a repurposed Cool Whip container and filling it up with raspberries so deep red they were almost purple (and about half of what I picked went directly into my mouth). I remember the juicy, sweet tomatoes we grew and how they tasted so much better than the ones we bought at the grocery store. Everything about growing and harvesting our own fruits and vegetables was absolutely intoxicating to me.

When I was twelve, my family and I moved out of that house with the big yard and into an apartment, and from that point forward, I spent the next thirty years living in multifamily dwellings with no outdoor space for gardens.

But recently, my partner and my forty-two-year-old self bought a house with a half acre of land, so I finally have space to grow my own fruits and vegetables. And wow did I dive into gardening wholeheartedly my first year here! My partner and I planted four apple trees, four raspberry bushes, two blueberry bushes, several ornamental perennials, lots of vegetables, sunflowers, tulips, daffodils, and crocuses, plus a vertical planter full of herbs. I pumped my friends for advice on permaculture and growing in the Maryland climate, and I did a sun study of my property to find the most ideal places to plant things. My partner watched a ton of YouTube instructional videos on gardening and cultivating fruit trees. My friend taught me how to make hugelkultur-style beds, and my partner and I built two raised beds in that style.

And as I'm writing this, I'm midway through the growing season for my first attempts at gardening, and about half of what I've planted has died, and none of the vegetables I've planted have produced anything edible that hasn't been immediately devoured by the local wildlife, despite my best efforts using organic deterrents.

Though this is very common for first-time gardeners and people gardening in a new place for the first time, I think I made the mistake of planting way too many different things rather than focusing on a few I could tend more carefully. I was so excited to finally have the opportunity to garden, and I wanted to grow *all the things*, all at once. I had a long list of things I wanted to grow, and I planted almost all of them. As a result, I exceeded my bandwidth for being able to give each plant the attention and consideration it deserved, didn't take the time to listen to what the land wanted, and didn't take the opportunity to learn to grow specific things well. And now I have a lot of dead and stunted plants as well as a lot of wasted time, money, and effort as a result.

I'd love to say this is an isolated incident in my life, but to be honest, this same pattern is also showing up in the form of me taking on way too many commitments. I run a coven. I write books. I host a podcast. Until very recently, I was in a band that rehearsed and performed together regularly for ten years. I have a partner and a full-time day job. I have two cats in my care. And with the new house, there are all sorts of maintenance and caretaking responsibilities that I didn't have to worry about during all my years living in apartments, and my partner and I are trying to figure out how best to fit all of that into our lives.

As I'm writing this, everything has become pretty overwhelming. I've spent this year madly trying to keep up with it all and finding that I have to keep pushing projects back later and later in the year, no matter how much I focus and crunch through them. (Heck, I'm writing this piece one week before the deadline, despite having had the contract for months. Life has been *a lot*.)

When I take on too much, I stymie my growth opportunities. I get so laser-focused on knocking out my to-do list that I don't take enough time for friends, my partner, much-needed rest, anything new that crops up, or doing my various projects to the best of my ability. I spend so much time *doing* that I forget the importance of *listening*.

So how does all this tie back into Ostara?

Consider Your Seeds

If we look at the Wheel of the Year from a personal-development perspective, Ostara is the time when we can begin pushing forward as our energy returns with the strengthening sun. It's a prime time to set goals and take the first steps toward achieving them. The contemplative, restful time of the dark half of the year is ending, and with the spring comes hope and the promise of new growth and new opportunities.

Most of us acknowledge the importance of setting goals and creating things, but how much effort do you spend considering if you're setting the right goals and creating the right things at the right time? I'm not saying you should put a ton of pressure on yourself to set the best goals or create something perfect, but I do want you to consider what the best use of your precious and limited time is.

We can't do all the things we want to do. We are not Barbie: No human can simultaneously be a doctor, an astronaut, a vet, and a supermodel. We have to choose, and in so doing, it's just as important to choose the optimal things as it is to *not* choose the less-optimal things. By choosing to do one or a few things right now, you are choosing not to do other things right now. You can circle back to those other things at another time, of course, but the point is that you need a point of focus to pour your heart into, and you have to be okay with not pouring your heart into absolutely everything.

Those who know me personally may laugh at me giving this advice. They know I'm always madly juggling way too much and chasing too many passions! But until this year, I felt like I mostly had the juggling routine working. I have always ruthlessly prioritized my passions and responsibilities, and I have said no to tons of stuff to keep up with all the things that are important to me. But even with years of experience doing this, as I look out my window today at my garden full of dead or stunted plants, and then at my calendar yelling my ever-approaching deadlines at me, I realize that I simply have too many competing priorities. And, frankly, that's a bit scary for me. I don't like feeling overwhelmed and out of control. That's not how I roll.

I'm choosing to look at this as a learning opportunity, though. Over this past year, I have learned to be more comfortable with the fact that not everything I do will be done to perfection, or even to my own satisfaction. For example, on particularly chaotic days, I've made some embarrassing mistakes at my day job, I have misspoken and inadvertently started a fight with my partner, and I've forgotten to do things I promised I would. And, though those mistakes bring me a bit of shame, on the balance, all of that is okay.

None of us can be perfect at all the things, all the time. What we need to do is prioritize which things we want to put our best effort into most of the time and accept that we won't be 100 percent perfect. (I'm looking at you, Virgos and fellow gifted kids.) On the flip side of this, it's also important to make sure you don't lean so hard into the "I'm not perfect" mindset that you end up constantly dodging accountability and shifting burdens to those who didn't sign up for them. (I'm looking at you, fellow Sagittarians.)

Breathe and Allow Your Seeds to Reveal Themselves

One way I am learning how to make better priorities is by allowing wisdom to arise rather than forcing it. If you work with the concept of a multi-part self, the ego (the middle self, the conscious mind) is only one part of self, and it is not superior to any of the other parts. Good discernment includes conscious, logical decision-making, of course. But it also includes tapping into the wisdom of your higher self (the spark of you that is eternal and connected to all of the cosmos) and the needs of your lower self (that part of you concerned with your survival and meeting immediate needs).

Allowing wisdom to arise from someplace other than my own head does not come naturally to me, though. As someone who owned a Franklin Covey planner at age fourteen (yes, really, and I was mega-stoked about it and carried it absolutely everywhere for years), it's not a stretch to say I can be a bit of a control freak. I like to be in charge and choose what I need to focus on, and I don't always make the best choices because I get so far up in my own, er, head that I lose the larger picture of what is needed in a given situation. When I get too deep in my own thoughts, I disconnect from the rest of the universe and from my higher and lower selves. I become so certain that my own mental logic has shown me the truth that I stop listening to see if I may be wrong or if there's more information to consider.

What I'm trying to practice more of in my life right now is pausing to breathe. Especially when things are at their most hectic, it's better if I step back, breathe for a minute, and allow my next step to arise, rather than try to force it.

As I write this, I've just had an unusually hectic week at my day job, where I've barely had time to go to the bathroom, much less take a lunch break. I've had to-dos upon to-dos, and thankfully I was able to complete it all, though it did involve working longer hours than I usually do. Part of how I've managed to get through it was by taking periodic, intentional pauses to quiet my mind and breathe for a minute, even amid all the hecticness. I'd breathe deeply, let it out slowly, and ask myself, "What is the best next thing to do? What am I missing?" and in a moment, the answer would come to me. Though it was an intense week, I was able to make it through without a breakdown, causing any inadvertent fires, or making any huge mistakes, because I allowed myself those small moments of breathing and quieting my mind.

When I think about my garden, this is a classic case-in-point where I should've spent more time quietly listening to my other parts of self and the land around me as I determined what to plant and where, rather than barrel in with my own agenda that was purely based on what *I* wanted and thought needed to be done.

Next year, I'm going to do a lot more meditating, a lot more listening, and a lot more honest assessment of what I have time and bandwidth to care for before I choose my seeds. As you celebrate Ostara this year, I encourage you to learn from my mistakes and approach this time from a place of quiet contemplation, listening, and honest assessment of your time and other priorities. Choose carefully the seeds you decide to plant, and make sure you have the time and space to give them what they need so that they can flourish...and so can you.

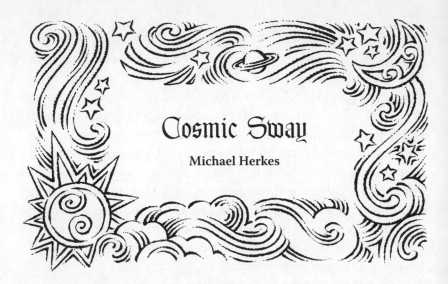

Cosmic Sway

Michael Herkes

OSTARA, CELEBRATED ON MARCH 20, marks the arrival of spring and the vernal equinox. This ancient festival holds deep historical and energetic significance, making it a joyous occasion for many. Rooted in Pagan traditions, Ostara is a celebration of rebirth and renewal. It symbolizes the awakening of nature after the long winter months. As the vernal equinox occurs, day and night are in perfect balance, representing harmony and equilibrium.

Not only does this mark the first day of spring, but it also welcomes Aries season with open arms, as it aligns perfectly with the essence of this astrological sign. Just as nature begins to awaken from its winter slumber during Ostara, Aries brings forth a surge of energy that propels us forward into action. The combination of these two energies creates a potent force that encourages us to embrace change and embark on new endeavors.

Ostara's celebration of rebirth and renewal harmonizes with Aries's dynamic spirit to create an atmosphere ripe with possibility. It is a time when we can tap into our inner strength and courageously pursue our passions. As we welcome both Ostara's arrival and embrace Aries's influence, we are reminded that this season serves as an invitation for personal growth, transformation, and embracing new beginnings.

Celebrating Ostara

To celebrate Ostara, there are many meaningful rituals and activities one can partake in. One popular tradition is creating an altar adorned with fresh flowers, colorful eggs, seeds, or any other symbols of nature you prefer. This serves as a focal point for reflection and gratitude for the abundance that spring brings. Another way to celebrate Ostara is by participating in egg decorating. The egg has long been seen as a powerful symbol of rebirth and fertility. By painting or dyeing eggs with vibrant colors or intricate patterns, we can connect with this symbolism while also engaging in creative expression. Taking walks in nature during this time can be especially rewarding. Observing the blossoming flowers, budding trees, and chirping birds allows us to connect deeply with the energy of growth and rejuvenation that Ostara embodies. Additionally, hosting gatherings or feasts with loved ones can be an enjoyable way to celebrate Ostara. Sharing seasonal dishes made from fresh ingredients not only nourishes our bodies but also strengthens our connection to nature's cycles.

Big Aries Energy

On March 23, Venus is cazimi in Aries, and this occurs during the Venus retrograde. This is an intensely powerful time when the energy of the Sun illuminates the power of Venus, conjuring a powerful day to work on any magic that inspires love, beauty, abundance, passion, and social status.

Then on March 29 at 6:58 a.m., we will experience a New Moon in Aries solar eclipse. Just weeks after the Full Moon in Virgo lunar eclipse, now is a time to harness the fiery energy of Aries by performing rituals that focus on courage, passion, and self-empowerment. This could include lighting red candles, using crystals such as carnelian or garnet, or engaging in visualization exercises that ignite your inner fire.

While eclipses can indeed be chaotic and unpredictable, they also offer a unique opportunity for transformation. It is advisable to approach this time with caution and mindfulness. Use the eclipse energy to release any negative patterns or limiting beliefs that no longer serve you so that you can spring ahead into Aries season with a newfound sense of freshness.

Venusian Balance

April 12 is full of Venusian energy. It not only marks the final day of Venus retrograde, but also welcomes the Full Moon in Libra at 8:22 p.m. As Libra is ruled by Venus, this celestial event presents an opportune time to crucially take stock of the lessons learned throughout the Venus retrograde period. For the past weeks, we have been examining and reevaluating our relationships, self-expression, and what holds value within our lives. Now it is time to instill a renewed sense of clarity and balance. The Full Moon in Libra urges us to seek harmony and fairness while addressing any imbalances that may have arisen during the retrograde phase. By acknowledging and addressing these issues, we can foster healthier connections and strengthen emotional bonds.

Self-expression also comes into focus now and invites us to explore how we communicate our thoughts, feelings, and desires to others through our identity. This is an ideal time to find ways to express ourselves authentically while maintaining diplomacy and tact in our interactions.

This energy magnifies with the Mercury-Neptune conjunction five days later on April 17 at 12:11 a.m. This event heightens intuition, creative inspiration, and communication abilities. Boundaries between reality and fantasy become blurred, allowing for innovative ideas to flow effortlessly. During this conjunction, you may find yourself drawn to artistic pursuits, such as writing, painting, or music. This Venusian energy is maximized with the start of Taurus season on April 19—bringing about a time to engage the senses in the blossoming natural world.

April 24 brings another Venus-Saturn conjunction. The combined energies of Venus and Saturn merging can bring about a sense of seriousness when it comes to matters of the heart or creative endeavors. It encourages us to take a realistic approach toward relationships or artistic pursuits by assessing their long-term potential. This conjunction invites us to evaluate our commitments carefully while also fostering growth through patience and dedication.

A New Moon in Taurus on April 27 at 3:31 p.m. signifies new beginnings, stability, and grounding. Taurus is an earth sign known for its practicality, determination, and appreciation for beauty. During this time, we are encouraged to set intentions related to abundance, financial stability, self-worth, and sensual pleasures. It is a wonderful opportunity to focus on cultivating a sense of security and harmony in our lives. To celebrate this Moon, engage in activities that align with its energy. Consider spending time outdoors surrounded by nature's beauty or indulging your senses with comforting foods or luxurious self-care rituals. Take this opportunity to reflect on your values and set clear intentions for what you wish to manifest during this lunar cycle.

During this time period encompassing both the New Moon in Taurus and the Venus-Saturn conjunction, we have an opportunity to work with these energies synergistically. By aligning our intentions around abundance with practicality and commitment, we can lay a solid foundation for our desires to manifest. It is a time to reflect on our values, nurture our relationships, and pursue creative endeavors with dedication and a long-term vision in mind.

Tales and Traditions

Lupa

Spring has arrived, and although the land may not be fully awakened, it's a time of increased activity in the world of nature. The first buds will soon be apparent on trees and other plants, and the first young animals are being born. Some fungi are even sprouting mushrooms to spread spores on chilly mornings and warming afternoons.

It is not always an easy time, though. For many there is still little to eat compared to the abundance of summer and fall. Farmers may sow seeds, but it will be months before they come to fruition. This is a time to balance out waning reserves while rejoicing in the potential for new growth and future security.

Coyote (*Canis latrans*)

I love coyotes, and I also feel bad for them. They're often overlooked in favor of their larger cousins, the wolves, and are not viewed in such a noble light. Yet in areas where they have strengthened their numbers in the wake of wolves' extirpation, they end up receiving the same hatred and violence that was once reserved for those larger predators. It's not uncommon to see trucks and other vehicles in backwoods areas with bumper stickers sporting the saying

"Smoke [kill] a pack a day," and many of these people would happily shoot a coyote as quickly as a wolf.

In spite of this ongoing persecution, coyotes thrive in both rural and urban areas. Whether they're pouncing on mice and rabbits in a mountain meadow, or hunting rats in city alleyways, these resourceful, clever canids are expanding their territory with each year. No longer subject to competition from wolves, they have taken over their relatives' niches and help to keep prey animal populations in check wherever they go.

Part of the coyote's success is its ability to eat just about anything. Far from being an obligate carnivore, coyotes can consume a wide variety of both animal and plant foods. In the middle of summer, for example, coyote scat can reveal a diet almost exclusively made of berries. And while they may not be able to climb the way a raccoon can, they're able to work their way into surprising places to make the most of opportunities for a meal. An urban coyote may supplement its diet of rats and house mice with pet food and garbage, and coyotes in any setting will prey on free-roaming cats (so it's best to keep your kitties safely indoors!).

Their resourcefulness does not save coyotes from being endlessly hunted, and they still draw a level of hatred that other predatory animals do not. Yet they manage to balance misfortune with luck and skill, and this spring will see many new litters of coyotes ready to learn how to make the most of a mixed bag.

Skunk Cabbage (Western *Lysichiton americanus* and Eastern *Symplocarpus foetidus*)

There are two different species of large wetland flowering plants in North America that carry the common name "skunk cabbage." Both plants feature very large green leaves and stalks of flowers surrounded by protective chambers called spathes. But the western species' spathe is bright yellow, while eastern spathes start out green and deepen to a dark maroon with pale flecks.

Skunk cabbage is usually among the earliest native wildflowers to bloom; in some areas it may be the only flower around during Ostara. The spathes are the first to emerge from wetland soils and are followed soon by the leaves. Large skunk cabbage plants may be several feet across once fully grown.

Even if there is still snow on the ground, the skunk cabbage has a secret: It is among the few thermogenic plants. The spathe of both species is able to generate heat, which melts snow and ice around it, making the flowers more accessible to the first pollinating insects to awaken in the spring. This heat may also help to spread the skunk cabbage's characteristic "skunky" odor which gives it its name, and which brings in the bugs too! Since insects cannot generate their own heat, the warmth inside the spathe gives them extra incentive to land on skunk cabbage flowers, carrying pollen as they go.

This harbinger of spring offers an additional benefit to another early riser: The western skunk cabbage has laxative properties, and black bears may be seen eating their leaves. This helps their digestive systems get moving again after months of hibernation—quite a relief!

When I see western skunk cabbage begin to emerge in the wetlands around my home, I know spring has arrived. These flowers may never find themselves in a florist's bouquet, but their early beauty is something I have associated with Ostara for many years now.

Lichen Agaric (*Lichenomphalia umbellifera*)

Walk through the conifer forests near my home on the West Coast of the United States around Ostara, and you may see a wealth of tiny, cream-colored mushrooms popping up out of old logs and stumps. With shapes reminiscent of little petunias, they are quite lovely little things to behold, though easily overlooked due to their size.

But look closer! All around the base of these mushrooms, you'll see what looks like wet, green algae forming a film over the rotting wood—but that's actually part of the same organism. Most lichens have a dry appearance, and you won't be able to see the photosynthetic partner that's safely encased within the structure created by the fungus. The algal partner in lichen agaric, on the other hand, can be easily seen amid the fungal mycelium growing over its woody substrate.

Unlike most lichens, lichen agaric is unique in that the fungal partner produces a distinct mushroom. Like other mushrooms, this one only lasts a few days to a few weeks, just long enough to produce spores. It's a fascinating look into how lichen partnerships may have started out when the process first evolved hundreds of millions of years ago. In most lichens, the partners are so intertwined that they essentially become a new organism, but in this case they still display some individual traits as well.

Here on the cusp of winter and spring, it seems appropriate that we can catch a glimpse of a similarly liminal being. It is neither solely a fungus nor an algae, and the partners are neither independent nor completely merged. The seeds of possibility that we plant at this time are full of potential, and we wait on the brink to see what wonders they will produce in the weeks and months to come.

Feasts and Treats

Dallas Jennifer Cobb

A CELEBRATION OF THE goddess Eostre, goddess of dawn, fertility, spring, flowers, and rebirth, Ostara is the celebration of spring, renewal, birth, and resurrection. Occurring on the equinox, Ostara is the beginning of spring, a time when the length of day and night are equal, and when the balance tips. From this day on, the day will grow and become longer than the night, until Litha, or the Summer Solstice.

The goddess Eostre once turned a bird into a hare, and so the recognition of chicks and rabbits have become part of the celebration of Ostara. Another reason that rabbits are associated with Ostara is because of their propensity for fertility.

Feasts at Ostara rely on seasonally available goods, and often include eggs, honey, sprouted greens, asparagus, and fiddleheads, which are beginning to push up through the soil, depending on where in the world you live. Because fresh lamb is often available at this time of year, I have included it in the Ostara feast, which includes Rabbit's Food with Lemony Dressing, Spring Lamb Chops with Buttery Green Beans, Mint Sauce, and Traditional Oatcakes with Honey. Because they take a while to bake, make your oatcakes earlier in the day or a few days before. They are hearty and stand up well over time. You can also make Mint Sauce and Lemony Dressing in advance and keep jars in the refrigerator for easy access.

Traditional Oatcakes with Honey

My grandmother used to keep a big glass jar on her counter. When I was there, my first stop in the kitchen was to see if there were oatcakes in the jar. Apparently, as the story goes, one of my early words was "Oatie-akes," my childish, mispronounced request for oatcakes. Because food is such an easy way to show love and provide nourishment, so many of us have deeply sustaining memories of favorite foods. Whenever I make oatcakes, I take my sweet time eating them, savoring the remembrance of my grandmother.

Prep time: 5 minutes
Cooking time: 15 minutes
Resting time: 5 minutes
Servings: 8

2 cups rolled oats
1 cup oat flour (You can use all-purpose or baking flour, but using oat flour makes these gluten free.)
¾ cup brown sugar or monk fruit/erythritol sweetener for those sensitive to glucose spikes
1¼ teaspoon sea salt
¼ teaspoon baking soda
¾ cup unsalted butter, or use a vegan substitute if you choose
¼ cup boiling water
Optional: honey and butter

Preheat your oven to 375°F.

In a large bowl, combine the oats, oat flour, brown sugar or erythritol/monk fruit sweetener, salt, and baking soda. Mix well. Add butter or vegan substitute and use a big fork to work it all together. When you have the butter mostly mixed in, add the boiling water and keep mixing to form a sticky ball of dough.

Flour a rolling board and rolling pin, then transfer dough to the board and roll. You can cut the dough into shapes using cookie cutters and place them on a baking sheet to bake, or make a pie plate full of oatcakes that are wedge shaped. They will rise and snuggle into one another but are easy to separate after they are baked.

Pop them into the oven and bake for 12–15 minutes, until golden brown. Traditional oatcakes are baked longer (20–30 minutes) at lower temperatures (300°F). This produces a denser, chewier version that also happens to soak up honey better.

Let sit for 5 minutes before serving, or serve them cooled, days later. Plate the oatcake and add a teaspoon of honey on the plate. If you are in need of a real treat, add butter and honey to your oatcake.

Mint Sauce

I was never a big fan of mint sauce when I was small. After all, it was green and looked a lot like vegetables. I don't remember how the mint sauce first found its way onto my plate, but once I tasted the way it highlighted the delicious flavour of the lamb, I was a fan. Not only does mint sauce taste great, but the color adds contrasting visual beauty to the plate.

Prep time: 5 minutes
Servings: 8

¼ cup mint leaves, finely chopped
2 tablespoons apple cider vinegar
2 tablespoons sugar
¼ teaspoon salt
⅛ teaspoon pepper
¼ cup boiling water

Rinse mint leaves and pat dry. Finely chop and place in a bowl. Add vinegar, sugar, salt, and pepper.

Pour boiling water over and let steep for 20 minutes before serving.

Rabbit's Food with Lemony Dressing

Rabbits are a traditional part of Ostara celebrations, and rather than eat a real, live rabbit, I like to give a nod to them in the feast by including "rabbit's food," a salad made from fresh greens. It is easy to buy prewashed, mixed baby greens, and I encourage organic wherever it is available. I prefer baby romaine leaves, and when I have children at the table, I always avoid the spring mix with arugula and radicchio, which is a bit too bitter and fibrous for most kids.

Prep time: 5 minutes
Servings: 8

Prewashed baby greens
⅓ cup fresh lemon juice
¼ cup of olive oil
4 cloves of garlic, finely diced
1 teaspoon of sea salt
½ teaspoon of black pepper

Place all ingredients in a jar, and screw on the lid. Shake until well combined, and serve with the baby greens. If you choose to pre-dress the salad, use about one teaspoon of dressing per person.

Spring Lamb Chops with Buttery Green Beans

I love spring lamb. I live in a rural agricultural area and watch for the "Fresh Lamb" signs along the road each spring. Many farmers flash freeze spring lamb so it is available year round, but it's best in the spring.

The easiest preparation is to marinate the lamb, prepare the mint sauce, begin cooking the lamb, and midway through put the pot for the beans on to boil. Done in the right order, it is easy to produce a meal that is properly cooked and hot when it reaches the plate.

Prep time: 15 minutes
Marinating time: 30 minutes or more

Cooking time: 11 minutes
Servings: 8

Lamb Chops

1 large onion or 4 shallots, finely diced
4 cloves of garlic, finely diced
2 tablespoons of fresh rosemary, finely diced (or a teaspoon of dried rosemary)
4 tablespoons olive oil
2 tablespoons honey
2 tablespoons Dijon or grainy mustard (the bigger the mustard seeds, the better)
16 lamb chops, two per person

Green Beans

8 cups fresh green beans, washed and de-stemmed (I like to leave the bean whole, so they are long and elegant on the plate.)
¼ cup salted butter

Finely chop up the onion or shallots, garlic, and rosemary. In a separate container, mix the olive oil, honey, and mustard.

Coat the lamb with the oil mixture using a brush, then rub the savoury bits of onion, garlic, and rosemary all over. The oil and honey mixture will help the savoury herbs stick to the lamb.

Marinate for at least half an hour at room temperature before cooking, but you can prepare this earlier and let it marinate longer for more pronounced flavour.

While the lamb is marinating, make the mint sauce and prepare the green beans, washing and removing the stems. Set up a steamer pot and bring the water to a boil in preparation. Once boiling, turn it down to simmer.

Broil the lamb on high in the oven or barbecue it. Cook for 6 minutes on one side, flip, and cook for 4–5 minutes on the other. You want the lamb cooked but not overcooked.

When you flip the lamb to the second side, turn your steamer pot back up to high, and add green beans to the steaming pot once the water resumes boiling. Steam for 3–5 minutes depending on how crisp you like your beans. Remove beans from heat and add the butter. Now remove lamb from oven or barbecue.

Plate lamb and green beans and garnish lamb with Mint Sauce. Serve Rabbit's Food with Lemony Dressing on the side.

Crafty Crafts

Elizabeth Barrette

Spring has sprung! Ostara is far enough into the warming season that signs of life are everywhere. Trees and bushes are starting to leaf out. Early flowers like daffodils and tulips are blooming. Rabbits and chickens are reproducing. Day and night stand equal, and daytime is increasing. Warming weather entices people outdoors, although spring skies are unpredictable at best, so cold winds and pouring rain may appear without warning. Ostara decorations celebrate these signs of returning life, full of chicks and bunnies, eggs and flowers.

Upcycled Sock Bunny

You've probably seen sock monkeys, which have been around for a long time. It's also possible to make other stuffed animals, such as this upcycled sock bunny. These make great decorations for Ostara rituals. They're also ideal as gifts for children or adults.

Materials
Pair of large socks (preferably wool or wool blend)
One extra ankle sock or piece of felt
Polyfiber, wool, or upcycled stuffing
Embroidery floss

Sewing thread to match socks
Sewing machine or assorted sewing needles
Fabric pins
Washable fabric marker or sewing chalk
Scissors
Stuffing tool (blunt craft tweezers, chopstick, or pencil)
Optional: 2 buttons or sew-on animal eyes, ribbon
  Cost: $5–$10
  Time spent: 1 hour or more

Design Ideas

Large socks made of wool or wool blend make excellent craft materials. In case of allergies, consider cotton, bamboo, or hemp fiber instead. Synthetics like nylon or acrylic don't hold their shape or last as well, but can work. Avoid things like Tencel or microfiber that tend to hold static electricity and attract fluff that doesn't want to come off. Rabbits come in all natural colors—black, gray, white, brown, tan, etc.—either solid or patterned. You can also use Ostara colors such as pink, yellow, turquoise, or lavender. Patterned socks make exciting rabbits.

Use a lone sock to make the ear lining and the nose. It doesn't have to be as big as the pair for making the body. In most cases, pink works best for this, but if your rabbit is pink, then you might want a contrast color like red or purple. If you don't have a lone sock, then a 12-inch square of craft felt will work fine.

Eyes can be made in several ways. You can upcycle two buttons from your button jar or buy a pair of sew-on animal eyes. Rabbits made for small children should have embroidered eyes.

Choose a soft, huggable stuffing. Polyfiber is cheap and easy to find at any craft store. Wool stuffing is available but usually through special order only. You can also upcycle stuffing by saving snips of thread, yarn, and tiny fabric scraps; the different materials and textures keep it from compacting.

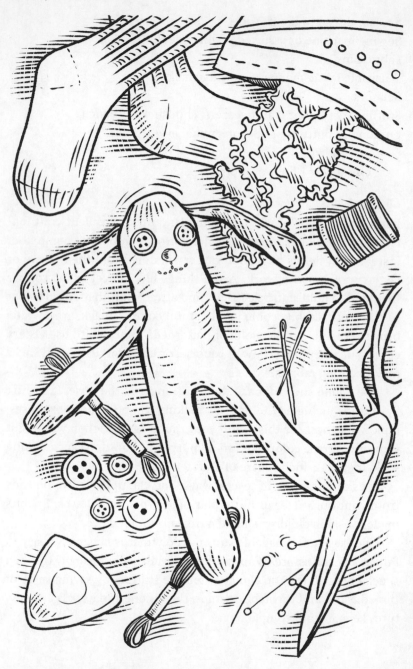

You will need an assortment of embroidery floss and sewing thread. Pink and black are good colors to embroider the face. Sewing thread should match the body sock color(s).

Assembly

If the socks have folded hems, cut off or open up the hems. Turn the body socks wrong side out, then press each flat with the sole and heel facing up. Draw on the pattern for the arms and legs; in both cases, make a double line down the middle of the sock leg.

One sock will use its foot as the head and body, while its leg becomes the rabbit legs. Sew two lines up the middle of the sock leg to the heel, then cut between them, splitting it into two leg sections. Leave a hole between the legs for stuffing later. Close the foot ends of the legs.

The other sock will make the ears, tail, and arms. Cut off the top of the foot above the heel for the ears and cut off the heel for the tail. Sew a double line up the middle of the leg, then cut the leg in half for the arms. Close the hand ends of the arms.

Flatten the two ear socks sideways—the foot part of one main sock, and the liner sock with the heel pointing out to make an angle. Cut off the heel and leg from the liner sock so you have a foot piece that matches the main one. Then cut each foot piece into two pieces by cutting around the side edges. Pin together a body sock piece and a liner sock (or felt) piece, right sides together. On the wrong side of each body sock piece, mark an oval shape, wide at the toe and slightly narrower at the top where it reaches the cut end. Sew along the line, then trim off the excess material.

Turn all pieces right side out. Stuff each arm and close the ends. Stuff the body and the legs through the hole between the legs. Use your stuffing tool to push the stuffing all the way to the ends. Then sew up the hole. Sew the arms to the body below the head, turning under the cut edges of the shoulders to hide them. Scrunch the body in your hands a few times to work the lumps out of the stuffing and shape the rabbit.

Sew around the edges of the ears to make them flatter. Sew the ears to the sides of the head, turning under the cut edges of the ear bases to hide them.

To make the tail, sew around the edge of the heel piece. Pull the thread slightly to form a pouch, stuff it, then pull tight to form a ball. Sew the tail to the backside just above the heel, which now forms the rabbit's seat.

Mark where facial features belong. To make the nose, cut a thumb-sized oval from the liner sock or felt. Sew around the edge and pull the thread, tucking the cut edge into the middle, forming a tiny ball. Sew the nose on the face.

Embroider a bunny mouth below the nose and whiskers if you want. Embroider or sew eyes on the sides of the head.

Optional: Tie a ribbon bow around the neck, cinching it down a bit to define the head better. You can also put bows at the base of the ears. To avoid losing the ribbons, sew the knots to the rabbit.

You may wish to finish your rabbit with a cute Ostara outfit. If you don't want to make your own, then you can measure the height of the rabbit and look for doll clothes in a similar size. Dresses and overalls are fairly forgiving in size.

Ostara and Oomancy

Charlie Rainbow Wolf

EGGS AND REBIRTH ARE often associated with the spring, so it seems fitting to explore this little-known but quite ancient form of divination at this sabbat. If you're a Harry Potter fan, this might sound familiar to you! Professor Trelawney taught it as *ovomancy* to her students. It's not limited to Potter's wizarding world, though. In *Robin Hood: Prince of Thieves* (Warner Bros., 1991), the witch cracks an egg and drags her long fingernails through its yolk to see the future. While it makes good onscreen entertainment, it is actually a valid form of divination and perhaps one of the oldest methods of seeing into the future. I've heard that ancient Celts and Druids used it, but because of the lack of written history about oomancy (*ōon* from the Greek word for egg, and *manteia*, to prophecy or divine) there's no way to actually prove this.

According to John Hale (1636–1700) in his manuscript *A Modest Enquiry into the Nature of Witchcraft* (published posthumously and still available), eggs were often used for divination in a method known as the "Venus glass." Here, an egg white was slowly poured into warm water, and the shapes it made were interpreted. Questions were often centered around how someone might die or who they might marry.

The Evil Eye

Eggs were used to ascertain the presence of the "evil eye." This was done by rolling a whole raw egg over the person suspected to be affected. It was then cracked into a clear glass bowl half filled with water, and the reader examined the egg to determine whether or not the evil eye had been cast on the person. It seems to me the outcome of the reading largely depends on the mindset of the reader!

Reading the Symbols

Another oomancy method is comparable to tea leaf reading. A question can be asked, or the images that appear can be noted and then interpreted later by either the querent or the reader. A whole raw egg is cracked and the yolk separated from the white. The white is then dropped into a pan of water just hot enough to start to color the egg white, and the images that appear in the white as it solidifies can be read similarly to the shapes made by the leaves on the sides of a teacup. A more detailed look at the egg white is possible if the water is heated in a clear glass bowl in the microwave, because then the white of the egg is available for examination from all sides, and even the bottom. This could also be done by piercing a small hole in the egg and letting the white slowly run into the warm water, interpreting the images as they appear and change.

Egg Rolling

Egg rolling is especially fun when done in a group setting, but it can be done as a solo activity too. It requires a plain hard-boiled egg and a waxy marker, such as a crayon or wax pencil. If you enjoy using vegetable dyes to color eggs, this could be added to the divinatory work.

Pick four new things you would like to see come to fruition or four areas of your life you want to improve. Be definitive, but don't get bogged down with there only being one way this could come to pass. For example, if you would like to see a romantic attachment develop, focus on finding the right love, rather than trying to lure a particular person. If job satisfaction is being sought, focus on finding it as opposed to landing a specific position.

At the pointed end of the egg, write your initials with the crayon and draw a circle around them. At the round end of the egg, draw a symbol of the deity you're working with and draw a circle around it. Connect the two circles with four lines going down the egg, dividing it into four equal parts. Write one desire in each of these segments.

When I've done the egg rolling, I've simply colored the segments: blue for mind and thought, yellow for action, green for income and financial matters, and red for relationships. Another method might be to divide the egg into three sections: blue for mind, green for body, yellow for spirit—or upper world, middle world, lower world. If you are trying to decide between two options, make two segments rather than four, each segment representing one of the choices. Let your intuition guide you; there's no right or wrong way to do this.

Find a good space to do the egg rolling. It does not have to be outside, but if working in a group, it's rather fun to collectively take the eggs outdoors to a mossy knoll or other sloping area and roll them together. The same success will occur if working solitary or indoors on a carpet or floor. The main thing is to roll the egg!

Quiet your mind and really focus on the areas of the egg. Ask for signs to be revealed and answers given so that your life may be enriched. Then stoop to the ground or floor, place your egg on it with the rounded end to the left and the pointed end to the right, and give it a gentle but firm push.

Watch the egg as it rolls. (Hopefully you can now appreciate how much fun this is if you're with a group and you have a good hill!) Don't lose track of it; you want to find it after it has come to a halt! Notice what sign is facing up. What sign is down? Did the egg land so that there's more than one sign upright? Note the markings and how you felt about things.

Putting Things to Rest

The rest of the egg's journey is up to personal preference. It can be left as an offering, buried in the ground so it can "grow," or eaten as a sacred food. If you do choose to eat it, make sure you're not allergic to eggs (which should go without saying), and also keep a reverent headspace. The egg has taken part in a divination rite; be mindful and grateful for that with each mouthful.

Ostara Ritual

Enfys J. Book

OSTARA IS THE SPRING equinox, one of two days of the year when day and night are very nearly equal in length at all latitudes. The spring equinox is the tipping point between when the nights are longer than the days to when the days are longer than the nights. It is therefore an ideal time to harness the strengthening sun energy to plant seeds, both literal and metaphorical, in the hopes of reaping a harvest later in the year.

A Seed-Choosing and Planting Ritual

In this ritual, you will connect with the energy of Ostara through a guided meditation, which will lead you to listen and consider an intention for the months ahead. Following the meditation, you will commit to your chosen intention and plant a seed as a focal point for your magical work to bring that intention to fruition. Note that if you are performing this ritual alone, you may wish to record yourself reading the guided meditation portion ahead of time and play it for yourself during the ritual. Alternatively, you can review it ahead of time and work to remember the key points. I recommend performing this ritual in the morning, if possible.

Supplies

A small paper cup or plantable pot

Enough dirt to fill the cup

A seed (Be sure to read up on it ahead of time so you know what depth to plant it and how much sunlight and water it needs.)

A small cup of water

Materials for a spring-focused altar (This could include fresh flowers, pictures of plants or baby animals, decorated eggs, etc.)

Cleanse

Begin by cleansing your ritual space in whatever manner befits your practice. If you're unsure what to do, simply tidy the area, sweep, and dust with the intent to cleanse any unwelcome energy from the space, or ring a bell with focused intent to cleanse the space.

Energetically cleanse yourself. You may waft incense and sprinkle saltwater on yourself to represent the four elements, or you may simply wash your hands, being aware of all the elements present in that experience: the water, the air around you, the minerals in the water for earth, and the heat of the water for fire.

Set Up Your Altar

Fill the paper cup with dirt. Set up your altar in the middle of your ritual space. Place on the altar all the ritual materials and any spring-related imagery or tokens you wish to include.

Ground and Center

Ground and center yourself. Breathe deeply and feel yourself present in your body, in the moment. Become aware of the earth energy beneath you. Become aware of the celestial energy above you. Feel those two kinds of energy intermingling within you. Breathe.

Cast the Circle

Using the index finger of your dominant hand, scribe a circle of blue astral fire energy clockwise around your ritual space, beginning and ending in the east. Focus your intent to create a container for your magick. If it is part of your practice, call to the elements in each quarter as you scribe the circle.

When the circle is cast, call in any spirits, deities, or helpers you wish to include, using your own words.

Preparing for the Journey

Pick up the seed and hold it in your hand. Make yourself comfortable. Close your eyes. Take three slow, deep breaths. With each exhalation, let go of any tension you're holding in your body. Become present in the moment, conscious of where you are sitting, how clothes feel on your body, and so on.

Guided Meditation

You are traveling down a misty pathway through the woods at twilight. The trees emit a slight bioluminescent glow. They seem to sparkle in the low light with deep blues and purples. The mist obscures the path, so you can only see a few feet in front of you. You proceed slowly. You can hear the crunch of rocks and gravel as you move, and faint noises of insects buzzing and small animals scurrying away from the path.

After some time, you find yourself in a clearing, and the light shifts from twilight to a late-afternoon orange glow. In the clearing there is a garden, full of vegetables ready for harvest. As you proceed toward the garden, you can smell the damp soil and decomposing autumn leaves. The air is warm but not hot, and occasionally you feel a brisk breeze blow past.

Examining the garden, you realize these crops are connected to your future. These are the fruits of your labor, results you can grow depending on the choices you make today, tomorrow, and throughout the year. Each of these vegetables requires specific kinds of work to make them flourish. See if you can find the connection within yourself to the plants you see before you.

(Pause.)

If you are drawn to a particular plant, approach it and examine it. Listen to what it has to say to you.

(Pause.)

Consider what you have learned. Is this something you wish to grow? Spend some time moving around the garden, listening to other plants that catch your attention.

(Pause.)

Based on what you have learned, select a vegetable connected to results you'd like to see in your life, or one that simply feels right. Pick it, and hold it in your hands. Note the texture of the skin, the scent, the weight of it. Listen to what it has to say to you.

(Pause.)

As you hold your chosen vegetable, the light in the clearing grows brighter, the warmth more intense. The vegetable you're holding begins to shrink. Gradually the air becomes cooler, the light dimmer, and as you look around, you realize it is early spring, and now, instead of a fully grown vegetable, you hold a seed in your hand. It glows softly in your palm. Feel the power it holds. Carry it with you as you turn back to the misty pathway through the woods. The light wanes, and your path becomes lit by the eerie glow from the trees around you.

Gradually you return from your trance into ritual space. You can feel the seed in your hand charged with power. Take a deep breath, shift around a bit to remind yourself of your physical form, and open your eyes.

Charge the Seed and the Water

If needed, take a few moments to listen and clarify the intention your seed represents. When you're ready, hold the seed in your nondominant hand, palm facing up, and place your dominant hand over it, palm facing down, with enough space between your hands so you can still see the seed on your palm.

Chant several times:

Ostara bright, returning light,
Charge this seed within my sight.

As you chant, focus on your intention. How will you feel when you achieve this goal? What will this look like when it's manifested? Imagine the seed in your hand growing. When the seed feels empowered, stop chanting.

Next, hold your dominant hand over the cup of water and visualize or feel that water being charged with powerful bright light, the quickening energy of spring.

Plant the Seed
Plant your seed in the dirt in the paper cup at the appropriate depth (determined by the seed's instructions). Cover it with dirt, and give it a bit of water.

If it aligns with your practice and feels right in the moment, say, "So mote it be" or "And so it is."

Give Thanks and Open the Circle
If you invited deities, spirits, or other helpers to join your rite, thank them in your own words.

Beginning and ending in the east and moving clockwise, use the index finger of your dominant hand to trace the blue astral fire circle you created earlier, feeling the energy flow up into your finger, through your body, and back to the earth. If it is part of your practice, acknowledge and thank the elements or directions at each quarter.

Ground and Reflect
Eat and drink a little something to help you ground and return to your body. Journal about your experience as soon as possible after the ritual, and continue to reflect on your chosen intention in the coming days as it continues to take shape in your mind.

Continue the Work
Water your seed regularly, make sure it gets adequate sunlight, and when it's big enough, transplant it into a larger pot or into your garden, following the directions for that specific type of seed.

If the seed doesn't grow, be patient and double-check the instructions to make sure you aren't overwatering it or giving it too much sun. If it still doesn't grow, consider if that's a reflection of how you're approaching your intent in the mundane world. You may need to do some other things to help your intention manifest.

Notes

Notes

Beltane

Returning Again to the Spring

Dodie Graham McKay

WHAT COULD BE SWEETER than a warm spring day? What potential does it hold? What can be grown from the promise of a new beginning? For every sabbat there is a mystery at play—what is the divine mystery of Beltane?

The celebration of this sabbat is commonly held on the first day of May in the Northern Hemisphere or on the first of November in the Southern Hemisphere. This sabbat is more than a date on the calendar; it is the tide of the seasons as we cross from ripeness of spring into the richness of summer. Beltane falls between Ostara (the Spring Equinox), and Litha (the Summer Solstice), marking the midpoint between them. It is sometimes referred to as a cross-quarter day, and its literal occurrence actually falls a few days after the first of the month. For example, in 2025, the Beltane cross-quarter date will fall on May 5 in the Northern Hemisphere, EDT. This is handy to know, as it offers you the opportunity to stretch out your celebrations over a longer span of time, and just like you can find the timing for the precise moment of a solstice or equinox, you can find this also for a cross-quarter date and time by consulting an almanac or doing a search on the internet.

In my own practice, I appreciate the ability to work with the tide of the seasons and the flexibility to celebrate the sabbat on a day within this timespan that works best to gather the coven together. That way, our celebration won't conflict with attending our local public Pagan community event that is held every year on the first Sunday after May 1.

Historically, Beltane was celebrated in the Gaelic-speaking counties of Scotland (where it is called *Latha Bealltainn*), on the Isle of Man (where it is known as *Laa Boaldyn*), and in Ireland (where the festival day as well as the entire month are known as *Bealtaine*). Fire was considered to be a key element of the celebrations, and it represented the growing power of the sun after a long winter and the revitalization of the land and people. These fires also offered protection from the mischief of fairies and the workings of malevolent witches. In some regions, a pair of bonfires would be lit, and cattle would be driven between them in order to purify them and make them fertile.

The feasting and dancing that were part of these festivities have echoed down through time along with the association with fertility for both the land and the people. Dancing around a Maypole crowned with flowers and festooned with brightly coloured ribbons has been adopted by many celebrants of Neopagan traditions from British folkloric practices. This is a holdover from the earlier custom of bringing in greenery from the countryside to decorate for the season. Likewise, the wearing of floral crowns or wreathes of leaves on the heads of folk participating in modern Pagan rituals echoes this theme, bringing the freshness and vitality of the season into the sabbat celebrations.

The public Pagan community I entered as a teenaged seeker in the late 1980s presented the rites of Beltane as a celebration of the divine pairing of the Maiden Goddess and the virile Horned God, the mystery of the sabbat being their courtship, leading to romantic love with fertile results. In this interpretation, the burgeoning spring and fertility of the land is seen in the pairing of this divine couple. This trope has been a popular one in Neopagan groups, but as our communities become increasingly aware of the diversity that thrives within them, this vision of a heterocentric, cisgendered Beltane is limited and does not take into account the diversity of the people who celebrate it. There is room for more than one Beltane story, and for many of us, there is a hunger for one that is relatable to the human experience and that still honors a cornerstone of what witches and Wiccans believe. I believe that to ignore this hunger is a mistake and that we have the opportunity to examine Beltane and explore deeper into the mysteries of this time of year. To begin to dig into this, let's roll the Wheel of the Year back about six months.

Sitting on the opposite side of the Wheel of the Year from Beltane is Samhain, the sabbat that is arguably one of the most fun and popular among witches and Pagans, and thanks to its partnership with Halloween, it is widely appreciated by anyone who enjoys the witchy themes, ghosts, goblins, and free candy. This is a time for honoring the dead, remembering our ancestors and the spirits of those whom we respect. The rituals of magical folk may include setting up an ancestor altar, visiting the grave of someone you cared about, or doing divination or necromantic work to communicate with spirits.

My coven takes this opportunity to go on an annual retreat to a cabin in the woods for two consecutive evenings of ritual, the first being the naming of ancestors, the second being a ritual to aid in the passage of souls from this world to the next. This sort of witchcraft has a certain type of attraction to it, and it feels natural for those of us who practice magic to work with the dead this way, but this is where I would get stuck. It felt like something was missing. The Wheel of the Year, as it is popularly interpreted, speaks of rebirth at Yule, when the sun is seen as being born again into the world at the solstice. This comes close but does not consider the concept of reincarnation as it applies to life on earth directly. At Imbolc and Ostara we have growing anticipation as light and warmth return, then the culmination of this vitality at Litha, followed by the reaping and reward of the harvest festivals of Lughnasadh and Mabon. But what of Beltane? Sitting opposite the Wheel of the Year from Samhain, it feels like it should be about so much more than the popular trope of human mating. This is indeed a part of it, but is it really the whole story? In this Wheel of the Year, there is a key piece of the witchcraft I fell in love with missing, one that is not being celebrated with the exuberance that it deserves: the concept of reincarnation. Could this be the mystery at Beltane?

Reincarnation, or at least the idea that death makes way for new life, is fairly universal in witchcraft and Pagan traditions. It was the hook that caught and steered me firmly into exploring witchcraft and then into the Wiccan tradition I am an initiate of. Wicca is a coven-based system, and this provides me with a religious framework and group structure to celebrate the changing of the seasons and mysteries of life and death, including the concept of reincarnation. When I practice my witchcraft alone, I look to the practice of Green Witchcraft and the examples I witness in the natural world to further lead me into this mystery of spring. As a Green Witch, I see the promise of reincarnation in the verdancy of my environment. I see every seed, bud, embryo, or new sprout of life as a potential new body for a reincarnated spirit. For every spark of new, radiant life, there is a beacon calling the life forces of the beloved dead back into creation. The warming of the land in the spring quickens the body of the earth, producing an explosion of new life that gives corporeal form to spirits of the ones we have loved and lost. New life hosts old souls; the cycle of birth, death, reincarnation, and rebirth turns once more.

In trying to figure out if this witchcraft was for me, I read books by the early writers on the subject and kept finding references to reincarnation. I found my first hint of what was to come as a young teen reading Sybil Leek's *The Complete Art of Witchcraft* in which she dedicates a chapter to reincarnation. She describes reincarnation as a "tenet of witchcraft," stating that "if the witches of the world ponder on reincarnation it is not because they consciously desire to meditate on death in a macabre fashion, but simply because it holds the same meaning that life itself holds" (Leek 1971, 146, 139). I was initially resistant to this concept, but my opinion changed when I came upon a quote in *The Meaning of Witchcraft* by Gerald Gardner about how witches believe that it is possible to experience "a reincarnation into your own tribe again, among those whom you loved and who loved you, and that you would remember, know, and love them again" (Gardner 1999, 25). This, to me, speaks of the longing we all feel for a sense of hope that there is something good and rewarding on the other side of death, a reward or comfort that we will be with our loved ones again and that we will be received with love and recognition when we are reunited.

This joy, this sweetness and magic, this exuberance of rebirth, reincarnation, hope, and love is the very essence of Beltane, and it is inclusive of all beings. In celebrating the return of those we have loved or at least the potential of it in the future, we revel in the knowing that we will be able to love and be loved by them again. This loving can and does, under some circumstances, lead to the divine mating that is more popularly associated with Beltane, but it also extends to all ecstatic, joyous love that is inclusive of everyone.

I believe that this version of reincarnation happens, that it has happened to me, and that it is not all that rare. Have you ever met someone for the first time and felt like you have known them forever? Have you ever been introduced to a stranger and felt like you were looking into the eyes of a long-lost friend? I have found this to be true with the Wiccan tradition I am a part of. I have joyously been introduced to a fellow Wiccan only to look into their eyes and know that we are seeing each other again, and that it shall happen yet again in our next incarnations. These small moments of magic are part of our human experience, and they are confirmation that the never-ending cycle of birth, death, reincarnation, and rebirth is active and revealing itself to you.

References

Gardner, Gerald. *The Meaning of Witchcraft*. Lake Toxaway: Mercury Publishing, 1999.

Leek, Sybil. *The Complete Art of Witchcraft*. New York: Harper & Row, 1971.

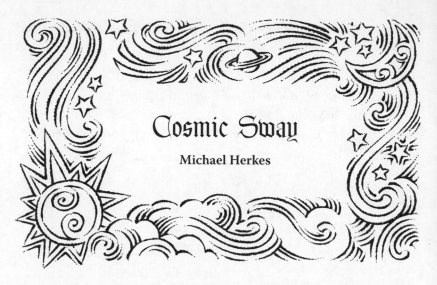

Cosmic Sway

Michael Herkes

BELTANE IS A VIBRANT and ancient fire festival marking the half-way point between the spring equinox and the summer solstice, symbolizing the blossoming fertility of nature with the approaching arrival of summer. It is traditionally observed on May 1; however, astrologically, it is when the Sun reaches 15 degrees Taurus, which will occur on May 5. Anytime between the two dates is a great time to celebrate the festival. By honoring this ancient festival's rich traditions or adapting them for contemporary times, we can connect with our roots and find joy in the ever-changing rhythms of the natural world.

Both Beltane and Taurus are deeply rooted in nature's rhythms of fertility, renewal, and indulgence. Beltane celebrates the blossoming of flowers, the return of warmth after winter's cold embrace, and the union of reproductive energies. Similarly, Taurus embodies these themes by symbolizing growth in nature as well as personal growth and prosperity in the material realm. Additionally, the two also emphasize sensuality. Beltane rituals often involve dancing around Maypoles or bonfires to honor fertility deities like Aphrodite or Venus—aligning with Taurus's ruling planet Venus, further emphasizing love, beauty, pleasure, and the arts. Similarly, individuals born under the sign of Taurus are known for their appreciation of physical pleasures such as good food and artistry in all forms, including music or painting.

Celebrating Beltane

As a fertility festival, all rituals and spellcraft for love and pleasure are welcome now. Feast on seasonal foods such as fruits, vegetables, honey cakes, or mead (a fermented honey beverage associated with ancient rituals). Decorate your home or altar with fresh flowers and greenery to represent the abundance of nature's beauty now. A common practice during Beltane involves creating floral wreaths or garlands, and it is a cherished tradition that brings an air of enchantment to any celebration. Gather colorful flowers, leaves, ribbons, or any other natural elements that resonate with you, then weave them together into beautiful headpieces to symbolize growth, fertility, and vitality.

Beltane is a time that is traditionally associated with lighting bonfires. These fires are believed to have cleansing properties that drive away negative energies, making way for positive ones. People often gather around these fires, dancing, singing, and leaping over them as a symbolic act of purification and transformation. If having a large bonfire is not feasible for you, light white or pastel candles around the house to celebrate the transformative flame. (Be sure to practice fire safety and never leave candles burning unattended.)

Maypole dancing is also a common Beltane celebration. A tall pole adorned with colorful ribbons is erected in an open space, around which people weave intricate patterns by holding onto the ribbons as they dance in circles. This lively dance symbolizes unity, community spirit, and harmonious connections between individuals. Alternatively, you could host a festive dance party with friends or head out and paint the town red.

Conjunctions and Retrogrades

On May 2, we experience another Venus-Neptune conjunction at 1:07 p.m. This merger of energies plays in well with the themes of Beltane as the realms of love, pleasure, and beauty align with dreams, fantasy, and inspiration. Utilize this time to tap into inspiration with love and your connection to all relationships—romantic, platonic, and familial.

Pluto retrograde begins on May 4 at 11:27 a.m. and lasts until October 13. This time provides unique and powerful energy that can have a profound impact on our subconscious emotions. Be prepared for an emotional journey during this time. It may bring up unresolved issues from the past and force us to confront them head-on. This can be challenging but ultimately liberating, as it allows us to release old patterns, confront fears, and transform with self-discovery.

Three Lunar Celebrations

The next major cosmic events center on three lunar celebrations. First, expect emotions to run high with hidden truths coming to the surface with the Full Moon in Scorpio on May 12 at 12:56 p.m. Scorpio, as a water sign, is known for its deep emotional intensity and passion. When combined with the illuminating power of a Full Moon, this energy becomes even more potent. In classic times, Scorpio was ruled by Mars; however, in contemporary astrology, it is ruled by Pluto, making this Moon a particularly intense occurrence with the planet's retrograde.

Use this lunar phase to delve deep into your subconscious mind and confront any buried emotions or unresolved issues. Journaling or meditating to explore your innermost thoughts and feelings can help release any emotional baggage that no longer serves you. Since Scorpio is a water sign and the Moon is deeply connected to water, consider connecting with that element by taking a bath with essential oils aligned with Scorpio, like myrrh, patchouli, or vanilla. Scorpio is also known for its deeply sensual energy, which will resonate in the post-Beltane fertility celebrations. Engaging in sex magic for manifestation through physical pleasure is appropriate now.

Gemini season begins on May 20 and is shortly followed by a New Moon in Gemini on May 26 at 11:02 p.m., bringing a swirl of vibrant, dynamic, and intellectually stimulating energy into the mix. Gemini, an air sign ruled by Mercury, is known for its curious nature and versatility. When this energy combines with the transformative power of a New Moon, it creates an atmosphere that allows you to plant a seed to inspire new ways to communicate, learn, and adapt. This is also a powerful time to express yourself and communicate with words. Embrace your inner wordsmith by writing poetry or start a journal to capture your thoughts during this transformative lunar phase. Connect with friends or loved ones through meaningful conversations or engage in group activities that foster connection and intellectual stimulation.

The energy of a Full Moon in Sagittarius on June 11 at 3:44 a.m. is vibrant, expansive, and adventurous. This celestial event brings forth a sense of enthusiasm and optimism, encouraging us to embrace new experiences and explore uncharted territories. In contrast to the intense and transformative energy of Scorpio, which precedes Sagittarius in the zodiac cycle, the Full Moon in Sagittarius offers a lighter and more jovial atmosphere. It encourages us to embrace our inner wanderer and seek new experiences that broaden our perspectives. To celebrate the occasion unique to the Full Moon in Sagittarius, one can engage in activities that align with its energetic qualities.

As Sagittarius is associated with travel and exploration, use this time to plan your next adventure or embark on a spontaneous road trip if possible. This Full Moon encourages you to step out of your comfort zone and embrace unfamiliar territories. Expand your mind by diving into books or courses that align with your interests or explore new subjects that pique your curiosity. Engaging in deep conversations with friends or loved ones for an evening filled with laughter and stimulating dialogue is also a good idea.

Tales and Traditions

Lupa

Beltane brings with it longer days and warmer temperatures, and even in the most northerly climes, winter's grasp is loosening significantly. The Northern Hemisphere is full to bursting with young animals of all sorts, and plants burst forth with new leaves and flowers, while spring mushrooms flush on the forest floor. If Beltane is a festival of fertility, then the beings of nature have fulfilled that theme quite nicely.

Gone, too, are winter's hunger pangs, as wild greens and the earliest crops offer up a variety of fresh food. Here along the Columbia, spring salmon run upriver while the hatchlings of fall's spawning prepare to venture out toward the ocean. The sky smiles in sunshine and showers.

Pacific Tree Frog (*Pseudacris regilla*)

If Beltane had a theme song here in the Pacific Northwest, it would be the Pacific tree frog. These little amphibians sing all night (and often into the daytime too) in search of mates. In fact, you're more likely to hear one than see one because they have such effective camouflage. They can change between two color phases, one bright green and the other an earthy brown, and both have dark brown "masks" over their eyes. They generally don't get more than about two inches long, which helps them stay hidden from predators even as they call out to potential mates.

Pacific tree frogs may have been active for weeks by the time Beltane rolls around. While they don't sing as vigorously in the early spring chill, if it's warm enough for them to come out of brumation, they will get started on their feeding and mating efforts. Soon enough, freshwater like ponds and slow streams in this area will be full of eggs and then tadpoles, representing the new generation of tree frogs. It normally takes about two months for the tadpoles to metamorphose into adult frogs, though some individuals may delay this for almost half a year. And a very lucky frog may survive to be eight years old.

Every species has strategies for surviving the hard times, and for many cold-blooded animals, brumation or hibernation are necessary parts of their winter lives. But they make up for it by living life to the fullest once it's warm enough. Beltane is similarly a milestone for a lot of people: gardens that couldn't be planted earlier can now be sown, and foraging for wildflowers and other plants begins in earnest. For many, winter challenges like reduced travel opportunities or seasonal affective disorder are replaced by more ways to engage in one's inner and outer worlds.

Salmonberry (*Rubus spectabilis*)

Another important spring marker in this area is the ripening of salmonberries. These are the first native berries of the year, and their bright orange and red coloration makes them an attractive sight against spring green foliage. The Chinook, on whose unceded land I live, even tied salmonberries into their seasonal First Salmon Ceremony. While the first salmon might be caught as early as late April depending on location, the people would severely restrict harvest until the salmonberries had ripened late in May or June.

It can be difficult sometimes to wait for a good thing, especially after lean times. But not even the hungriest birds or bears will chow down on salmonberries until they're ripe, for the unripe berries can be hard and sour. Beltane marks the middle of spring, and the pressure is off with warmer temperatures and longer days. But many food sources need time to finish developing, and so the relief must be mixed with patience.

Still, I enjoy seeing the lush foliage of the salmonberries along streamsides and in forest understories. They often play host to songbirds, who build their nests within the thorny branches of these shrubs. Deer, caterpillars, and other herbivores may browse on the leaves. Around Beltane, I often enjoy seeing the bright pink flowers being visited by bumblebees and other pollinators, feeding animals long before they ever produce their tasty berries.

I may have to wait a little longer for the first true harvest of the year, but for now I am so incredibly fortunate to be surrounded by such beauty. Salmonberries provide so much to their ecological communities, and I do not mind waiting my turn for their gifts.

Morels (*Morchella* spp.)

If there is one mushroom that can be considered the "king of spring," it is the morel. There are several dozen species found throughout the Northern Hemisphere, often divided into groups by color, such as yellow or black morels. They all have a markedly honeycomb-like texture, with cone-shaped caps, and are completely hollow inside when cut open. They tend to have mycorrhizal relationships with trees, both conifers and hardwoods, though which trees depends on the species of morel.

It is fire adaptation for which many morels are best known. Wildfires are common in North America in summer and early fall, and they may burn hundreds or thousands of acres of forest. This may seem like complete devastation, and it is true that climate change has caused fires to burn larger, hotter, and longer than in the past. But from the ashes, life still rises in spite of the destruction. In the springtime after a wildfire, it is common to find an enormous number of morels bursting forth from the charred land, spreading their spores to and fro, and contributing to the renewal of life.

Beltane occurs right in the middle of morel season, and this fungus is a fitting symbol of the sabbat. None of us can completely escape challenges in this life, though it is true that some face greater hardships than others. The morel, then, is an important reminder that no matter what happens, life goes on. It may be within a deeply changed landscape, and that will take some adjustment—sometimes easier said than done. But fall's wildfires are soon followed by spring's pioneering species like the morels, and nothing stays completely burnt down forever. Let Beltane's fertility be not only about new birth, but rebirth as well.

Feasts and Treats

Dallas Jennifer Cobb

BELTANE LITERALLY TRANSLATES AS "bright fire" or "lucky fire." Halfway between Ostara, the vernal equinox, and Litha, the Summer Solstice, Beltane is celebrated on May 1, and has also been called May Day.

Because Beltane was traditionally a festival to celebrate fertility and the returning solar fire energy, it is also a celebration of passion, sexuality, and the fire of the life force that dwells within each of us and our animals.

Not just an animal blessing, the fires of Beltane also blessed couples who, after dancing around the Maypole, made their way to the forest to sleep outdoors and engage in the sacred rites of pleasure.

Traditionally a time to protect cattle and crops, fires were used to bless and protect the folk and their animals, who walked around or between the fires, or leapt across them. Just imagine trying this with a cow!

Because pork is naturally fatty, it creates lots of smoke and sizzle on the barbecue. Remember to invite your guests to walk through the smoke as you are grilling, and to carry or lead animals through if they can, calling in the bright blessings and protection of Beltane upon them all.

Our Beltane feast includes Pork Sizzlers on Steamed Baby Bok Choy with Mixed Berry Crumble for dessert. Because it takes the longest, make the Mixed Berry Crumble ahead of time. It can be easily warmed in the oven or microwave.

Mixed Berry Crumble

In some areas there will be an abundance of berries in season at Beltane. In other areas, you may need to get berries imported from somewhere warmer or use frozen berries. This recipe can work with fresh or frozen berries equally well. We will celebrate Beltane with the luscious fruits, which are symbols of passion and fertility, made into a crumble. I like a mix of raspberries, blackberries, and blueberries, but you can use whichever you prefer or are available. If you like a tart fruit crumble, add some cranberries to the mix. I generally avoid strawberries in the crumble because their texture changes so much, and they become mushy. If you love strawberries and choose to use them, dice them up small and mix well with other berries.

Prep time: 20 minutes

Cooking time: 30 minutes

Servings: 8

Crumble

1 cup oat flour (I use oat because it's gluten free.)

¾ cup rolled oats

½ cup of brown sugar (Substitute monk fruit sweetener if you are Keto or allergic to sugar.)

¼ cup white sugar—see above

1 teaspoon cinnamon

½ teaspoon of salt

⅔ cup cold, unsalted butter, diced into tiny pieces

Filling

6 cups mixed berries, washed and de-stemmed

2 tablespoons oat flour

¼ cup white sugar (I use monk fruit sweetener as an alternative.)

Heat the oven to 375°F. Oil or butter (it tastes better) a large, 11 × 7-inch baking dish.

In a bowl, mix flour, oats, brown and white sugar, cinnamon, and salt. Add the butter, working it in until the mix is crumbly. Chill the crumble mix in the fridge while you prepare the berries.

Sprinkle berries with flour and sugar and mix carefully, gently coating all berries.

Take the crumble out of the fridge, and use a little less than half of the chilled mix and press it with your palms into the bottom of the dish. Spread all the berries on top. Sprinkle the rest of the crumble mixture evenly over the berries. Bake for 35 minutes.

Pork Sizzlers

I love these easy, quick, and yummy seasoned brochettes. A *brochette* is a dish of chunks of meat, poultry, or fish threaded onto skewers and cooked. I like to use pork because it has fat marbled through it, is relatively affordable, and grills up very nicely on the barbecue. Best of all, it creates some Beltane blessing smoke as it sizzles and cooks.

Prep time: 10 minutes

Marinating time: 1 hour or more

Cooking time: 10 minutes

Servings: 8

2 pounds boneless pork (Try to choose a marbled, fatty cut like shoulder or boneless side ribs. If you need to, you can use tenderloin or pork chops.)

⅓ cup olive oil

3 tablespoons Chinese five spice blend (I like the ready-made version, but if you can't find it, the ingredients are cinnamon, fen-

nel seed, sea salt, garlic, black pepper, coriander, anise seed, star anise, and cloves. It's way more than five ingredients, so I am never quite sure about the name, but it adds yummy, authentic flavour to the pork.)

2 cloves garlic, finely diced
1 teaspoon salt
½ teaspoon pepper
1 teaspoon dried thyme
1 large onion, cut in 1-inch squares

Cut your meat into 1½-inch cubes. In a large, sealable container, drizzle with olive oil and stir to coat the cubes. Sprinkle all the herbs and spices in and stir well to cover evenly.

Put a lid on the container and let it marinate for at least an hour, or overnight for exquisite flavour.

After marinating for at least an hour, preheat barbecue to medium-high and wipe some olive oil on the grill so the skewers don't stick. You can also cook these indoors on a cast-iron frying pan at medium-high heat.

Thread pork onto the skewers, alternating with a slice of onion in between pieces. For skewers, it is possible to buy disposable wood or bamboo skewers in most grocery stores, or look for the stainless steel reusable skewers. These don't catch on fire when used on the barbecue. If you use wood or bamboo, soak the skewers in water before using to reduce their flammability. You can also coat the ends of the skewers in tin foil to prevent burning.

Barbecue or cook until pork is well cooked on all sides. Onions will be tender and almost translucent.

Serve the Pork Sizzlers on top of Steamed Baby Bok Choy.

Steamed Baby Bok Choy

I love baby bok choy because it is small, cute, and easy to cook. Of course, if you can't find the "baby" version, you can use regular bok choy. It is larger and takes just a little longer to cook, and you'll follow the same instructions.

Prep time: 5 minutes
Cooking time: 5 minutes
Servings: 8

1 tablespoon olive oil
1 tablespoon fresh ginger, grated
2 cloves garlic, finely diced
1 small onion, finely diced
16 small heads baby bok choy
1 tablespoon soy sauce or tamari
Water as needed

Put oil into a large frying pan on medium heat. Add ginger, garlic, and onion, then sauté until translucent.

Rinse and trim the stems off of the baby bok choy. Throw the baby bok choy into the heated frying pan. Add soy sauce or tamari and a splash of water to create steam.

Cover with a lid and let steam for about 2 minutes, then remove from heat.

Arrange the baby bok choy on the plate, and serve with Pork Sizzlers placed diagonally on top.

Crafty Crafts

Elizabeth Barrette

LATE SPRING BRINGS A flourish of life in every direction. Trees and bushes leaf out. Fragrant flowers like lilacs and peonies are blooming; so are many types of fruit trees. Birds are building nests. Other animals that breed during the warm season are courting or giving birth. Days are notably longer than nights. The beautiful days draw everyone outside for yardwork, rituals, or just sheer enjoyment of the season. Beltane rituals often focus on sex and romance, but they can showcase the greening world in general, with decorations based on the growing season or more suggestive symbolism.

Miniature Maypole

If you don't have room for a full-size Maypole or the weather is unpleasant, then consider a small-size one instead. A tabletop Maypole makes a great altar decoration.

Materials
Wooden dowel
Wooden finial or top button
Wooden square or round base
Wood glue or hot glue

Craft paint or finishing oil
2 colors of ¼-inch ribbon
Ruler or measuring tape
> **Cost:** $10–$15
> **Time spent:** 15–20 minutes

Design Ideas

Wooden dowels are readily available at craft stores. Aim for about ½ inch wide and 12–18 inches tall, but a little smaller or larger is fine. Use what you can get.

You need a top to hold the ribbons. There are end buttons (without holes) and finials (a decorative point) for woodworking projects.

For a base, choose a square or round piece of wood about 6–8 inches wide. This should weigh enough to keep the Maypole from tipping. If it's too light, get two and glue them flat together for a thicker and heavier base.

You can paint your Maypole in ritual colors if you wish. To keep the natural wood color, use a finishing oil instead. For ribbon, choose any two contrasting colors: green with yellow or gold are popular.

Assembly

Paint the base, dowel, and top piece, or polish them with finishing oil. You can make them all the same color or contrasting colors. Some people like to paint a spiral up the pole or flowers around the rim of the base.

Cut four lengths of ribbon, two of each color. They should be just over twice the height of the dowel. Fold each ribbon in half to find the middle, then glue that middle over the top of the dowel. This gives you eight ribbons hanging around the Maypole to represent the eight sabbats. Let that glue dry. Next, glue the top piece over the ribbons to hold them firmly in place. Let that glue dry too.

Use a ruler or measuring tape to find the center of the base piece. Glue the bottom of the dowel to the center. Let the glue dry.

Check everything to make sure it's secure. Touch up the glue if necessary. Then check to make sure you haven't missed any spots with the paint or finishing oil. Touch that up if necessary.

Seed Bombs

Seed bombs consist of wildflower seeds enclosed in a ball of clay and compost. They're small enough to carry easily and heavy enough to fly well when thrown. Rain melts the clay so the seeds can sprout.

Materials

Newspapers or butcher paper
Compost

Clay (locally dug or purchased)
Wildflower seeds
Bucket for mixing
Trowel or other stirrer
Water
>   *Cost:* $0–$50
>   *Time spent:* 1 hour or more

Design Ideas

Compost provides nutrients for the seeds to grow. Composted manure or mushroom compost work well.

Local clay is best because it won't change the soil where it lands. You can often find clay along waterways, so if you know someone with a pond or creek, ask if you can look there for a bucket of clay. Otherwise, you can buy clay powder at a garden store.

Wildflower seeds are the most important component. First, make sure to avoid invasive species. The best approach is to choose species native to your area, bought or gathered locally. They will be best adapted to your environment, need no care, and fit the ecosystem. "Weedy wildflowers" like milkweed are good for colonizing barren or disturbed ground. Prairie plants such as echinacea or yellow coneflower can break heavy soil and survive droughts. If you are making seed bombs for a specific area, you might choose a species for sun, shade, or other known conditions. For most purposes, however, a "regional wildflower blend" for your locale will work best. These are available from many nurseries in packet, pouch, or bulk sizes and are more affordable than buying individual species to mix together. Avoid using a general wildflower mix because some species may misbehave in the wrong habitat.

Assembly

First, cover your work surface with newspapers or butcher paper. You can work on a counter or table.

Put some compost in the bucket. It helps to use a scoop so you can measure the parts. This way, once you figure out the proportions, you can mix up more. Moisten the compost with water until it's damp but not dripping. Squeeze a handful to see how well it sticks together. Pure compost usually won't form a stable ball.

Add clay one scoop at a time, stirring it into the compost with the trowel. If you have powdered clay, you'll need to add more water. If it's wet, you'll need to cut it in with the trowel. Then test the texture again. Continue adding more clay until you have a mixture that is like a stiff dough, which holds together well but is not too sticky. This is often 2–3 parts compost to 4–5 parts clay, but it depends on the consistency of your materials.

Pinch off small amounts of clay mixture. You want enough to make a small ball between ½ and 1 inch across. Flatten the blob of clay and put a pinch of wildflower seeds in the center. Then close

the clay around the seeds and roll gently to form a smooth ball. This method prevents seeds from escaping the ball prematurely.

Allow the balls to air dry until the surface is no longer tacky to the touch. Don't let them sit out too long, because seeds can die if they dry too much.

Carry the finished seed bombs in a cloth pouch to keep from getting clay dust in your pockets. For best results, distribute the seed bombs shortly before a predicted rain, which will melt the clay balls and disperse the seeds to sprout. You can drop or toss seed bombs along roadsides or medians, in empty lots, or anywhere else that needs some native plants. You can also stand on a sidewalk or trail and lob them as far as possible.

Beltane and Scrying

Charlie Rainbow Wolf

I REMEMBER BACK IN the 1970s when I first stuck my toe in the realm of magic and I first heard the word *scry*. (I had been an energy worker in the church for years prior to that, but it was around 1978 when I started really exploring things.) I thought it was one of the most mystical and ethereal words I'd ever heard! I associated it with gazing into a crystal ball, but soon learned that scrying can be done in a number of different ways: crystal scrying, water scrying, dark mirror scrying, fire scrying, and more. The main thing to keep in mind when approaching any kind of divination is to focus on the question or situation at hand. "What does the Universe want me to know" is also a very valid question if it's just general guidance that's being sought.

Crystal Scrying

"Gaze into my crystal ball" is the stereotype when crystal scrying is mentioned, and there's some truth to it. Metaphysical shops sell crystal balls for the purpose of *crystallomancy*, but I've always used a quartz stone. It is a multifaceted cluster, and I call it "the seeing stone" because when I give it to people to gaze into and tell me what they see, they nearly always see some kind of an animal. Discussing that animal's properties and magic with them opens the divination.

To scry into a crystal ball or polished stone (I find clear quartz with some inclusions in it works best for me), it is important to position it so it catches the light. This is another matter of preference. Some use moonlight, others use sunlight. I just use the available light, even if it is a lamp or a flame. Keep gazing into the stone until your eyes go slightly out of focus, and then make a note of what images appear.

Water Scrying

This is easy because water can be found nearly everywhere, and no special tools are needed. I have a big blue mixing bowl that I have used for scrying before! Some people add a silver coin to the water in the bowl, some add ink or dye or even herbs, but it's not necessary.

Successful water scrying is done by angling the surface of the water so the light dances across it. Rest your eyes on the surface of the water and let them go out of focus a bit (like with the crystal scrying). Make note of what you see, then either drink the water so the experience really becomes a part of you, or offer it to the earth with gratitude.

Any water can be used for scrying. I've done it on the surface of a lake while camping, in puddles while walking, and in a ceremony using a dancing water bowl. Also called a Chinese spouting bowl, this is a metal bowl that looks like an old porcelain wash basin, with two handles on the sides. The bowl is half filled with water, and the handles rubbed with the palms of the hands. This makes a resonance—similar to a wet finger rubbed around the rim of a wine glass—and the vibration of the sound causes the water to ripple.

When scrying, the two most important factors are not to focus too intently with the eyes, and to let the mind wander to see what it will find in the ripples and reflections.

Dark Mirror Scrying

This makes for an interesting and enjoyable group practice, making the dark mirrors and then scrying in them. (Of course, it is just as rewarding when done solo.) Black mirrors for scrying are manufactured for purchase, but it's easy to make one with a few simple supplies:

- A picture frame—charity shops, thrift stores, and rummage or jumble sales often have nice ones, but make sure the front is glass and not acrylic or plastic.
- Black paint—craft paint from art supply shops or even samples of household paint from hardware or home improvement stores work well, as will a can of spray paint.
- A reasonable quality paintbrush (if not using spray paint)—I like to use artist's fan-type brushes.

Remove the glass from the picture frame. Paint one side. Once the paint is dry, place the glass with the paint on the inside back inside the frame. This produces a very shiny but black surface.

Scrying with the black mirror—a form of *catoptromancy*—is similar to scrying with water or a stone. Let your eyes rest slightly out of focus on the surface of the mirror, and pay attention to any patterns or shapes that appear. If doing this as a group, it's interesting to have everyone make their own black mirror and then report what they see, maybe even swapping mirrors with others to see what different results are produced.

Fire Scrying

Beltane is a fire ceremony, so fire scrying—a type of *causimancy* or *pyromancy*—is most appropriate at this time. It's also perhaps one of the most difficult scrying to explain, because it is more like a meditation than an activity. We do it in the sabbat bonfire, but it can be done in a campfire or a fireplace. I like the fullness of a fire as opposed to a single flame for scrying, which is why I don't necessarily recommend a candle. It can be done, and I have done it, but I find a fire where multiple flames are dancing together seems more gratifying.

Sometimes fire scrying does not even seem like scrying, because it's really just fire gazing. Go into a meditative state and just gaze into the blaze as the sparks dance and the flames flicker. What is the fire saying? What do the patterns in the smoke say? (This form of divination is called *capnomancy*.) Some of my best fire gazing has been done with the smoke rather than the actual fire.

Different additions to the fire produce different results. Epsom salts make the fire burn white, borax makes it a light green color, table salt makes it burn more yellow than orange or red. Calcium (found in antacid tablets) also produces an orange flame, while potassium will turn the fire a light purple. These are entertaining and add another depth to fire scrying activities.

Beltane Ritual

Dodie Graham McKay

IN THIS RITUAL WE are taking responsibility for nurturing the growth of new plants and seeing them as vessels that will fill with the returning spirits, souls, or energy of living things that have died. A small Beltane fire will be lit, and its power of purification will be evoked as participants jump over its smoke and flame, sealing the commitment to look after the development of the seeds. The powers of the elements will bear witness to the pledges we make and the actions we take. This ritual should be approached with a sense of hope and optimism for the future and tender concern for the new, young growing things that are emerging throughout the tide of Beltane.

Nurturing Reincarnation and Rebirth

This ritual can be performed by yourself or with a group, and it is ideal to do this outdoors, if possible. Adaptations for indoor ritual are included below.

Decorate your ritual space with fresh flowers, potted plants, and boughs of greenery cut from trees on your own property or from trees that you have permission from the landowner to harvest from. Bedding plants that you intend to plant in your garden, a bouquet of hand-picked wildflowers, or a bouquet from the supermarket are all great options. Use what you have naturally in your environment and that you can access without causing undue damage to the local flora.

Set up an altar and include any ritual tools that you would normally use. You will also need a watering can with water in it, packets of seeds for each participant, and a basket to hold them. If you are doing this ritual outdoors, you will need a cauldron and some kindling to start a small fire inside of it. You may also light a small fire in a firepit, but it must be small enough to safely jump over. If indoors, you can place a tealight or votive candle in a large jar, making sure the candle is secured to the bottom of the jar and that you have a long match or BBQ lighter to light it.

When selecting the seed packets for this ritual, try to choose either seeds that you will plant in your garden or seeds for wildflowers that will grow happily in your bioregion. If you are doing the ritual solo, you may want to bless some extra packets of seeds to send to friends (see "Extra Seed Packets: Mail a May Envelope" at the end of the ritual).

When your ritual space is set up as you like it, start by standing in a circle with your unlit cauldron on the ground in front of you and your basket of seeds beside it. The watering can may be placed on your altar. Take a moment to close your eyes and listen to the sounds around you. Notice the birdsong, the rustling of the wind in the trees, or the faraway sound of small animals scurrying. If you are indoors, allow yourself to visualize a green and growing landscape, secluded from civilization.

When you have had a few moments to savor these natural sensations, turn to the north and say:

> *Spirits of the north, powers of air,*
> *blow out the darkness, the tired, the stale, and the stagnant.*
> *Grant us fresh perspective and the promise of a new way of thinking.*
> *Release us gently from the gates of death*
> *and allow us into the dawning light of life anew!*

Bless our magic and witness this rite.
Hail and welcome!

Turn to the east and say:

Spirits of the east, powers of fire,
warm us with the vital life force of the dawning spring.
Grant us fire in our blood and the brilliance to activate
our potential as new life explodes all around us.
Fuel our actions as we welcome new growth and the arrival of life
anew!
Bless our magic and witness this rite.
Hail and welcome!

Turn to the south and say:

Spirits of the south, powers of earth,
sustain and ground us as we nurture these regenerated life forces.
Grant us the ability to be resourceful and patient as we care for
the young and growing things.
Manifest your bounty and benevolence so that we may be grate-
ful for life anew!
Bless our magic and witness this rite.
Hail and welcome!

Turn to the west and say:

Spirits of the west, powers of water,
fill our hearts to the brim with love for the sweetness of the small,
newborn things.
Grant us the ability to care for the well-being of regenerated be-
ings as they develop their own ways of understanding the world
they are being reborn into.
Send us dreams of a future to strive for, and rock us gently along
the tides of life anew!
Bless our magic and witness this rite.
Hail and welcome!

Return to the altar and take up the watering can and consecrate the water by saying:

I do consecrate this water; it is life.
Without this, we all shall wither.
With this, we all shall thrive.
May all we touch with our hands
flourish under our care.

Move around the circle and ask each participant, "Do you see the cycle of birth, death, reincarnation and rebirth around us? Will you take part in the mystery of reincarnation and rebirth?" If they answer yes, "water" the hands of each participant with a few drops from the watering can. If you are working this ritual alone, state out loud, "I see the cycle of birth, death, reincarnation, and rebirth. I will be an active participant in the mystery of reincarnation and rebirth." Then sprinkle some water on your own hands. Saying these words out loud allows the spirits around you to hear your commitment, and more importantly, hearing your own voice speaking is empowering, and it reinforces your will to do the work.

Move around the circle and offer the seeds to each participant and ask them, "Will you share the responsibility for nurturing these seeds and offer them the potential to host new and returning life?" If they say yes, allow them to take a packet of seeds. If you are alone, state out loud, "I will share the responsibility for nurturing these seeds and support their potential to host new and returning life."

When all present have their packet of seeds, light a small fire in your cauldron or firepit, ensuring that it is easy to jump over. If jumping is not an option, participants can hold their packet over the smoke. Each participant should have a turn jumping the fire to bless and purify themselves and their seeds and confirm their commitment to them.

After everyone has had their turn, starting in the West, thank the spirits and powers of the directions for their presence at your ritual and pour out any remaining water from the watering can on the ground as an offering.

In the days that follow, plant your seeds. If you do not have a garden of your own, find a friend, family member, or neighbour in your community who will let you sprinkle the seeds on their property, and check in on them periodically to ensure they are thriving.

Extra Seed Packets: Mail a May Envelope

In the nineteenth and early twentieth century in the United States, there was a sweet custom of anonymously leaving a May basket on the doorknob of friends, neighbours, and sweethearts. These baskets would be handmade and could be as simple as a piece of colored paper folded into a cone, decorated with ribbons and stuffed with flowers, candy, baked goodies, and small tokens of affection. The baskets would be delivered on tiptoe, the benefactors quietly sneaking up to a house, slipping a basket over the doorknob, then knocking loudly and running away. In some accounts, if you caught someone leaving a basket at your door, you were allowed to kiss them, so not every basket delivery person made too much of an effort to run away. This tradition has all but died out, so this is an opportunity to revive it—with a bit of a twist.

So many of us now live in apartment buildings or in places where a cute gift could go missing if it was left unattended on a doorknob, and chasing down delivery people to kiss them is generally not a good idea. So with safety and practicality in mind, why not create May envelopes and mail a more discrete and thoughtful treat to someone instead?

You will need:
Extra seed packets that you blessed in ritual
Envelopes and greeting cards (Handmade Beltane cards are fun to make and add a personal touch.)

Fun and colorful paper gifts like photographs, stickers, temporary
     tattoos, or bookmarks—things that fit easily into an envelope
     that don't weigh much
Appropriate postage stamps
Addresses of your recipients

Write a little note in your card explaining that these seeds have
been ritually blessed to welcome in the new and returning life this
spring and that it is your hope that the recipient will join you in
planting the seeds and nurturing them. Tuck the card, seed packet,
and any other small tokens of affection into the envelope, address it,
decorate it as much as you like, and affix appropriate postage, then
pop it in the mail. While this may not be an old-fashioned basket,
it will still be a delight for your friends and loved ones to receive
something in their mailbox that was sent with such sweetness and
affection from you. With a little effort on your part, you can make
someone truly feel loved and blessed at Beltane.

Notes

Notes

Litha

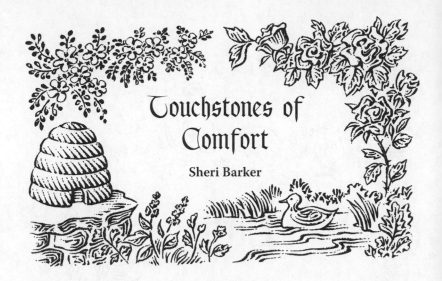

Touchstones of Comfort

Sheri Barker

THE RISING ENERGY OF late spring had me up and out of bed in time to greet the sun today. The rhythms of my body are in tune with the turning of the Wheel of the Year, and I feel that connection more than ever in these days that are softly tumbling toward Litha.

I remember my first slow and lazy summer of freedom. After school let out, I was allowed to play outdoors and travel the neighborhood without adult supervision. Timekeeping that tethered me safely to home territory was relegated to three sources: the noon fire whistle, a cowbell, and streetlights. The first signaled that it was time for lunch, the second was my mom's way of calling me to dinner, and the third meant it was time to go home for the night. I needed the touchstone comfort of home that those signals provided, but the in-between times mattered to me most.

Touchstones are a familiar constant that allow one to measure or test the genuineness of other beings or experiences. As a small child out in the bigger world, checking into my safe place kept me in tune with my intuition. The enthusiastic, bubbling, ripening energy that the earth holds at this time of year might easily have overwhelmed a child unused to connecting with it; having the security provided by my touchstone helped keep me safe. As an adult, I now believe it is important when beginning any new magical or spiritual practice to have a touchstone at hand for that same reason.

At that point in my life, I had no real experience with religion or spirituality, had never heard of a solstice, and my family did not talk about nature as anything other than a setting for sports, camping, or other outdoor activities. Yet, with each day I spent outside, my own relationship with the natural world continued to grow. During that time, I became aware of a presence that I perceived as a lady whispering to me from the other side of a doorway. She told stories that I could not quite hear but understood nonetheless, and they filled my mind with a kaleidoscope of images of nature that awakened a deep sense of curiosity and belonging.

It did not matter that I did not have words to explain that my in-between time was somehow different or that my place in the world was crossing into liminal space. I would lie in the grass and watch ladybugs, butterflies, and ants moving about and, in doing so, become part of their journey through the season. I wandered through the nearby woods and green spaces and began to see and understand my environment differently—again, no words, but I accepted my experiences because they felt not only right but also safe.

The elementary school I attended was not far from my home, and the playground was on my adventure route. On the edge of the school fields was a little ring of trees, just large enough for two or three small children to sit inside. I noticed that I could hear the whispering lady more clearly whenever I sat within the circle, so I began to spend more time there. One morning, she told me a story about the sun and how he had his own journey through the seasons. I do not remember much of the story, but she showed me images of a party celebrating the sun, and I wanted to have a party for him too.

Before the noon whistle even sounded, I skipped all the way home to ask my mother if I could have my own picnic lunch that day. I tried to explain about the party, and she said that it sounded like a nice idea. She made a peanut butter and grape jelly sandwich for me, cut it into triangles, put it in a lunchbox with a thermos of Kool-Aid and an apple, and told me to have fun with my party. Lunchbox in one hand, my stuffed dog friend tucked under the other arm, I returned to the park and the magical circle.

I put the lunchbox on the ground inside the circle and left Spot to guard it while I picked some flowers to decorate. Three or four handfuls of bright yellow dandelions, buttercups, red clover, and violets set carefully around the edge of the inner circle of the trees was festive and bright, and I arranged a little bouquet of dandelions in the cup from the thermos. Memory tells me that I sang "Happy Birthday" to the sun (it was the only celebration song I knew) then offered around bites of my lunch and sips of grape Kool-Aid. I lingered in that space, looking at spiderwebs and sun-dappled leaves. Eventually, I grew sleepy, so I scattered the bread crusts I had saved for the birds and put the apple core in a little nook in a low-hanging branch, then left to go home for an afternoon nap.

I was five or six years old, and that was my first time celebrating Litha as a solitary practitioner. The memory of that tiny witch using the materials and knowledge she had at hand to honor the sun on his special day fills my heart with gladness. The only gatekeeper she encountered was a being who held the gate open and invited her to join in, and that experience has informed my practice for decades.

What Feels Right for You?

My awareness of Litha and other holy days as they mark the turning of the Wheel of the Year has changed over time. I have read articles and books, studied by myself and with teachers, joined in rituals and celebrations with others, and continued to honor and deepen my relationship with nature and the spirit realm. In that accumulation of knowledge, perhaps the most integral part of the learning process has been observing how others celebrate.

The geography, flora, fauna, and spiritual energies of upstate New York and western North Carolina are my primary points of reference for choosing materials to prepare an altar or craft a ritual. Secondary to that has often simply been where I was in my life. Did I have access or the physical ability to gather natural supplies like flowers, seeds, shells, rocks? What about the means to purchase items like colored candles, if I could even find them in local stores?

Practitioners who live in other areas of the United States or other regions of the world might associate different plants, animals, or available foods with Litha or another sabbat. It is important to use what feels right and true to oneself and the environment. Thanks to my early introduction to Litha, I have always been comfortable using what I had available and whatever inspired me. Thanks to the generosity of others who freely share descriptions of their celebratory choices in conversation or in images, I know the possibilities are endless.

Be Creative When Adapting Rituals or Making Your Own

Two items commonly used in Litha celebrations are flowers and flames. This year I will be using flowers picked from my own gardens and candles purchased in a local metaphysical shop. I have reached a point of practice where I prefer to use locally available or supportive items for magical purposes, but over the years, I have also made use of artificial flowers and greenery, LED flameless candles, and battery-operated lanterns. I have attended bonfires in the past but no longer have local social or spiritual connections to access that type of ritual, and my dog is still too young and rambunctious for a firepit in the private space on my property to be safe or practical. Sometimes I have a nostalgic longing for the fireside, but I know it is not a requirement for honoring the sun.

Other materials I have seen used to create flower and flame are drawings done in pencil and crayon, images created in watercolor or home-crafted inks, clay or playdough sculptures, pipe cleaner figures, solar-powered lights, construction paper, and fabric art. And oh, the kitchen-crafted ceremonial objects people have shared! A cookie, cupcake, bread loaf, or pie decorated with colors or images makes for a powerful altar piece and offering. So does a ritually crafted cup of tea made with ingredients like honey, chamomile, and lavender.

One of my friends draws their altar scenes. Another asks her little children to color flowers and hangs them behind the altar. Still another once used a Litha ritual that called for carving symbols into a yellow candle, which she did not have. She did have a battery-powered tea-light candle, so drew a circle, colored it yellow, then drew her symbols into the circle before placing the candle in the center.

The Natural Connection

As the semi-retired keeper of a tiny homestead, I no longer pay much attention to keeping track of time or seasons by clocks or calendars. One of the few timekeeping pieces in my life these days is the flock of chickens that I keep, and they are as much a touchstone of comfort as the ones from my childhood. Even without a rooster crowing, they still squawk and fuss for their needs to be met in the morning and must be put up every evening.

It is easy to mark the turning of the year and the power of the sun by paying attention to the way they keep increasingly longer days between Yule and Litha. Chickens keep their own time by the light of the sun, and by Litha, they stay in their run until 8:45 p.m. or so (by human time standards). After Litha, they retire earlier each evening. At Lammas, they will be in the coop by 8:30 and at Mabon by 8:00. In the dark days of midwinter, they will turn themselves in by 5:30 p.m., only to begin keeping longer days once Winter Solstice has passed.

I have developed a habit of taking an evening stroll around my property before I do the work of gathering eggs and putting the birds up, and this evening is no exception. The light in the north yard is especially nice at this point in the day, so I headed up to place a fresh tomato as an offering to the land spirits on the habitat fence that bounds part of the northern property line. While walking through the tall grass, I flushed out a plump and healthy-looking eastern cottontail rabbit. He bolted past the hawthorn and across the greenway, a fuzzy streak of brown, gray, and white. As always, my inner child was delighted by the sight of a wild rabbit, and while I was admiring his beauty and speed, I could not help but smile.

His presence is a sign that this land is recovering a healthy eco-system and that the natural abundance I am striving to foster here is taking hold. In my own Litha ritual, I will be celebrating the cycle of seasons that is allowing that to happen. I will also honor the sun for his life and death part in that cycle. The more my relationship with this tiny bit of land and the land spirits develops, the more I understand the meanings and importance of the turning of the wheel.

The evening bird chorus is singing the day asleep as the light fades from the sky. A red fox calls from somewhere up the mountain and another answers. I see random flashes of light along the tree lines as the fireflies wake up, and I amuse myself by thinking about them, rabbit, fox, and other neighbors attending a Litha celebration together. What a lovely story that is.

In the coming days of the approaching sabbat, I will likely wander outside many times without any intention other than to feel the earth under my body, dirt and good green stuff in my hands, and the warmth of the sun on my skin for as long as I can. The days will soon grow shorter, and the slow progression through the darkling days of the year will begin.

Litha. Midsummer. Summer Solstice. Speaking the names is a conjuration that makes my tongue tingle with power promised and remembered. Through years of spiritual adventuring, I have celebrated this holy day using each of these names at different times, and I shiver at the thought of once again standing with toes on the edge of all things possible, leaning into the liminal space that enfolds them.

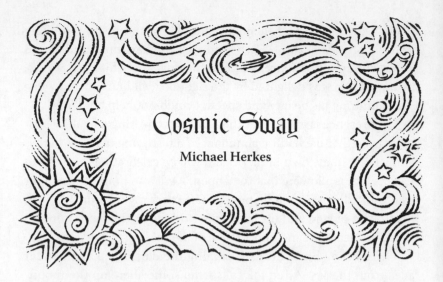

Cosmic Sway

Michael Herkes

JUNE 20 WELCOMES LITHA, also known as Midsummer or the summer solstice, celebrating the arrival of summer and the longest day of the year. This is also the first day of Cancer season, highlighting our emotional depths and encouraging us to nurture ourselves and those around us.

Litha represents a time of abundance, growth, and vitality. It is a celebration of the Sun's power and its ability to bring life to all living things.

Cancer embodies qualities such as nurturing, emotional sensitivity, intuition, and a deep connection to nature. During this time, we may find ourselves more attuned to our emotions, seeking comfort in close relationships, family bonds, and creating a safe haven for ourselves. Just as Litha encourages us to embrace the warmth of the Sun's rays, Cancer season urges us to embrace our vulnerability and connect with our inner selves on a deeper level. By aligning with these energies during this period, we can tap into our intuition, cultivate meaningful connections with others, and create an environment that fosters growth both internally and externally.

Celebrating Litha

Many people also choose to create altars or sacred spaces dedicated to Litha. These can be adorned with fresh summer flowers, herbs, and symbols representing the Sun. Lighting yellow, orange, or gold candles and frankincense, orange, or cinnamon incense can add an extra touch of reverence during this special time. Embracing nature through outdoor activities such as hiking, swimming, or simply taking a leisurely walk in a park helps in connecting to the energy of this festival. This allows you to soak up the vibrant energy of summer while appreciating the beauty of your surroundings. You may even wish to organize a small gathering with friends and loved ones for a bonfire or outdoor picnic to bask in the warmth of the Sun while enjoying good company and delicious food.

New Moon in Cancer

The New Moon in Cancer on June 25 at 6:32 a.m. presents an opportunity to connect with our emotions and intuition, and create a foundation for personal growth. The energy of this Moon is all about finding comfort within our own vulnerability and embracing the power of self-care. It encourages us to dive deep into our emotions, understanding them on a profound level and using them as guides for our journey ahead.

One ritual you may wish to embark on now begins with creating a sacred space by lighting candles or burning incense that evokes feelings of warmth and security. Next, take some time to reflect on your emotions and desires. Write them down on paper or speak them aloud, allowing yourself to fully express your intentions for personal growth during this lunar cycle.

You may also choose to meditate or engage in visualization exercises to further connect with your inner self. As you do this, focus on self-care practices that resonate with you personally. This could include taking soothing baths infused with essential oils aligned with Cancer, such as jasmine or gardenia, or engaging in activities such as journaling or painting that allow you to express your emotions freely.

Conjunctions and Retrogrades

A Saturn-Neptune conjunction on June 29 at 4:20 a.m. brings together the energies of structure and spirituality. Saturn represents discipline, responsibility, and practicality, while Neptune embodies dreams, intuition, and imagination. When these two planets align, it creates a unique blend of grounded spirituality. This conjunction encourages us to find harmony between our material, real-world responsibilities and our spiritual aspirations. It prompts us to bring our dreams into reality by applying practicality and discipline.

On the other hand, when Venus meets Uranus in a conjunction on July 4 at 8:45 a.m., we experience an electrifying energy that ignites excitement and unpredictability in relationships and creativity. Venus symbolizes love, beauty, and harmony, while Uranus represents innovation, rebellion, and freedom. This combination infuses relationships with an unconventional spark that challenges traditional norms or brings sudden changes. It encourages us to embrace individuality within partnerships or explore new artistic expressions outside conventional boundaries.

Later that day at 5:34 p.m., Neptune goes retrograde until December 10. When Neptune goes into retrograde motion—the planet associated with dreams, illusions, and spirituality—its energy becomes more internalized. This period invites us to examine our belief systems or illusions that may be clouding our judgment or hindering personal growth. It is an ideal time for self-reflection to gain clarity on spiritual matters or dissolve any illusions that no longer serve us.

Full Moon in Capricorn

The energy of a Full Moon in Capricorn on July 10 at 4:37 p.m. is characterized by a sense of ambition, discipline, and practicality.

Capricorn is an earth sign known for its strong work ethic and determination. During this lunar phase, you may feel a heightened drive to achieve your goals and take on responsibilities with a focused mindset. This Moon also helps encourage you to be more organized, diligent, and goal oriented. It may also bring about a desire for recognition and success.

To celebrate the Full Moon in Capricorn, one can engage in rituals or practices that align with these themes. It is a perfect time to set intentions for the coming months, particularly in terms of career advancement or long-term goals. Write out a structured plan or strategy to achieve these objectives and burn it under the light of the Full Moon to amplify your ambition, career success, and financial stability. Try working with crystals like black tourmaline for grounding and protection or malachite for ambition, focus, and prosperity. Essential oils such as cypress, oakmoss, or vetiver can provide stability and promote focus during ritual or meditation practices.

Mercury Retrograde and Leo Season

On July 18 at 12:45 a.m., Mercury goes retrograde again until August 11. Starting in Cancer season and ending in Leo season, this retrograde will likely see communication mishaps relevant to ego and selfishness. During this time, be sure to make empowered decisions that allow you to radiate your light without snuffing others' out.

The energy of a New Moon in Leo on July 24 at 3:11 p.m. is vibrant, passionate, and full of creativity. Leo, being ruled by the Sun, brings a fiery and confident energy that encourages self-expression and individuality. This celestial event is an opportune time to tap into your inner courage and embrace your unique talents.

To harness the powerful energy of a New Moon in Leo, consider performing a ritual or spell to boost confidence and creative self-expression. Begin by finding a quiet space where you can connect with your intentions. Light a candle in the color associated with Leo, such as gold or orange, to symbolize the radiant energy of this sign. Take a moment to reflect on what areas of your life could benefit from increased confidence and self-assuredness. Write down your desires or goals on a piece of paper, focusing on how you want to shine brightly like the Sun.

As you visualize yourself embodying the qualities of Leo, recite affirmations that align with this energy. Repeat phrases such as "I am confident in my abilities," "I embrace my uniqueness," or "I radiate joy and creativity." To further enhance this ritual, incorporate elements that represent Leo's ruling element: fire. You may choose to safely burn the paper with your intentions in a fireproof dish or release it into a bonfire while visualizing your desires manifesting. Remember to express gratitude for the opportunities ahead and close the ritual by extinguishing the candle while expressing gratitude for Leo's empowering energy.

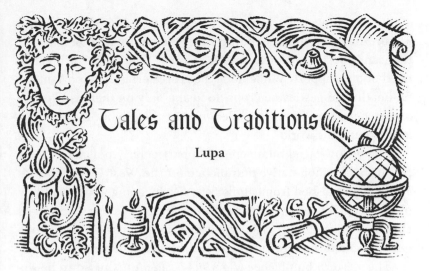

Tales and Traditions

Lupa

THE SUMMER SOLSTICE IS here, and this is one of the most active times in nature! Young animals have figured out the first things they need to know and are now refining that knowledge to gain skills and understanding that will help them survive to adulthood. Flowers abound, and the first fruits and seeds ripen on vines, stems, and twigs.

Yet not everything that grows this time of year is here for the taking. Even at a time of seeming abundance, there are species in peril, and there are those that need not validate their existences by being useful to us humans.

Yellow-Faced Bumblebee (*Bombus vosnesenskii*)

As summer arrives, the trees, bushes, and meadows are full of pollinators. Butterflies, diurnal moths, beetles, and hummingbirds travel from flower to flower in search of nectar, transporting pollen as they go. Bees are probably the best-known pollinators, but sadly their numbers have been decreasing in recent years.

"Save the bees!" has been a clarion call among environmentalists and other nature-lovers for years now. Originally prompted by the collapse of domesticated European honeybee hives in the early

2000s, this movement to protect bees has since blossomed into a more nuanced understanding that it is wild native bees—four thousand species in North America alone—that are in the greatest need of our support. While honeybees are certainly important for pollinating domesticated crops, focusing only on them is like saying we need to save cattle while ignoring the plight of wild ungulates around the world.

The yellow-faced bumblebee is a particularly poignant example. It's a common native bumblebee on the West Coast, and it's easily distinguished from similar species by being almost entirely black except for yellow on its head and a narrow yellow stripe on its abdomen. Like other social bees, it lives in colonies consisting of a queen, a couple hundred workers, and a handful of drones.

The western bumblebee (*Bombus occidentalis*) used to be the one of the most common native bumblebees here, but intensive use of this species in commercial pollination introduced European bee diseases from honeybees that caused western bumblebee numbers to crash hard. Other native bees have also seen declines due to diseases introduced by honeybees, as well as habitat loss and increased use of pesticides.

And it is the yellow-faced bumblebee that seems to have been filling in the gaps left behind. While it may seem like a good thing that a native bee is moving into empty niches, their expansion is not coupled with the return of other native bees, and it remains to be seen whether rarer species will make a comeback.

Ghost Pipe (*Monotropa uniflora*)

Another sensitive species for this Summer Solstice is the ghost pipe, formerly known as the Indian pipe. It's named for its translucent white coloration that makes it look like a little phantom floating above the forest floor, and its drooping flower often looks like a bowed head on the stem. Often mistaken for a fungus, it's actually a parasitic plant. It draws nutrients from nearby trees using the mycorrhizal mycelium of nearby *Russula* and *Lactarius* fungi, and therefore does not need to develop the chlorophyll that gives other plants their green hues.

Ghost pipe's range is large, and it is found in large areas of eastern North America and the Pacific Northwest. However, individual colonies of this plant may be few and far between, and because it requires specialized habitats that support *Russula* and *Lactarius* fungi and their tree partners, habitat loss is a major risk. Moreover, rampant harvesting of ghost pipe by herbalists for tinctures and other remedies further cuts down their numbers. While not considered endangered on a national level, several states list ghost pipe as a species of concern, and in some cases "critically imperiled."

After the long months of winter and spring when there may have been little to nothing to harvest, it may be tempting to ramp up one's foraging efforts once summer arrives and take every opportunity available to us. Yet caution is advised, as overexploitation has led to the extinction of more than one species and threatens many others. Sometimes the best thing we can do for the ongoing health of the nature around us is to exercise some restraint and leave special treasures like the ghost pipe where we found them.

Northern Red Belt (*Fomitopsis mounceae*)

Walk through the conifer forests near where I live, and you'll see both live and dead trees festooned with large, shelf-shaped mushrooms that have various bands of brown and red, and an outer rim of white. These are the fruiting bodies of the northern red belt fungus, one of the few fungi whose mushrooms last more than a few days. In fact, each one may persist for years, producing a new set of spores each year.

Northern red belt is a saprophytic fungus, meaning that it helps to decompose decaying matter, particularly wood. It is responsible for breaking down cellulose in dead wood, and can even affect the dead heartwood of live trees that have received an injury. A healthy tree can thrive in spite of the internal decay so long as the live tissues that convey sap throughout its body are unaffected.

This isn't such great news for the timber industry, as the "brown rot" caused by northern red belt and other cellulose saprophytes can make the wood of the tree commercially useless. Moreover, this species of fungus isn't edible, nor does it have widespread medicinal uses. I've run into more than one person who dismissed this mushroom entirely simply because we can't eat it or otherwise extract anything of commercial value from it.

Yet as summer sees life kicking into high gear, it's important for us to remember that it isn't all about us. There are many species that have no extrinsic value to humans, yet they are important not only for their ecological interconnections, but because—like all living beings—they are marvelous simply for existing. Litha is a good time to meditate on the intrinsic value of all organisms within the vast biodiversity of the planet, and not just estimate their value in board feet, gallons, or dollars.

Feasts and Treats

Dallas Jennifer Cobb

THE LONGEST DAY OF the year and the shortest night are ours to celebrate at Litha. Known also as the Summer Solstice and Midsummer, Litha is a time to celebrate fertility and abundance. The crops are growing, and the garden is filled with flowers, herbs, and lots of leafy greens. Honouring the element of fire, we greet the mythical "sun" king, or young god.

Some traditions celebrate Litha with a labyrinth walk, contemplating what needs to "come to light," meditating and seeking spiritual answers as they walk the path in, and hearing the illuminating message from spirit as they walk out.

Our Litha feast includes Cedar Plank Salmon, Herbed Rice, and Edible Flowers Salad. To invoke the fire element of Litha, we will cook the salmon on the barbecue. With a harvest that begins as early as April in some areas, salmon is readily available for Litha. Look for wild salmon or explore farmed salmon, depending on local availability.

This is a relatively quick feast to prepare. Remember to marinate the salmon in advance, and when it is close to feast time, start the rice. While the rice cooks, you can prepare the salmon and salad so that your meal comes together easily. The quick preparation and cooking time, combined with the easy-to-clean grill, means you can enjoy the long hours of light sitting outside with your friends, family, neighbours, and magical circle. Delight in the warmth of the sun's fiery energy and in the abundance of fresh foods so readily available.

Herbed Rice

I like this recipe because it brings small flecks of greenery into the white of the rice—a great metaphor for the abundance of green available at this time of year, especially here in Ontario, Canada, when we have just come through a long, white, and snowy winter.

Choosing your favorite flavours, or perhaps noticing what is available in your garden or locally at the farm stand, this Herbed Rice offers infinite variety. Every time I make it, the recipe shifts a little depending on which herbs I use. The end result is a subtle shift in flavour. Let experimentation be part of the practice, and note the magical results.

Prep time: 5 minutes
Cooking time: 15 minutes
Servings: 8

3½ cups water
½ teaspoon sea salt
1 teaspoon butter
½ cup mix of either parsley and thyme or dill, finely chopped
2 cups basmati rice
Optional: squeeze of lemon juice if using dill

Rinse the rice to remove starch, then drain. Add water, salt, butter, fresh herbs, and optional lemon juice to the pot.

Bring the pot to a boil. Put a lid on it, and turn it down to simmer for 15 minutes. Then turn the heat off. Resist the urge to look in the pot; leave the lid on and let the steam finish cooking the rice as it rests for 10 minutes.

When you open it to serve, you will see the beautifully green, speckled, fluffy white rice. On the plate, the green and white accent the pink of the salmon and are dressed up by the colors of the edible flowers. This is a feast dish that looks as gorgeous as it tastes.

Cedar Plank Salmon

I started making this after finding the recipe on Once Upon a Chef. I have modified the recipe slightly but give credit to its origins. Cedar planks are widely available these days because many cooks have realized the wonderful smoky flavour that they impart. I like that the plank makes it way easier to clean up the barbecue after. Just remember to thoroughly soak your cedar plank before cooking with it. The last thing you want is a flaming cedar plank scorching your salmon.

I add soy sauce to the marinade for a distinctly "teriyaki" flavour, or alternately, one tablespoon of maple syrup for a sweet and zingy taste.

Prep time: 5 minutes
Marinating time: 30 minutes
Cooking time: 15 minutes
Servings: 8

A well-soaked cedar plank used to grill (These are widely available in grocery and kitchen stores.)
½ cup olive oil
3 teaspoons lemon zest, grated
4 cloves garlic, finely diced
2 tablespoons soy sauce
2 tablespoons fresh rosemary, finely diced
1 tablespoon fresh thyme, finely diced
1 teaspoon sea salt
1 teaspoon black pepper
8 (6 oz) salmon fillets, skin removed
8 lemon wedges

Remember to soak your cedar plank(s) in water before cooking with them. Turn the barbecue on to a medium-high heat (400–450°F).

In a big bowl, mix olive oil, lemon zest, garlic, soy sauce, rosemary, thyme, salt, and pepper. Stir everything together. Then place salmon in the bowl and roll it around to coat evenly. Cover the bowl and refrigerate, letting the salmon marinade for half an hour, though longer periods of marinading definitely add more flavour.

Dab your cedar plank dry and put the well-marinated salmon on it. Then put the plank on the barbecue and close the lid. Grill 10–15 minutes or until it is softly pink and flaky.

Remember to keep an eye on the cedar plank and quickly extinguish it with water if it begins to burn.

Slide the salmon off of the cedar plank onto the plate, add Herbed Rice and the Edible Flowers Salad, and serve with lemon wedges.

Edible Flowers Salad

I love edible flowers. Not only do they lend interesting and complex flavours to food, but they are colorful and add to the visual appeal of the plate. I make sure that the edible flowers I like best are planted in my garden so I have quick and easy access to them.

If you have a garden or a window box, consider planting calendula and nasturtium from seed in the spring, and gather their seeds when they are dry. These seeds can be replanted next spring, or you might find some volunteers have self-seeded and sprout and grow again.

Pansies are cold tolerant and widely available in the spring. Gifting yourself with a basket of pansies will ensure you have the pretty, edible petals to use throughout spring and summer.

I have also dressed my salads with chive flowers when they are in season. Big, purple, and pretty, they add to the colorful palette.

Prep time: 3 minutes

Servings: 8

8 cups of lettuce or mixed baby greens, washed and torn to bite size
1 cup of edible flowers (calendula, nasturtium, chives, or pansies),
    washed and removed from stems
¾ cup olive oil
¼ cup balsamic vinegar
Salt and pepper to taste

In a large salad bowl, combine the mixed greens. Sprinkle the edible flowers on top.

In a glass jar with a lid, combine all salad dressing ingredients. Seal the jar and shake vigorously until the dressing blends together.

When you are ready to plate the feast, place about 1 cup of salad on each plate. Make sure everyone has some gorgeous edible flowers on their salad. Drizzle with 1 tablespoon of dressing, or more to taste.

Any leftover dressing can be labelled with name and date and kept in the fridge for future use.

Reference

Segal, Jenn. "Cedar Planked Salmon with Lemon, Garlic & Herbs." Once Upon a Chef. Accessed January 3, 2024. https://www.onceuponachef.com/recipes/cedar-plank-salmon-with-lemon-garlic-herbs.html.

Crafty Crafts

Elizabeth Barrette

WITH LITHA COMES HIGH summer. The sun is at its greatest strength, and the longest day is at hand. Everything is green and growing. Fruit begins to ripen on trees. Gardens are bursting with produce. Flowers spill over fences. Young animals frisk in the fields. Litha rituals often focus on the sun's power, using solar imagery. Sometimes they celebrate the flowers and fruits of the season. Bright, bold colors predominate the decor.

Pressed Plant Bookmarks

Every Book of Shadows deserves a beautiful bookmark. It's easy to make your own using leaves and flowers from your garden. These also make lovely gifts for ritual attendees.

Materials

Flower petals and leaves
Paper towels
Heavy books or other weights
Clear contact paper
Scissors
Hole punch
⅛-inch or ¼-inch ribbon

Cost: $5–$10

Time spent: 30–45 minutes to gather and prepare plants, 3–7 days of drying time, and 10–15 minutes per bookmark for assembly

Design Ideas

If possible, choose flowers and leaves from your yard or a coven-mate's. Otherwise, you could buy some. Consider looking up the symbolic meanings of flowers, herbs, trees, and other plants to suit your Litha theme.

Paper towels and books or other weights enable you to press plant parts for no extra cost. If you already have flower-pressing tools, however, you can use those.

Clear contact paper is smooth on one side, sticky on the other. Putting two sticky sides together makes a great seal. Craft stores often have several varieties in sheets or rolls.

Narrow ribbon works well for finishing the bookmark and ensures that it doesn't get "lost" inside the book. Choose colors based on your Litha ritual; solar colors are popular. Alternatively, match the flower petals chosen.

Assembly

Pick flowers and leaves on a clear, dry day in midmorning after any dew has dried but before anything starts to wilt in the heat. Choose things that will press flat easily, not things with too much texture.

Set up your pressing area with paper towels and weights. Tiny flowers or those not divided into petals can be pressed whole, as can most leaves. Most flowers should be picked apart so you can press the petals separately to make them completely flat. Place them between two paper towels, then press between two weights.

Wait several days to a week, checking every other day, until the flowers and leaves are dry.

Lay out dried petals and leaves on a table to find a design you like.

Use scissors to cut strips of contact paper larger than you want the bookmarks to be. Peel the backing paper off one strip at a time.

Transfer the petals and leaves to the contact paper. Press another strip over the top. Trim the edges of the bookmark, keeping plant parts at least ¼ inch from the edges.

Punch a hole in the top of the bookmark. Cut a ribbon twice the length of the bookmark. Double it, thread the fold through the hole, then pass the free ends through the fold. Pull the ribbon into a lark's head knot to stay secure.

Ice-Dyed T-shirt

Ice dyeing uses powdered dye and ice cubes to create beautiful, unpredictable works of art. You can combine it with any tie-dye techniques, such as using rubber bands to make concentric circles or folding into accordion pleats to create stripes.

Materials
Plastic dropcloth
2 or more colors of powdered dye (commercial dye or colored drink mix)

100 percent cotton T-shirt (or another item)
Bucket of ice cubes
Cooling rack
Large tray or tub
Optional: rubber bands or other tie-dye accessories, rubber gloves,
    long cardboard strip
    Cost: $15–$50
    Time spent: 15–20 minutes for the craft, 24 hours setting time,
2 or more hours for washing and drying finished T-shirt

Design Ideas

Powdered dye comes in a huge range of colors and qualities. If you're experienced with tie-dye, consider investing in top-notch dye powder from a business like Dharma Trading Co. It costs more and is more complicated to use, but gives brilliant, colorfast results. If you're inexperienced, powdered drink mix like Kool-Aid is safe and easy to use, though it doesn't give colors as bright. Choose rich colors like black cherry, grape, or blue raspberry for best results. Cheap powdered dye like Rit falls in between. For commercial dye, you'll want protective equipment like gloves.

Most dyes work best with natural fibers, and 100 percent cotton is readily available and dyes well. Cotton also wicks incredibly well, so colors will blend on it; if you use yellow and red dyes, you'll also get orange. T-shirts are the most popular, but you can also ice dye other things such as socks or an altar cloth.

Assembly

If you're working with commercial dye, read the instructions on the box and follow them, because different dyes have different steps. With powdered drink mix, you can just dump it over the ice.

Cover your work area with a plastic dropcloth.

Prepare the T-shirt based on what dye you have. Powdered drink mix requires no setup, but some commercial dyes need a mordant or other preparation.

Scrunch the T-shirt or use rubber bands to make tie-dye patterns. Place it on the cooling rack and put that in the tub. You can wrap a long cardboard strip around the T-shirt to create a collar for keeping the ice in place. Pile ice cubes over the T-shirt, covering it completely.

Open a dye packet and sprinkle dye over the ice cubes. Then follow that with the other color(s). You can make an ombré design by putting one color over half the ice and a different color over the rest, or you can make wide stripes or random patterns—whatever you like. Cover as much of the ice as possible with the dye so you get good color saturation.

Place the tub in a sunny location. Watch the power of the sun melt the ice. The meltwater will activate the dye and distribute it onto the fabric, creating beautiful and unique designs as it flows. Once the ice has melted, let the T-shirt stay in the tub for twenty-four hours to set the dye, but you can bring the tub indoors.

Next, wring out the T-shirt. (It will look like a muddy lump, but that's normal.) Rinse it in the sink with cold water to remove excess dye. Then run the T-shirt through the washing machine using gentle detergent. Then run it through the dryer on hot.

If you're not using high-end dye with its own complete process (which you should follow carefully) on the box, consider soaking your T-shirt in water with a splash of vinegar, then re-wash and re-dry it. This helps set a variety of dyes and stains.

Litha and Lithomancy

Charlie Rainbow Wolf

CRYSTAL DIVINATION IS VERY popular these days. All kinds of divination sets and cards are readily available everywhere from online to metaphysical shops to even booksellers and craft stores. When I first started learning how to read the stones over thirty years ago, I initially learned parrot fashion: this means this, that means that. I then started working with a casting cloth—the same cloth I mentioned in the Samhain section. There are so very many different ways to read stones, and people who are wary of the stigma attached to crystal balls or tarot cards may not be quite so hesitant to work with rocks!

Different Stones Mean Different Things

I had five stones when I first started working with crystals: amethyst, aquamarine, carnelian, rose quartz, and tourmaline. They covered the main areas of life quite well. Amethyst referred to spirituality, creativity, and fairness. Its function was to simply receive the energy of the reading. Aquamarine indicated mental agility, happiness, and clear thinking. Its function in the reading was to help me understand the message being given. Carnelian pointed to the self, which really is the only viewpoint any of us can ever have because we perceive things through our own reality. Its function in the reading was to ground it so that we don't blow things out of proportion. Rose quartz is the crystal of love, but not the "I love you. Do you love me? How much do you love me? Will you always love me?" that comes from ego. Rose quartz represents pure unconditional love. Its function in the reading was to convey the messages in a way they could be accepted. Finally, tourmaline referred to power, determination, and purpose. It brought focus and discipline to the reading.

I got wonderful readings using just these five stones for several weeks, but I got hungry. I obtained a copy of *The Crystal Workbook* by Ursula Markham (Aquarian Press, 1988) and started exploring the meanings of other stones and adding them to the mix, eventually doing without the casting cloth. Some of the first stones I added were Venus's-hairstone, a type of rutilated quartz, which I associated with creativity and latent artistic talent; snakeskin agate, which I associated with major life changes; tektite, which spoke to me of challenges and upheaval and other demanding situations; and bloodstone, which I used as a health marker.

No Crystals? No Problem!

If you want to do a stone reading but you don't have the crystals to do it, a fun and very workable set can be made with some river rock or crushed stone, and either tempera paints or crayons. Paint or mark each stone with a different color, with each color representing a different energy. If you are working with smaller stones and already have a casting cloth, you may use that, or use the grid below for another way of interpreting the stones.

We've had great enjoyment doing stone divinations using larger painted rocks and a hopscotch-type grid drawn on the pavement. The different squares on the grid referred to different things. The stones were gathered in the hands and tossed into the grid. Stones that did not lie in the grid were not counted; only the stones that fell in the squares were part of the reading.

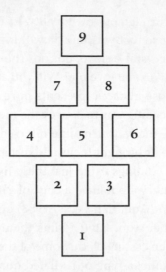

Interpreting the Stones

It's not important to ask a particular question here because the meaning of each stone and the box in which it lands will provide the guidance. However, this method of divination can easily be adapted to answering specific questions should direction be needed for a particular situation.

- Box 1 is closest to where the person tossing the stones will stand because it represents them. The stones that land here reveal what's important at the moment and what the immediate issues are. If this box is empty, then it means the person is more focused on things that are happening to other people rather than to themselves.
- Box 2 represents the stone thrower's feelings, where happiness might be found, or where joy is possibly being stolen by other people and circumstances. If this box is empty, either the querent is unconcerned about things, or perhaps they are trying to hide their emotions.
- Box 3 reveals where growth is concerned and what areas of the questioner's life are changing. Look to the stones that land here to see how that growth is unfolding: a growing family, a

growing wallet, a growing spiritual practice, etc. If this box is empty, growth could be stagnant.

- Box 4 concerns everything that is beyond the caster's control, and often if box 1 is empty, then there will be action in box 4. These circumstances don't necessarily have to be bad things, but they are things that happen to the person, not things that the person instigates. If this box is empty, usually the questioner is very independent.

- Box 5 shows how the stone thrower communicates, and this includes all kinds of communication, such as their social media pages, their education, and more. If this box is empty, it may be indicative of hidden talent or not living up to their full potential. It could also mean that there is some kind of a communication breakdown somewhere in their lives that needs to be dealt with.

- Box 6 points to romance and love life and creativity in all forms, including artistic pursuits and even children. If this box is empty, then the questioner may be hurting in some way, either unhappy with their relationship or feeling lonely and uninspired.

- Box 7 is where intuition, dreams, wishes, psychic energy, and things paranormal might be found. If this box is busy, then the person is probably very psychic. If it is empty, either they're very practical, or they have not awakened into their psychic potential yet.

- Box 8 is where the questioner might be struggling. This is not the happiest of placements, and it is one of the boxes where it is good that it is empty. If this box is busy, then the questioner may feel trapped somehow or may feel that they are downtrodden and things are spinning totally out of their control. Please do *not* try to miss this box when you throw the stones! This and box number 4 may not be the most joyful placements, but they are important. We all have struggles, and we all have challenges, and stones falling in these boxes reveal what they are and how to overcome them.

- Box 9 may be the final outcome box, but I like to interpret it as the "how can we help?" box. The stones here indicate where the questioner can look for help.

It's interesting to compare grids when working as a group. For example, the stone in box 1 represents the person who is getting the reading. Box 9 represents how others can help. Do any of the stones match? If my box 1 stone is the same as your box 9 stone, then it might indicate that I am the person to help you with your situation. If my box 1 stone is the same as your box 5 stone, perhaps there is something we need to talk about. This exercise is a great way to get people talking!

Litha Ritual

Sheri Barker

THERE ARE A VARIETY of symbols and colors associated with Litha that make creating an altar and performing a ritual a wonderful opportunity for expressing your relationship with nature, the sun, and the environment.

Celebrating the Sun

This simple ritual is designed for solitary practitioners or groups. If you are setting the altar for group participation, ask each attendee to bring an item that represents timekeeping to them. Determine ahead of time how formal or informal your ritual will be. Inform those attending of expectations for behavior and dress code, if there is one. Flower crowns or paper sun crowns can certainly add to the celebratory air!

The first step in setting an altar is determining the location and what the altar will be made of. Because I live with cats who love to explore everything I do, I usually set up ritual altars on my desk. That way, I can herd cats and clean up quickly once the ritual working is complete. Weather permitting, I might set an altar outdoors. Choose a place where you will have privacy (if you need it) and where you will be comfortable working. If you have a regular altar space you can use, just add some extra items or reset the altar. A windowsill, dresser top, dinner plate or tray, open spot in your yard, a park, or even a picnic table make good temporary altars.

Items needed for this ritual

We have all seen the fancy, overdone, stage-dressed altars in movies and tutorials. Please do not let those images overwhelm you. Remember that this is your altar, created to serve your purpose. The most important thing is that the items you choose to include have significance for you. Suggested items for this ritual are:

Altar Cloth

It is customary (but not necessary) to use an altar cloth that corresponds to the colors of the sabbat. The colors most often associated with Litha are those that represent the sun or fire and other colors of summer. Yellow, orange, red, white, pink, and purple represent the sun and many of the flowers in bloom during this season. You can also use blue, green, and brown to represent the sky and earth. The cloth can be a solid color or something printed in a pattern that appeals to you. I have used tablecloths, wall hangings, dish towels, and nothing.

Candles

For this ritual, only one candle is required and can be any size and any color that represents the sun (such as yellow, orange, red, white). If you are unsure of options, refer to the discussion in my introduction article at the beginning of this section.

Of course, you may choose to use candles to represent the quarters and a divine presence if you are calling one in. Note: if you are going to include any deities in your version of this ritual, you can add a statue or other depiction of them to your altar.

Timekeeping

Choose something that represents timekeeping for you. Suggestions are a watch, a clock, the written lyrics to your favorite lullaby, an hourglass, or a sundial. For this ritual, I will be using a fresh egg from my chickens because they are the most basic timekeeping element in my life. Note: if performing the ritual as a solitary practitioner, you will need one timekeeping piece on the altar. If this is to be a group ritual, you will need one piece for the altar, and each participant will need their own piece.

Altar Decorations

Select flowers in colors that represent the sun: marigolds, sunflowers, calendula, clover, dandelions, and daffodils are a few. Add flowers or herbs that are symbolic of the season, such as lavender, roses, chamomile, bee balm, St. John's wort, yarrow, or rosemary. Anything that grows locally to you and is in bloom or leafed out in this season is appropriate to use.

Select items that you are drawn to or that seem significant to you for this time of year or for celebrating the sun. The pieces on my altar will include flowers, acorns, a rabbit figurine, a candle shaped like a baby chick, and something to represent bees. There will also be a few small stones I have picked up over time while walking or adventuring.

Remember that whimsy and humor are acceptable as long as used respectfully or with reverence. If a plastic statue of a ladybug wearing sunglasses represents your joy for this sabbat, then by all means, place that on your altar!

If you choose to use crystals, I recommend researching those that are local to the area in which you live and acquiring one of those. Crystals can be cleansed and used repeatedly, so you do not need to acquire one for every altar or ritual. I am generally not a crystal witch and tend to choose altar pieces by intuition, color, or the shiny factor. I have also set many pretty altars using the colored glass pieces available in craft stores.

Place one item on the altar to represent the sun: a yellow flower in a vase or glass, a pressed flower, a small figurine, or anything else that says "sun" to you. If you want to draw or craft a sun from construction paper or other material, do so as part of your ritual preparation.

Honey

Prepare a small dish of honey with enough spoons or popsicle sticks for each celebrant to use. You will also need a receptacle for the used ones out of sight at the end of the altar.

Altar Setup

Drape the altar with the cloth. Then place the single sun candle near the back center edge of the altar. If using quarter candles or a deity image, add those to the altar next, spaced as you are accustomed.

Put the timekeeping piece on the altar to the left of the sun candle. Leave an open space for it to the right of the sun candle. Note: in group ritual, each celebrant will hold their own timekeeping piece.

Place the honey dish and spoons in front of the sun candle. Place the receptacle for used items at the far right end of the altar.

Finally, take your time decorating the rest of the altar with the other items you have gathered. While there is no specific order for their placement, you should be thoughtful and considerate in preparing the altar to honor the sun.

Ritual

The table is set, the guests have arrived, and it is time for the celebration to begin.

As you are accustomed to doing, cleanse and bless the ritual space, then cleanse and bless each celebrant as they are welcomed into the space. Cast the circle, call the quarters, and call in deities if you choose. Celebrants may stand or sit, as you choose, but should be organized in a circle.

For solitary ritual, you can silently read or speak these words. For group ritual, read out loud:

Since Yule we have traveled with the sun halfway around the Wheel of the Year to arrive at this point in time. Litha is the longest day of the year. The sun has nurtured us, warmed us, and given his light to us over all these days. On this day, he reaches the peak of his power.

At this point, light the sun candle.

Let us celebrate and remember the sun in gratitude and love as he has carried us here to the threshold of the sweet days of summer, to the threshold of abundance, setting us up for success and growth through the coming season and into the darkling days.

For a solitary ritual, pick up the altar timepiece and hold it in your hands. For group ritual, each individual will hold their own timepiece, and the altar timepiece will remain on the altar.

The world we live in has altered our understanding of time, forcing us to conform to routines and schedules that are unnatural to our bodies and to our spirits.

The sun is the true keeper of time and always has been. The natural world around us remembers this, and regardless of the imposition of the human construct of time, it is imperative to our well-being that we remember.

The timepiece that you hold today will become a touchstone of comfort to the true and natural order of life. Let go of societally imposed expectations and definitions of success or achievement, and remember how sweet it is to move in the natural order and time of your life.

Looking at the light of the sun on your altar (or the light of the sun around you!), move your hands over your timepiece to fold and press the time truth and natural energy of the sun into the timepiece. What does the sun's energy mean to you on this day, when he is at the peak of his power? What are you grateful for? What is the sweetest thing in your life? Think about the people, animals, and natural scenes that bring you happiness and peace, and store those good feelings inside your timepiece.

Spend about five minutes on this exercise or as long as you need. When you are finished, hold your timepiece close until you are sure you will remember its new significance. (Note: For a group ritual, participants may either leave their timepiece on the altar until the circle is opened or continue to hold it when they return to their seat or place in circle. The officiant should make this decision before ritual begins.)

For a group ritual, the officiant will read the following instructions out loud to participants and guide them through as necessary before taking action themselves. For solitary ritual, follow these instructions:

When you are ready, approach the altar. Stand to the left of the sun candle, holding your timepiece. Close your eyes and settle yourself into this present moment with the sun. Think of his natural movement. When you open your eyes, step sideways so that you are directly in front of the sun candle. In your own words (out loud or silently), express your gratitude to the sun for all that he does, and ask his blessings on your timepiece.

Again, when you are ready, step to the space to the right of the sun candle. Take a deep breath, then release it. You may leave your timepiece in the empty space (if previously determined) or carry it with you as you move on.

Pick up a spoon and take a taste of the honey that is on the altar, savoring the sweetness of being in this moment and remembering the sweetness of the sun.

Return to your seat or place in circle when you are ready.

For group ritual, when all participants have completed their sun journey, the officiant will thank the sun for his efforts and blessings. When you are ready, extinguish the sun candle if you cannot leave it to safely burn down.

Release any dieties you called, release the quarters, and close the circle as you are accustomed to doing.

Keep your timepiece in a place where you can see it and touch it as you need to throughout the year.

Notes

Notes

Lammas

Assembling the Wondrous Head

Ian Chambers

HE STANDS LAZILY LILTING in the warm breeze, the beating rays of the midday sun, once effulgent emanations of fecundity, now turned torrid and searing. The land smoulders beneath piercing heat of punishing solar crown, a baneful gaze cast upon the green earth like a callous king whose vibrant visage is inescapable, whose hand once gentle and kind is now turned enervating. The groan of abundance heralds the reaper's blade as the shadow of death creeps across the horizon. The promise made in the cold confines of cruel winter, witnessed in the quickening of spring, now ripens upon vine, stalk, and tree to be gathered and fulfil the tryst betwixt lovers locked in the verdant dance.

Head hanging, John Barleycorn can sense the swinging blade of the reaper. In one fell swoop, the dark, crooked shape severs the stalk legs and grasps him at the neck, crying aloud triumphantly. Raucous routing erupts from the field of the fallen, the cutter and his crew capering joyously toward the tall tor looming above, where the lone baleful eye of the sun casts its lingering, parching stare. As they ascend the crest of heaven's high hill, fatigue stabs at their legs, unnoticed in the savagery of the jubilance of carrying the head to the peak. As the solar sphere alights from the crown of the tor, the golden light turns red and spreads dusk-ridden hues across the fields shorn by the slashing of scythes. From the seed head, the future is fastened fast within the germ of the grain, the cycle of life secured within the swing of the reaper's sickle blade.

Atop the sacred summit, the revellers slake their thirst with the first of the barley-brewed beer before laying to rest the head of Barleycorn as offering to the Ancient Ones, pouring libation of that amber beer, sorcerous soma of intoxicating ale. The triple-faced stone idol watches this most hoary of rituals, the primordial agrarian god presiding over the commencement of the funerary festivities, for John Barleycorn is dead!

As the mood shifts, a solemnity stretches over the field as festivities pale before the shadow of the Lord of the Dead. The darkening shade of his fingers elongate over the land, replacing the fierce day-heat of the sun, his touch secreting away the fecund force of the earth. Here is Hades, come to collect his bride-price, to conduct Persephone to his dread domain, for the harvest marks the return of the vivifying essence of the queen to her chthonic realm—an end of growth and commencement of gathering-up. There she will tarry until time is once more ripe to return to the land as Kore (Maiden), in her the power of the quickening of the land. In the depths of the dark soil, the fertility of the world rests in repose, safeguarding the seminal head of the murdered king, now committed to the earth in the age-old custom.

In the court of the underworld, the head of the slain presides as oracle, singing such wondrous, keening songs. Once a golden king, since sundered at the hands of Dionysian revellers stupefied in celebration, inebriated on the ichor of the fallen, the loaf of the lord now croons for the leader of the chosen and his queen. Delighting and amusing in marvellous song, the Orphic oracular head is become the utterer of possibility, the disembodied voice and the vision enchanting all. The poetic portends potentiality, rooted in potency, ability, and availability. What dreams and desires, inventively imagined worlds of endless hope and risk, are housed within the coal-black cranial cavern.

Fire in the Head

Encased within the head of the poet is the seat of inspiration and initiation both, the sacred "fire in the head," where entire vistas of virtual realities reside, the focus of consciousness itself given face and interface to a shared world. Considering the generative capacity of the mind, uninhibited capability of conscious experience, we might rightly hold the head as seminal, the seed from which all worlds are rooted, reified dreams made reality in the field of belief. Everything humankind has made manifest has first existed within the imaginal, the head having literally and metaphorically seeded the world in which we navigate and enchant anew as we fashion around us our daily lives.

No idea, no philosophy, no invention, no religion or politic, no art or song, none of the wonderful or creative powers within the capability of humankind has not first found shape within the recesses of the mind. In truth, all we perceive of the world exists solely within the cave of the skull, the manifest and the imaginal both being possessed of equal reality within the experience of the intelligible. Ancient agrarian ancestors recognised the significance of the head, collecting the heads of enemies as trophies in the Celtic countries, and seeking oracle from the prophetic head of kings and poets.

The medieval Welsh book *The Mabinogion* recounts this in relation to the Assembly of the Wondrous Head and the decapitated king, Brân. The seven survivors of a battle to rescue Brân's sister, Brânwen, are told by Brân's head to travel to a miraculous hall. Within the confines of the hall, itself synonymous with the cranial walls of the Wondrous Head and its phantasmagoric enchantment, the company enjoy songs and festivities until one of the three doors is opened and they must return to the ravages of the temporal world. Until that moment, that dreamlike revery, time itself passes unnoticed; all stresses are forgotten and the delights of the imaginal are enjoyed in fulness. (Once, in a dream, I saw the philosopher Plato, who revealed the secret of "The Allegory of the Cave": the cave is your own head, the shadows on its walls are your own vision, and the light is your own consciousness.)

For our ancestors who celebrated the first harvest during the period we identify as Lughnasadh, or Lammas (*loaf-mass*), this was also a time of funerary rites and games, mythologically founded in Ireland to commemorate the foster-mother of Lugh, Tailtiu. Intimately tied to the agricultural cycles of the land, the sun, and the seasons, this time marked an acknowledgment that all life feeds upon death, that the gathering of fruits—whether grain, vegetable, or even honey and meat—meant destruction and cessation of life. Moreover, crops unharvested would die on stalk and branch, rot and decay—indicating the onset of the dark part of the year. The sun, like the baneful eye of Balor in Irish mythology, is put out at midsummer, and the day begins to shorten as darkness reclaims the land.

The seed head, then, is allegorically connected to the head of the poet, the oracular head of Orpheus or Brân. It is seminal, literally being possessed of the seed, generative and creative. The seed is the germ from which the next generation emerges. Therefore, the poetic inference is that the head of the corn is akin to the head of mankind, the casing of mind, creation, and rebirth, and the corn king survived from the old mythological cycle of Lugh and Balor (sometimes Crom Dubh or Crom Cruach) through to the rural folk customs of John Barleycorn. The ritual of slaying the king, the grinding of his bones for bread, and the fermentation of his blood to brew intoxicating wine or beer can be identified as an agrarian mystery found from early mankind: Orphic and Dionysian traditions and the Eleusinian Mysteries, surviving in the Eucharist and persisting in country traditions such as Crying the Neck in the West Country of Britain.

A number of Old Craft traditions, especially in Britain, recognise this time of the year when the Lord of the Waxing Year, the dark mask or twin of the Lord of the Waning Year, escorts the life-giving Rose Queen to the Land of the Dead. This withdrawing of the Goddess from the land heralds the decline of fecundity, of vitalising force that greens the earth and makes the sap rise. From this point, according to some Old Craft lineages, the earth enters its period of contraction into the darkness of the tomb, which will become the womb of the vernal quickening of the land.

For many Pagans, the name *Lughnasadh* represents the first harvest, signifying the first pause for appraisal of the year's progress and the cutting of the first corn, gathering of first fruits—a celebration of the bounty of nature. In folklore, a recurrent theme has a slightly darker aspect associated with the ritualised beheading of myth and ritual: the harvesting of the head and its revivifying essence as the seed crop for the next year's yield.

As the year ages and turns from the time of the longest day, the solar-crowned head of the sun king begins its slow descent. As the sun, the great luminary that was earlier fertilising, turns to a fierce, scorching face, the solar rays take on a more baneful mask. In Irish myth and folklore, this is the baleful eye of Balor, "the flashing one," whose gaze causes destruction upon all who fall under it.

The triumph of Lugh, through whom we see cognates in Lugus as well as the Welsh Lleu Llaw Gyffes, over the baleful eye of Balor was anciently associated with the Irish festival of funerary games mourning Lugh's mother, Tailtiu, whose death occurred in the clearing of Ireland for the introduction of agriculture. It is significant to note here that death, funerary rites, and beheading are thematic components of the harvest festival, denoting how early agricultural peoples to the British Isles were dependent upon and recognised the significance of death in life. At the heart of it, Lughnasadh is a festival that acknowledges that life feeds upon death, and the harvest is gathered in the knowledge that the vivifying energy of the sun that has gone into the crop is now ripe to feed the community.

Lugh and the beheading theme find themselves amid an occurrence of stone heads found in Ireland at locations related to the Lughnasadh festival, such as the Corleck Head. This first- or second-century idol depicts a three-faced deity found at Corleck Hill, a site tradition-ally connected to Lughnasadh, where it was likely buried as an offer-ing, committed to the earth to preserve the future of the clan and its harvests.

Crom Dubh, the "black crooked one," is an interesting name that is suggestive of the scythe, the traditional grain harvesting tool. In-deed, Crom Dubh is commonly associated with harvest and sacri-fice, assuming the character and appearance of the "grim reaper," the necessary and inexorable fate of all life. In Ireland, Crom Dubh Sunday was observed around Lughnasadh, during which time fam-ilies and clans gathered to enjoy the first harvest of meat, fruit, veg-etables, and grain. An associated god, Crom Cruach, is also some-times called Cenncroithi, interpreted to mean "head of all gods," an interesting name linking the beheading theme.

The discovery of the Corleck Head is a glimpse into earlier cus-toms and lore associated with Lughnasadh, connecting the first harvest with earliest arable farming of grain, the Celtic head cult, and the association of Lammas with funerary customs. This inti-mately links the festival with death and harvest traditions, signify-ing the importance of this time to European ancestors as a time of honouring death in life, gathering sustenance for storage in order to seed future crops, and identifying this analogously with the human head as the seat and seed of life and creative impulse.

For Old Craft folk and modern Pagans, this festival marks the beginning of a period of withdrawal, of death in life, directly mirror-ing the festival of Candlemas, or Imbolc, at the opposite side of the Wheel of the Year. It is a time of repose, of starting to become in-trospective, and gathering in the head to prepare to seed next year's crop. The fructifying essence has receded, and we are reminded to become conscious of our own harvests in our lives.

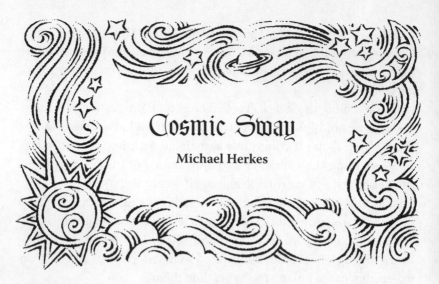

Cosmic Sway

Michael Herkes

AUGUST 1 MARKS THE festival of Lammas, also known as Lughnasadh, a time that marks the waning summer and beginning of the harvest season. It is a time to give thanks for the abundance of the earth and honor the hard work of farmers and agricultural communities. It is a time to celebrate the first fruits of the harvest and express gratitude for nature's bountiful gifts.

Celebrating Lammas

In ancient times, people would gather in fields or sacred spaces to perform rituals such as making corn dollies or weaving wheat into wreaths. These activities symbolized fertility and prosperity for future harvests. Additionally, feasting on freshly harvested foods was a common practice during Lammas celebrations.

In modern times, Lammas continues to be celebrated by individuals who embrace nature-based spirituality or have an interest in Pagan traditions. Many choose to honor this festival by engaging in activities that connect them with nature and reflect themes of gratitude and abundance. Now is a time to set up a sacred space with symbols representing abundance, such as grains, fruits, flowers, or corn dollies. Yellow, orange, gold, green, and brown candles mirror the seasonal colors. Take advantage of summer's warmth by going on nature walks or picnics in natural settings like parks or gardens. Visit a local farm or farmer's market to gather fresh produce. Prepare a meal using these ingredients as a way to connect with the spirit of Lammas. As bread is often associated with harvest celebrations, consider baking your own loaf using locally sourced grains or incorporating herbs like rosemary for added flavor. Take a moment to reflect on all that you are grateful for during this season of abundance. Consider keeping a gratitude journal or sharing your appreciation with loved ones.

The Full Moon in Aquarius and a Conjunction

The Full Moon in Aquarius on August 9 at 3:55 a.m. brings forth a sense of innovation, independence, and intellectual curiosity. Aquarius, an air sign classically ruled by Saturn and now in modern time ruled by Uranus, encourages us to embrace our individuality and express ourselves authentically. It is also deeply connected to technology and community.

One way to harness the power of this Moon is by curating a magical social media presence that aligns with your true self and resonates with your community. Start by setting intentions for your online presence: What message do you want to convey? How do you want to inspire others? Then, take some time to review your social media profiles and posts. Remove anything that feels out of alignment with who you are becoming. Embrace the power of social media platforms as tools for self-expression and connection with like-minded individuals. Use this time to cultivate an online presence that reflects your authentic self while fostering meaningful connections within your digital community. Consider downloading photo editing apps on your smartphone. Find or create sigils or symbols that align with your desired goal that you wish to project and place them over selfies. In doing so, lower the top layer to an opacity of 1 percent so it is nearly invisible to the naked eye.

On August 12 at 1:30 a.m., the Venus-Jupiter conjunction brings forth an energy of abundance and positivity. It can enhance our relationships by fostering love and harmony within partnerships. It also amplifies our ability to attract abundance in all areas of life, from financial prosperity to personal fulfillment. This celestial alignment inspires us to dream big and have faith in the possibilities that lie before us. It encourages us to embrace optimism and take risks with confidence. The energy of a Venus-Jupiter conjunction invites us to explore new experiences with an open heart and mind. During this alignment, we may find ourselves drawn toward creative pursuits or indulging in pleasurable activities that bring joy into our lives. It is a time when opportunities for growth and expansion are abundant—both personally and professionally.

Big Virgo Energy

Virgo season begins on August 22 and is met with the New Moon at 2:07 a.m., culminating in practicality, organization, and attention to detail. Virgo is an earth sign known for its analytical nature and desire for perfection. During this time, the energy encourages us to focus on self-improvement, setting intentions related to health, work, and daily routines.

To harness the power of a New Moon in Virgo, a ritual or spell that calls upon Virgo's meticulous energy can be performed. One such ritual involves cleaning the home with a magical floor wash. This ritual not only physically cleanses your space but also infuses it with harmonizing and purifying energies.

Start by mixing equal parts white vinegar and water in a bucket or container. Add the juice of one lemon along with a few drops each of lavender and pine essential oils. Finally, sprinkle some rosemary leaves into the mixture. As you clean your home using this magical floor wash, visualize negative energies being swept away while invoking Virgo's energy of orderliness and purification. Focus on areas that require special attention or areas where you wish to bring more organization into your life. Throughout the process, maintain mindfulness by repeating affirmations such as "I cleanse my space with intention" or "I invite harmony into my home." Allow the fresh scent of lemon and lavender to uplift your spirits as you connect with Virgo's energy during this New Moon phase.

Pisces Virgo Eclipse Season

On September 7, the Full Moon in Pisces at 2:09 p.m. coincides with a lunar eclipse, providing an undeniably powerful and profound energetic experience. A Full Moon in Pisces brings forth emotions, intuition, and deep spiritual connections. It is a time when our emotions are heightened and our intuition is at its peak. This lunar phase encourages us to dive into the depths of our subconscious mind, exploring our dreams, desires, and innermost thoughts. When this Full Moon coincides with a lunar eclipse, the energy becomes even more potent. Eclipses are known for their ability to bring about significant shifts and changes in our lives. They act as catalysts for transformation, urging us to release what no longer serves us and embrace new beginnings.

The combination of the Full Moon in Pisces with the eclipse energy amplifies these effects. It invites us to delve into the realms of spirituality, compassion, and empathy. This is a time when we may feel more connected to our higher selves and have heightened awareness of the interconnectedness of all things.

In terms of magical work during this celestial event, it is recommended to focus on rituals that involve releasing old patterns or beliefs that hinder personal growth. Harnessing the energy of this Full Moon in Pisces lunar eclipse can be particularly beneficial for practices such as meditation, journaling, dream work, or engaging in creative pursuits.

Then on September 21 at 3:54 p.m., another New Moon in Virgo will coincide with a solar eclipse. During this period, it is crucial to pay attention to our health and well-being. Virgo encourages us to prioritize self-care routines and establish healthy habits. This is an ideal time for introspection and self-reflection, as we can identify areas in our lives that require refinement or adjustment. However, it is important to approach this energy with caution as well. The intensity of the solar eclipse may bring unexpected challenges or disruptions into our lives. Be mindful not to get overwhelmed by perfectionism or become overly critical of yourself or others during this time.

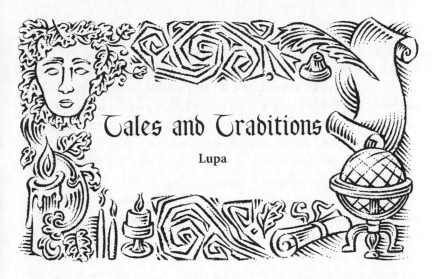

Tales and Traditions

Lupa

As we enter the first of three traditional harvest sabbats, summer's heat has dried out many of the plants, and birds become quiet as nesting season winds down and they no longer need to sing for their mates and territories. Fruit trees bow their branches with the weight of apples, pears, and more, berries create juicy packets of calories for birds and humans alike, and grains ripen in the sun. Wildlife may struggle with drought, and the water provided to live stock often becomes a lifesaver for their wild neighbors. It is a time of great wealth, but not without its drawbacks too.

Anna's Hummingbird (*Calypte anna*)

Hummingbirds are an absolute delight to watch on a warm summer's day. These speedy, agile little birds are not only able to maneuver through the air with amazing skill, but for their size they are surprisingly fierce little things. A hummingbird defending a nest or a food source will not only chase away other hummingbirds, but will even loudly stand its ground against much larger threats.

The Anna's hummingbird is no exception. These beautiful green hummingbirds live all along the West Coast from Baja California to southern British Columbia; males have an iridescent magenta throat patch that shimmers in the sun. At this time of year, they are likely done with nesting, or close to it. But where other hummingbirds prepare for fall migration to points south, some Anna's populations will be staying put for the winter. Originally confined to their range in Mexico and California, the proliferation of exotic late-flowering plants and hummingbird feeders not only caused this species to expand north, but allowed some individuals to spend all year in the same place as long as winter was relatively mild and artificial food sources were available.

It's certainly a trade-off. Those that stay behind avoid the long flight of migration, but must be ready to face scarcity and cold in winter. And a hummingbird's metabolism is so fast that they must feed nearly constantly; cold temperatures can cause them to burn off energy too quickly while staying warm. An Anna's hummingbird in peril can go into a state of torpor for a few hours, especially overnight, which temporarily lowers their metabolic rate. But they must find food again before too long.

This demonstrates the flexibility of this species; being able to make use of human-provided food sources caused a significant change in the life history of these little birds. Our responsibility to them now is to make sure that they have enough native flowers to feed from in the warm months, and supplement with feeders once the year turns to chill.

Pearly Everlasting (*Anaphalis margaritacea*)

At this time of year, most of the wildflowers have bloomed and gone to seed; trillium was followed by salmonberry, then lupine followed by fireweed. Now only a few intrepid native flowers bloom in meadows and pastures, mostly in *Asteraceae*, a very large family including daisies and sunflowers, among others. At Lammas, one of the most beautiful and evident of these is pearly everlasting. At first it appears to be a rather puffy white flower, but on closer inspection, it is a cluster of a dozen or more small, round white flowers. Technically the white "petals" are bracts that surround the flowers proper, but they're lovely all the same.

The dusty, pale-green foliage doesn't even get started growing in earnest until summer is well underway. A single stalk grows straight up, sometimes up to three feet tall. Alternating pairs of slender, lance-shaped leaves adorn the stem, which is crowned by a cluster of the white flowers. Unlike some blooms, these will not die away after a couple of weeks. The plant gets its name because the flowers stay remarkably intact even after fertilization, and they may dry out and remain visible well into fall—hence, "everlasting." This trait makes them popular in the florist trade, both fresh and dried.

While many species of butterfly and moth have had their mating flights and died away by now, late-summer species appreciate pearly everlasting for much-needed nectar. The leaves are an important source of food for local painted lady butterfly caterpillars, and even humans can eat the cooked leaves, especially when the plant is young. With its ability to tolerate drought, pearly everlasting is crucial to the survival of its local food web as summer begins to wind down for the year. While Lammas altars may be full of the ripe fruits and vegetables of the season, it's not out of place to include some late-blooming flowers too.

Chanterelles (*Cantharellus* spp.)

Fall is the premier mushroom season here in the Northwest, but some species get an early start while summer still reigns. Lammas is about when I'm able to pick my first Pacific golden chanterelles, and other species in the genus are revving up, especially at lower elevations. Chanterelles—of which there are several dozen species—are primarily found in the Northern Hemisphere, but a few species thrive south of the Equator as well.

Chanterelles will continue fruiting all through fall, and it's not uncommon to find a few stragglers into early winter too. This long harvest time means that intrepid mushroom hunters may be rewarded with this popular and tasty find for many months. The appearance of the first flushes around Lammas are a promise of greater abundance to come, not just within the genus *Cantharellus*, but other edible fungi as well.

Unfortunately, there is a dark side to the chanterelle harvest. Because these mycorrhizal fungi cannot be easily cultivated, they are in high demand by restaurants, grocery stores, and other market venues. This means that commercial mushroom hunters are often out in the woods in significant numbers. Should they happen across a patch of chanterelles—or any other marketable mushroom—they will take every single one, and then come back to pick later flushes as well. Not only does this take away opportunities for other mushroom hunters, but it robs the ecosystem of much-needed spores to help propagate chanterelles and other fungi in the future.

Yes, it is important to celebrate a fortunate harvest, but it's crucial to also remember moderation. We owe responsibility to both the land and our fellow foragers to not take more than we need and to always leave something for someone else—especially those non-human someones.

Feasts and Treats

Dallas Jennifer Cobb

LAMMAS IS THE FIRST of three harvest festivals and is celebrated at the midway point between Litha and Mabon. As with all sabbats, the calendar date assigned to the sabbat may be different from the astronomical occurrence. I prefer to celebrate on the astronomical date, when the sun sits at 15 degrees of Leo.

Here in Canada, August is warm and dry, and invites us to feast and celebrate outdoors. While I love the heat of summer in North America, I hate to create heat in my kitchen at this time, so most often, Lammas feasts are things easily prepared outdoors on the barbecue. I love to serve up healthy versions of old favourites for Lammas, including hot dogs on easy-to-load wraps, fresh corn on the cob with butter and salt, and fennel potato salad. I have happy memories of childhood cookouts on "the point," a piece of land that jutted out into the river we lived on. I lived there year-round, and the nearby cottage kids used to love to come over for a cookout, hot dogs roasted over the open fire. Carrying armfuls of wood and a big bowl of potato salad, my family members made sure everyone had lots to eat. When I plan a Lammas feast, I try to choose foods that might evoke a similar sense of joy and satisfaction.

There are so many versions of hot dogs available, from vegetarian to tofu, vegan, chicken, turkey, pork, and beef. Choose hot dogs that will suit your guests. Remember to keep vegan dogs separate from meat- or animal-based dogs on the grill.

I organize my Lammas cookout around the barbecue on my deck because I don't have a firepit with a grill. I like to put a large pot of water on one side of the barbecue, where I boil the corn. The other side of the barbecue is for cooking the hot dogs.

For this feast, prepare the Fennel Potato Salad in advance and chill in the fridge until ready to eat. The hot dogs and corn are both quick to prepare, and are both done outside on the grill.

Fennel Potato Salad

As a child, I didn't like most potato salads because they were mushy and lacked texture. The addition of fresh, thinly sliced fennel to a potato salad is the thing that finally won me over. A bit of crunch and that exotic flavour made me a potato salad fan. I suspect that once you try potato salad with fresh fennel in it you may never go back.

Prep time: 5 minutes

Cooling time: 30 minutes–1 hour

Cooking time: 10 minutes, but use a fork to gauge them

Servings: 8

2½ pounds fresh baby potatoes

1 medium bulb fresh fennel, chopped into bite size pieces

½ medium-size red onion, finely diced

1 bunch green onions, rinsed and patted dry

1 tablespoon fresh dill (Use a teaspoon if you use dry dill. It can be an overpowering flavour, so you may opt to skip the dill if you don't enjoy it.)

1 cup mayonnaise or vegan mayonnaise

2 tablespoons rice vinegar (I like the sweet tang it adds, but you can use white vinegar if you choose.)

1 tablespoon Dijon mustard

3 tablespoons olive oil

1 garlic clove, finely diced

Sea salt and black pepper to taste

Wash the potatoes and put them in a medium-sized pot. Do not cut them. Cover with cold water and throw in a big pinch of salt. Turn burner on high, cover the pot, and bring to a boil.

Then, turn the burner to medium-low, and simmer potatoes until they are tender but not mushy. After 10 minutes, use a fork to poke a potato. You want it to be soft, yet firm.

Drain the water from the pot, and rinse the potatoes with cold water. Drain again, and let the potatoes cool completely.

Cut potatoes into quarters. (Don't do this before cooking the potatoes because they will crumble and dissolve into the water, making for a mushy salad without distinct bite-sized bits.)

Use a clean cutting board and a sharp knife to slice the green shoots off of the fennel bulb. Cut the bulb in half lengthwise. Then flip the flat side down and slice the fennel into thin ribbons.

Peel and slice the red onion into thin ribbons. Chop green onions so they resemble tiny little circles. Dice the fresh dill.

In a large bowl, combine olive oil, mayonnaise, rice vinegar, mustard, garlic, dill, salt, and pepper and whisk the dressing until it is smooth.

Add the prepped potatoes, red onion, and fennel. Turn gently until the veggies are evenly coated, but be careful not to crush the potatoes. Sprinkle green onions on top of the salad.

Serve with Hot Dogs Fully Loaded on a Wrap and Boiled Corn.

Hot Dogs Fully Loaded on a Wrap

Since I stopped consuming gluten, I have learned to use coconut wraps instead of hot dog buns for hot dogs. Sana makes a great gluten-free coconut wrap that makes it easy to load up on condiments and really enjoy the hot dog. For those who are not sensitive to gluten, you could use wheat wraps, hot dog buns, or crusty rolls to put hot dogs in. Because this is a feast of abundance, I like to offer lots of different garnishes for hot dogs, so people can really pile it on.

I like to check on dietary sensitivities or restrictions with people in advance so I can provide options that suit their needs.

Prep time: 1 minute to heat the grill
Cooking time: 5 minutes for regular-size hot dogs
Servings: 8

16 hot dogs, 2 per person
16 wraps or buns, 2 per person
All the usual condiments, including ketchup, mustard, and relish, plus some fancy ones like dill pickles, braised onions, shredded cheese, pickled hot peppers, tomatoes, and lettuce. Really, the sky is the limit when it comes to condiments.

Preheat the barbecue to medium heat.

Keep meat and vegetarian hot dogs separate so they don't contaminate one another. Grill hot dogs on barbecue over medium heat until cooked.

Place a small pan on the grill and add butter and diced onion, letting the onions braise until translucent. When you serve the hot dogs, you can also offer the warm, braised onion.

Coconut wraps are remarkably sturdy and hold up to light grilling very well. I have, at times, lightly grilled the wraps and buns for 15 seconds per side to warm them, but find that by the time I load them up with condiments, they have cooled. You can decide whether you want people to load the wrap and then get the dogs on, or warm the wraps, add the dogs, and then add condiments.

I usually invite people to load their wraps with condiments first. Part of the beauty of using a wrap is that it literally holds three or four times the amount of condiments. Using lots of ingredients reminds us how abundant this time of year is and celebrates the harvest aspect of the sabbat. Once the wraps are sufficiently loaded up, they can bring their plates with them to the barbecue to get their hot dogs and boiled corn.

Boiled Corn

This recipe seems almost too easy, but I love to have corn as part of the sabbat feast. Not just a traditional Lammas food, corn requires shucking, and this is an activity to involve everyone in. It can be incorporated into competition and fun, which are a nod to the god Lugh and, in turn, help build community.

Do you remember the cookouts from your childhood? I remember that corn was a seasonal treat that we all wanted to eat and enjoy at its peak of flavour and freshness. I couldn't get enough.

For Lammas, cast a magical spell with food, and invite everyone to delight in the buttery munching of corn on the cob, revisiting the joys of harvest abundance.

Prep time: 1 minute
Cooking time: 5 minutes
Servings: 8

2 cobs of fresh corn per person
A pound of butter, on a separate plate, for rolling corn in
Sea salt in a shaker
Ground black pepper

Place a large pot half full of water on the barbecue, and add a generous pinch of salt to the water. Bring it to a boil.

While the water is heating, it is time to shuck the corn. You can make a game out of the task of corn shucking and invoke Lugh's traditional sacred games, which historically were part of the sabbat celebration. Let people compete to see who can shuck corn the fastest. It makes this work fun, invokes the young god Lugh, pays tribute to the grain goddesses, and engages people in the fun preparation of the feast.

Be sure to run your hand over the cobs of corn before they go into the pot, removing the fine filaments of corn silk.

When there are lots of people to feed at a sabbat feast, I place cleaned corn in a box near the barbecue. Because they take 5 minutes to cook in boiling water and you can see they are perfect when the kernels become bright yellow, you can continuously add cobs of corn to the pot while serving up the bright yellow cooked ones.

Remove the corn cob from the pot and drain.

Encourage people to roll the hot corn in butter and sprinkle it with salt and pepper to taste. Not only do these make the corn even more delicious, I find that butter helps me feel especially rich and blessed and raises my energy for the sabbat.

Crafty Crafts

Elizabeth Barrette

LAMMAS FALLS AT THE juncture between summer and fall. Late-summer gardens are bursting with produce like tomatoes, peppers, and zucchini. Hot-season flowers like echinacea, zinnias, and black-eyed Susans are blooming. Grain in the fields is ripening, but only the earliest varieties are ready to harvest, a precarious time for the rest due to late-summer storms. The first of the dessert apples are just beginning to appear, hinting at the harvest season yet to come. Lammas themes therefore touch on both summer and fall, bounty and risk, and sometimes sacrifice. Grain and its products such as bread and beer appear frequently in the decor. Colors include the deep greens and golds or wheaten tans of the season.

Cornucopia

The cornucopia, or "horn of plenty," is a popular harvest symbol that can appear from Lammas through Mabon to Samhain. So you can get a lot of use out of this craft. It consists of a curling horn usually made from straw, filled with the bountiful fruits and vegetables of late summer through fall. It represents all kinds of abundance.

Materials

Craft straw or raffia

Heavy button thread

Tapestry needle and thread or hot glue

Scissors

Assorted fruits and vegetables (long-lasting or artificial)

Optional: 2-inch-wide plaid ribbon

> *Cost:* $10–$15
>
> *Time spent:* 2 hours, plus soaking time if using straw

Design Concepts

Straw is more traditional but requires soaking to use; it may also give you grain heads for decoration. Raffia is easy to find and use, and does not require soaking. These can be natural color or dyed.

You will need heavy button thread to secure the braids for making the horn. Some people like to tie a big bow around the mouth of the cornucopia. A 2-inch plaid ribbon is popular, but any wide craft ribbon can work.

A cornucopia is traditionally filled with late-summer or fall fruits and vegetables. Some people add sheaves of wheat for Lammas or colorful leaves later in the season. You may find things like Indian corn and gourds for harvest decor. If you don't want to use fresh produce, there are plenty of artificial options to explore, such as foam or wood replicas.

Assembly

If working with straw, first remove any grain heads and set aside. Soak the stems for at least an hour (or according to the package), then let them dry a bit so they are damp rather than soggy. Raffia can be worked dry.

Gather a bundle of straw or raffia about as thick as your finger. Tie one end with button thread. Divide the bundle into three sections and begin braiding it. Near the end, add new strands a few at a time so you can extend the braid.

Once you have several feet of braid, put a temporary tie around the loose end. Roll the finished end into a tiny loop. Sew or hot glue the loop in place. Then work your way up the braid, coiling it in a spiral on top of the loop, thus forming the horn. Sew or hot glue each row in place as you work. Shape the horn into a slight curve. Extend the braid if necessary. Finish the rim with a double-thick braid. If you have grain heads, attach them just behind the rim to make a frill.

Fill the interior with a mix of fruits and vegetables. Allow some to spill out onto the altar in the overflowing horn of plenty.

Bread Warmer

A bread warmer is a cloth pad with a heatable filler. You microwave it briefly, then put it under the dishtowel in the breadbasket to keep the bread warm for longer. Seasonal printed fabrics make a cute choice.

Materials

100 percent cotton cloth

3–4 cups filler (depending on size of bread warmer)

Sewing machine or needle and thread

Spoon or small funnel

Optional: essential oil or ½ cup dried spices

   Cost: $10–$15

   Time spent: 30 minutes

Design Concepts

It is crucial to use 100 percent cotton cloth because it can withstand heat, whereas synthetics and even some other natural fibers cannot. Heavy quilting cloth and flannel are both sturdy enough to survive lots of use, and they come in many fun seasonal prints. Basketweave, leaf, or grain prints are good for Lammas themes.

Many fillers can be used. Among the best are crushed walnut shells, jasmine rice, and whole corn kernels (not popcorn). The latter two are cheap and easy to find in many stores. Walnut has the advantage of being inedible, so it won't attract pests, but you may need to order it from a craft supplier.

For scents, you can use food-based essential oil or dry spices. Oil doesn't always respond well to heat, so dry spices tend to work better, but some folks prefer the oils. Cinnamon bark chips, nutmeg chips, cardamom pods, whole cloves, or whole allspice berries work well, or use a blend of whole mulling spices if you can find that.

Assembly

Base the size of the cloth on the breadbasket you want to use it with. Most breadbaskets are either oval or rectangular. If you measure the inside of the bottom and double that area, then you should wind up with a bread warmer that fits in the bottom after you've folded and sewn the cloth. In general, a piece about 12 × 24 inches will fold to 6 × 12 inches and finish around 5 × 11 inches after sewing and filling it.

Begin by folding the cloth right sides together, wrong sides out. Sew the two ends closed, leaving the top (opposite the fold) open.

Turn the cloth right side out. Sew 2–3 straight lines from the fold upward to an inch from the top edge. This creates channels to hold the filler in place. The longer your bread warmer, the more channels it needs, about 2 inches apart.

Mix the dried spices, a few drops of essential oil, or both into your filler. Use a spoon or funnel to fill the channels, leaving about an inch of headspace below the top of the cloth.

Fold the raw edges of the cloth down toward the inside of the pouch. Press the folded edges together and sew the top closed.

To use the bread warmer, heat it in the microwave for one minute alongside a cup of water. Place the bread warmer in the bottom of a breadbasket. Line the basket with a dishcloth, put in the bread, then fold the edges of the dishcloth over the bread.

Lammas and Runes

Charlie Rainbow Wolf

RUNES ARE EASIER TO find these days thanks to the popularity of the different Norse and Viking series that have been on the television over the last few years, but there's nothing modern about runes. They've been around for centuries. In my quest to find the divination tool that spoke the clearest to me over thirty years ago, I explored runes too.

This is not an in-depth guide to what each rune means. There are very good books on that topic, and I highly recommend *Taking Up the Runes: A Complete Guide to Using Runes in Spells, Rituals, Divination, and Magic* by Diana L. Paxson (Weiser Books, 2021) as a good place to continue delving into the language and magic of the Elder Futhark. However, I do want to get you started, so here are very basic meanings. If you don't have a set of runes, you don't need to go out and buy some; just draw these symbols on stones or wooden discs for now.

| ᚠ | Fehu | Upright: wealth and prosperity | Inverted: failure and loss |
| ᚢ | Uruz | Upright: determination, tenacity | Inverted: hesitation, animosity |

ᚦ	Thurisaz	Upright: willpower and fortitude	Inverted: compulsion and weakness
ᚨ	Ansuz	Upright: divine messages and life	Inverted: misunderstandings and distortion
ᚱ	Raido	Upright: journeys and movement	Inverted: stagnation and rigidity
ᚲ	Kenaz	Upright: knowledge and creativity	Inverted: endings and disillusionment
ᚷ	Gebo	Always upright and means a gift, some kind of sacrifice, or reparation	
ᚹ	Wunjo	Upright: joyful satisfaction and wholeness	Inverted: hopelessness and discord
ᚺ	Hagalaz	Always upright and points to a crisis or a major disruption	
ᚾ	Naudiz	Upright: necessity and assessment	Inverted: deception and dishonesty
ᛁ	Isa	Always upright and indicates inertia or a standstill	
ᛃ	Jera	Always upright and reveals where there's achievement and maybe some kind of repercussion	
ᛇ	Eihwaz	Always upright and means purpose and inspiration	
ᛈ	Perthro	Upright: fate or luck	Inverted: risks and warnings
ᛉ	Algiz	Upright: safety and surety	Inverted: withdrawal and misgivings
ᛋ	Sowilo	Always upright and a very positive rune indicating completion and victory	
ᛏ	Tiwaz	Upright: authority and commitment	Inverted: doubt and weariness
ᛒ	Berkanan	Always upright and mostly a good omen, but take nothing for granted	
ᛖ	Ehwaz	Upright: teamwork and getting things done	Inverted: noncooperation and selfishness
ᛗ	Mannaz	Upright: awareness and self-confidence	Inverted: isolation and deception
ᛚ	Laguz	Always upright and usually reveals where growth is being made	
ᛜ	Ingwaz	Always upright and indicates growth and taking time to evaluate the next step	

ᛞ	Dagaz	Always upright and shows where a revelation is being made	
ᛟ	Othala	Upright: ownership and prosperity	Inverted: loss and instability

That's a brief introduction to the runes and should be enough to read them while learning the more in-depth meanings of the runes. I read runes differently to my runester friends, and I'm sure they read them differently to other rune masters they know. Ways of reading the runes go from simple to complicated; it's simply a case of choosing one.

Perhaps the easiest way to work with runes is to put them in a bag, jostle them around while focusing on the matter at hand, then choose one. There's the message! Most people want something a bit more meaty than that, so just draw more runes from the bag to provide clarification. It's your reading, so it's your rules!

Runes can be held in the hands and dropped onto a casting cloth, as in other methods we've discussed over these pages. Runes falling off the cloth are not included in the reading. Pay attention to clumps and clusters, runes closer to the middle, or runes that are separated or isolated in some way. They call attention to themselves and require a bit of extra interpretation.

This simple four-rune spread provides quite a bit of information:

- Rune 1 reveals where strengths and assets lie concerning the current situation. Here capabilities and the wherewithal to deal with things as they arise is found so that the best possible outcome might be created.
- Rune 2 indicates where obstacles and pitfalls lie, and what challenges may be coming up. It might even point to people who are hampering progress and creating blocks and challenges. This could even point to needing to get out of your own way, rather than indicating an outside issue.
- Rune 3 reveals vulnerability. There's actually great strength in vulnerability, because being vulnerable means, yes, it might all come tumbling down, but you have the strength to pick

yourself up and dust yourself off and continue to go forward, head held high. The rune that falls in this position will help to reveal the path of success.

- Rune 4 shows where support will come from and brings an understanding of what is necessary to achieve the desired results. There are going to be hindrances along the way; this rune provides insight on how to deal with them.

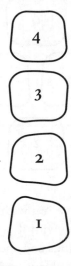

A seven-rune spread for a deeper interpretation of things looks like this:

- Rune 1 indicates the past and what hold it may have over things.
- Rune 2 reveals what's happening in the here and now to cause concern.
- Rune 3 points to potential future outcomes and how they influence things.
- Rune 4 provides advice on how to let go of the past.
- Rune 5 continues that advice with how to apply rune 4 to the current situation.

- Rune 6 shows what the potential obstacles and challenges will be along the way.
- Rune 7 reveals the potential outcome.

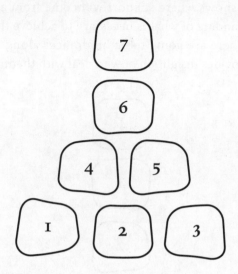

The main thing is to have fun with this. If it becomes a drag you're less likely to continue with it, and runes have so much to offer when it comes to readings and spellcasting and even magical writing. Work with them until you find something that resonates with you, a way of casting the runes that you feel comfortable with, and a way of understanding the meanings of the runes so you don't have to keep referring back to notes. The runes will speak loudly if they're just given a chance to do so.

Lammas Ritual

Ian Chambers

THE FOLLOWING RITE IS inspired by The Regency, a modern Pagan group of the twentieth century founded by Ronald "Chalky" White (1924–1998) and George Stannard (1912–1983), prominent figures of the Pagan revival in Britain. The Regency was a Pagan group that held open and public rituals during the late 1960s and into the '70s, culminating in large public sabbat celebrations in Hampstead Heath.

Incorporating mythology, folklore, and philosophies from diverse sources dear to its founders, including *The White Goddess* and Joseph Campbell's *The Hero With a Thousand Faces*, The Regency worked a mythos of the year cycle, observed by ritual plays where the mysteries of the seasonal festivals became dramatically revealed to the celebrants through participation. "Chalky" White compiled his thoughts and outline of The Regency rituals in an unpublished work, *The New Pagans' Handbook*—since made available through a website commemorating the legacy of White.

A Celebration of Death in Life

This simple and profound ritual uses only simple representations of universal truths. Overall, the theme is that of commemorating the necessary and all-purveying nature of death and its part in the cycle of life as expressed through the Wheel of the Year in modern Paganism. A token item, such as a corn dolly, takes the place of the sacrificial year king, the dying and resurrecting God of modern Paganism and Old Craft persuasions. Light signifies the hope of humankind, the gift of the gods that is the promise of renewed life.

Items needed
Corn dolly (one, to be carried by the principal participant if a group)
A candle in a safe holder (one for each participant if a group)
A loaf of bread
Beer
Forked staff
A blanket for placing items on the ground

For this ritual, it is necessary to make or acquire a corn dolly. This may be as simple or as complex as you like, and it is not imperative that your dolly be anatomically perfect. Indeed, there is something rustic and charming about the more creative dollies. This can be a fun activity, and it is one that can incorporate other people in the making.

Along with the corn dolly, you should have a candle that is placed within a jar or similar holder that affords safety when working outdoors. (If working as a group, then each participant should have a candle). Also, you will need some bread and beer. If you are so inclined, it is nice to make bread using local corn, and a plaited loaf is customary. Beer should also be used, not wine, as this is made from malted barley. Nonalcoholic beer is acceptable and is quite palatable these days. What is important to understand is that the bread represents the body of the corn king, the sacrificial offering of the body, while the beer is the ichor or sacred blood. A plate and cup are recommended but not entirely necessary. How elaborate or simple you keep things is up to you.

As for working tools, it is traditional to use a forked staff, or stang, for such a working. This commonly has associations with the agricultural pitchfork, which has ubiquitous function in agrarian activities and would have been common to farms and labourers. At this time of year, the pitchfork would have been used to shift hay or straw after the harvest into ricks, or stacks. In this ritual, the stang represents the Lord of the Dead, who presides over this rite. The forked staff will be fixed in the ground standing upright, and so a blanket is recommended to lay beneath it where you can place the candle, corn dolly, bread, and beer.

This ritual should ideally be worked outside, and therefore, it is most useful to find a location that is close to the earth, whether near fields or woodland. It is not compulsory to have access to a sacred hill or prominent mound, but where you feel comfortable in nature is best. The wild forces that we are invoking and gathering are more important than insisting upon a specific ritual ground. Indeed, the requirements of the site should include accessibility, rights of access, privacy, and safety. If you are planning to work alone, it is advisable to inform a close friend or relative of your exact location and how long you plan on being out. This rite doesn't require working in darkness, although this can help if you so choose. Please be responsible and have a care for your own and others' safety at all times. Being adaptable and conscious of how you can make this work your own is most important.

The timing in which you perform the ritual is, again, a matter of personal determination. Some prefer to observe seasonal indicators of timing, such as the ripening of wheat or barley fields, the sound of the first combine harvesters, the first ripe crab apples or blackberries. Others observe full moons or adhere to the calendar and the timings around the first of August. This author is not prescriptive and, while I prefer to use the season and locale as markers, each is perfectly acceptable to the individual or group as they choose.

Once at the location where you feel comfortable to perform this ritual, set up a space where you can mark or imagine a circle as widely as you feel appropriate and, at the centre, erect your forked staff. At the foot of the stang, lay out a blanket or cloth, then place your loaf and beer upon it. The purpose of this ritual, it should be becoming apparent, is to take the spirit of the corn, represented in the dolly, to the Land of the Dead and to enact the Lord's escorting of the spirit of the Goddess to the underworld realm, there to await re-emergence at Imbolc, or Candlemas.

With the unlit candle in its jar or other safe holder, and the corn dolly in your hand, move outside the perimeter of your circle or ritual space. At the outside, you are now without the circle of the Land of the Dead. If you are working this ritual alone, ignore the spoken parts written in parentheses. However, if you are planning to work this in a group, then somebody should speak these words of challenge from inside the edge of the circle. The lead participant should carry the corn dolly into the circle as the first respondent.

(We who in mourning lie, in the dread lands of the fair and departed, demand to know who would disturb our peace?)

If participating as a group, each individual should be asked and answer as follows before entering the circle. Otherwise, a solitary worker can simply speak this part alone:

In the name of the Lady, who brings all light and life, I come bearing Her now to this place of darkness.

Now, light your candle with the following words:

Know Her by this flame, that She is the one who oversees all light and darkness, the Pale-Faced Goddess that conveys life in death and death in life. All souls who wander know Her by this token and shall be drawn thereto.

The words being spoken, the participant now enters across the edge and into the circle, gathering around its perimeter.

When all are gathered within the circle, starting from the edge, begin a slow pace around the circle in a counterclockwise direction, gradually spiralling inward toward the staff at the centre. Take time to do this, and focus your eyes and attention upon the forked stick as Lord of the Dead, keeping the light close to your body as you escort Her into the heart of darkness. Again, the lead participant will also be carrying the corn dolly.

When arriving at the centre, stop to face the forked stick. Place the candle down at the foot of the stang and bow before Him. Place the corn dolly on the blanket alongside (but safely away from) the candle(s) and acknowledge thus:

The Summer King is dead; the Winter King shall rule the land. But, the seed of renewal has been sown in this dark soil; the sacrifice of the corn king shall revive the promised hope in me with His body and blood, this bread and beer.

Eat a piece of bread, drink some beer, and know that the fruits are partaken of at the cost of the sacrifice of the Summer King. Now that you have partaken of the harvest fruits, dance, sing, and play in the circle, bringing joy to the solemnity of the rite. Ritual joy is as much a part of this celebration as is the remembrance of death in life. In Irish Lughnasadh, games were enjoyed at this time. If you are working alone, do something vigorous that makes you happy, or enjoy the song of silence.

When you have concluded your time in the Land of the Dead, return to the perimeter of the circle or space. Turn to face the centre and the forked staff and speak:

In this dark place, we are reminded that all living shall die and that all death feeds life. Turning not from this truth, it is our duty to celebrate and continue our lives gladly in this knowledge, to honour the dead but remember the living.

Before you step outside of the ritual space, cast a piece of the bread preserved for the dead, and pour a libation of beer to remember the deceased. In the Old Craft, it is customary now that the rite is concluded to walk away and not look back as you depart.

When your ritual is concluded, blow out the candle(s) and recover any items—remembering to leave only footprints and take only memories.

Finally, don't let the simplicity of this rite deceive you. There is great scope for improvisation, and the participants should feel inspired to elaborate as they so desire or keep it concise as they feel appropriate.

Notes

Notes

Mabon

Gathering the Fruits of the Tree of Life

Nathan M. Hall

NO MATTER WHERE YOU live, be it in the Northern or Southern Hemisphere, in temperate, tropical, or arid climates, what is unmistakable about the autumnal equinox and in the traditions that celebrate it is a certain quality of light that triggers something very primal. In my own life, I felt it as a sort of *yearning*. For what, I couldn't always say, but it coincided with a need to draw myself in. The energetic outpouring and excess of summertime were gone, and in their place, a deep need for something. Safety? Security? Closeness to loved ones?

Autumn is an evocative time, and for many it's a time to reacquaint oneself with some favorite poets and their writings. Poetry always has been a close first cousin to spellwork, as both are capable of creation simply by the power held upon incanting them.

One poem by Robert Frost feels like it captures the impermanence of the season, that cast of light, the beauty of the fading leaves, that we're all wishing could stay around and we could visit just a little bit longer, if only we could freeze time on this jewel of a season:

Nothing Gold Can Stay

Nature's first green is gold,
Her hardest hue to hold.
Her early leaf's a flower;
But only so an hour.
Then leaf subsides to leaf.
So Eden sank to grief,
So dawn goes down to day.
Nothing gold can stay.

I love the classical, practically mythical, version of fall, an irony for someone who's spent almost twenty years in a subtropical climate. But no matter the location, when the sun begins to set in the autumn, you know it's time to start finishing what you're doing and prepare for the winter that comes just around the corner, even when winter simply means more darkness and not necessarily more cold.

With our rituals and our magick we also honor this gathering in. Though there was no autumn celebration called Mabon before the modern goddess movement and Wicca, there's plenty of evidence that the equinox was celebrated in various cultures around the world. In our present-day Neopagan traditions, we honor and celebrate Mabon as the second of three harvest festivals. While Lammas is the grain harvest, Mabon is the fruit harvest, and one of the images frequently used to depict this celebration is one of abundance—the cornucopia.

In my own observances, what I most closely relate Mabon to in the mundane world is the celebration of Thanksgiving in the United States and Canada. It's a time to gather with family and friends and share in the abundance of the harvest. By coming together in person, we are able to share the stories of our lives from the past year and enjoy a meal in good company. It's an intimate time filled with life and is a nice contrast to the Witches' New Year, Samhain, when we honor ancestors who cannot be *physically* present.

While the nuts and fruits on the actual trees are being harvested during this season, on the Sephiroth of the Tree of Life, I like to equate the fruits to what is manifested as we journey through each of the Sephirah from the divine inspiration of Kether, the crown, down all the way to Malkuth, where we find our sovereignty. What fruits have come from your energy and intentions over the previous year? Mabon as a metaphor for Malkuth is a great time to take stock of what you've put your energy into and see what fruit it has borne. Are you satisfied with what you're harvesting or are there changes that you could make to ensure better harvests in the years ahead? If you're not satisfied, perhaps it's time to consider investing some effort into a healing journey. Conversely, if you're happy with the way things are going, what seeds can you gather from the fruits of your labor that will be good for planting for the next year?

The Harvest and the Dangers of Nostalgia

Thirty years ago, and I swear I'm not crying admitting to that number, I remember autumn in northwestern Illinois as being a quite magickal time indeed. School had resumed, which for me at that time was not that exciting, but it did mean reconnecting with some of the people that I had fallen out of touch with during the summer. It was peak grunge era, so there were plenty of flannel and plaid-patterned shirts worn, naturally paired with black combat boots. It was a clothing style that was born from a colder climate and was perfect for nights that would dip into the 50s while we partied (sorry, Mom) around a fire and listened to music under the stars until the sun came up. We'd sleep the lazy weekend days away and go out to meet friends at the record store (CDs or cassette tapes, mostly), eat at cheap restaurants, or go hang out at the coffee shop, which had become a suddenly popular youth destination at the time. When you're young, you'll hang out anywhere they'll let you, and at that time it was a trendy destination where you could get too buzzed on caffeine and share your awful poetry at open mic nights.

Even as the days grew darker and colder, there was a magickal sense of timelessness that drifted lazily through those days, like so many multicolored leaves caught on a cool breeze. But are any of those memories actually real, or are they an amalgam of different events?

What are some of your best fall memories? Sometimes I like to write down my memories or vague recollections of what a time was like for me, even writing the same recollection repeatedly over the course of years and comparing how my memory has shifted. Part of the reason I do this is to see how nostalgia might be encroaching on my memory. The truth is that when I think back on more specific events, there were ups and downs during the fall season, just like any other. But the groove of my memory has associated strong and warm feelings toward what my life used to look like in the autumns I experienced in my youth. Nostalgia can be a dangerous drug because it begins to re-create the past into something that it never was. While I cherish the memories and the feeling of those autumns of yore, I acknowledge that there was a lot of struggle mixed in with the joy. The danger is that without a system of checks in place, you begin to yearn for something that never was. Beliefs like "Things were better back then" or "We need to go back to a better time" are disingenuous because *better* is a relative term, and the statements don't actually match with the daily reality that you or I ever experienced. We're just taking our idealism and placing it on a memory that we've pieced together. Some of this comes from real life experiences, but we are also influenced by media we've consumed, which was then reinforced by a general cultural fondness for fall. As an artist, a writer, and a witch, I can sit with all of these messy feelings and still experience joy and gratitude—joy for the ability to continue living and creating my life in the way that I desire and according to my will, and gratitude for the memories that I've cultivated and the knowledge that I don't have to be controlled by the emotions they evoke.

Libra Season and the Beginning
of Astrological Autumn

As we process into astrological autumn, Libra stands as the scales of equilibrium, a fitting symbol for this time of year, as the equinoxes strike the balance of day versus night, when each are represented in equal measure before tilting toward the dark half of the year. As a cardinal sign, Libra is the signifier of a new season; as cardinal air, it asks us to initiate creatively, to communicate readily, and to invest in our social groups. It's a time to solve problems and rekindle social bonds before the hardships of the winter months ahead.

For most of us, the day and night will not actually be equally divided, but it will be pretty close unless you're near the North or South Poles. What it does signify astronomically is that the sun is passing from the Northern Hemisphere to the Southern Hemisphere, crossing the celestial equator. Funnily enough, in certain years, the equinox will fall on the twenty-second, technically the last day of Virgo. This is happening because of the precession of the equinoxes, a sort of wobbling of the earth that cycles through every twenty-five-and-a-half thousand years or so.

Whether you're a Libra yourself or, like the rest of us, just moving through the season, invest in those qualities that represent what the sign is about. Libras love to invest in their relationships with others; indeed, it's one of the most noteworthy aspects of the sign. Libra is ruled by Venus as well, so take some pleasure in the sensual aspects of the season, whether that be a change to more comfortable weather-appropriate clothing, a warm drink (something pumpkin-y, perhaps? Don't shoot the messenger, PSL haters.), or a new friend to cozy up to. Make time for quick-witted conversation, friendly banter, and deepening communal ties.

The Hot-Weather Harvest

For the rest of us who live outside the boundaries of the traditional autumn landscape—who are certainly and most definitely not jealous of the abundant beauty that you lucky few just sit around and get bored with—we still mark the time and acknowledge the harvest that we bring into our lives. In South Florida, it's still mid-hurricane season, and most of the tropical fruiting trees have long since shed their fruit. In my small world, while I'm biologically attuned to the fact that the days will begin to grow shorter and hopefully, mercifully, we might have some cooler weather, I'm also busily in preparation mode. September is generally a time when I'm planning my garden because the winter is dryer and cooler and thus better acclimated to the summer crops of more northern climates. Tomatoes are the first to be put into seed trays because they take the longest to get transplant-ready, I'm often able to place them into soil only in November.

But while I'm occupied with that, there's another fall phenomenon that occurs with the steady southerly march of the sun. I like to call it Kitchenhenge because the orientation of my kitchen window is perfectly aligned to the rising sun on the morning of Mabon (and Ostara, on the opposite end of the year). I have a small altar set up in my kitchen to my house spirit, and on that day, the first rays of light that break over the nearby houses and trees will bathe it in sweet sunlight. It's become something that I look forward to each year and is an example of how even when you live in a different climate, you can still discover and observe the signs that mark the passing of days and honor them.

While my magickal activity and ritual observances tend to be geared around protecting myself and my family from hurricanes and putting energy into the vegetable seeds I'm planting, I still celebrate the harvest of another year. This may be a holdover from my youth, but there's a certain resonance to knowing that the celebration and energies that you're honoring are also being observed by countless others around the world. Even without decorative gourds, the deeper connection to a greater community is what keeps me feeling grateful for what I'm bringing into my life.

References

"About Our Seasons." Lunar and Planetary Institute (LPI). Accessed October 15, 2023. https://www.lpi.usra.edu/education /skytellers/seasons/.

Frost, Robert. "Nothing Gold Can Stay." From *New Hampshire: A Poem with Notes and Grace Notes*. New York: Henry Holt, 1923.

Cosmic Sway

Michael Herkes

MABON, ALSO KNOWN AS the autumn equinox, celebrates the balance between light and dark, as well as the harvest season on September 22. Symbolizing the second harvest, Mabon is a time to give thanks for the abundance of nature and reflect on the cycle of life. As day and night are equal in length during this time, it represents a perfect equilibrium between light and darkness. This energy encourages us to find balance within ourselves and our surroundings.

This day also coincides with the first day of Libra season on September 22, bringing forth a harmonious blend of energies characterized by a sense of balance and beauty. Libra is ruled by Venus and represented by the scales, symbolizing balance, harmony, justice, and beauty. During this time, Mabon's influence on Libra enhances its natural inclination toward fairness and justice. The energy of Mabon encourages one to seek balance not only in their personal relationships but also in their decision-making process. It prompts a time to evaluate situations from all perspectives and strive for harmony in our interactions with others.

Conversely, Libra's influence on Mabon adds an element of social grace and diplomacy to this seasonal celebration. As we enter into the autumn season, a time characterized by change and transition, Libra's energy helps navigate these shifts with poise and tact. It inspires us to foster harmonious connections with loved ones while embracing the transformative nature of this time.

Celebrating Mabon

Traditionally, Mabon was celebrated by gathering with loved ones to enjoy a feast made from freshly harvested fruits, vegetables, and grains. It was also common to create altars adorned with autumnal symbols such as gourds, cornucopias, and colorful leaves. Rituals involving bonfires or candle lighting were performed to honor the changing seasons. In modern times, some people choose to spend time in nature, taking walks through forests or parks to appreciate the beauty of autumn. Others engage in activities like apple picking or baking seasonal treats using ingredients from local farms. Participating in community events such as harvest festivals or volunteering at food drives aligns with the spirit of giving thanks for abundance while helping those in need.

Full Moon in Aries

The Full Moon in Aries on October 6 at 11:48 p.m. is associated with courage, passion, and assertiveness. When this fiery sign aligns with the lunar energy of a Full Moon, it creates a potent combination that can bring about transformative experiences, as Aries symbolizes new beginnings and taking bold actions. It represents the spark of inspiration and the drive to pursue our goals fearlessly. During this celestial event, this energy intensifies, urging us to embrace our inner warrior and step into our personal power.

To harness the energy of the Full Moon in Aries, one can focus on rituals or spells that align with its themes. This may include rituals for self-empowerment, manifestation of goals or desires, or letting go of fears and limitations. One ritual or spell that can be particularly effective during this lunar phase is to conjure ambition and energy to move forward in our goals.

To perform this spell, find a quiet space where you can connect with the lunar energy. Light a red candle to represent the fiery nature of Aries and place it in a fireproof bowl or cauldron. Take a moment to visualize your goals clearly and vividly. Feel the passion and determination within you as you envision yourself achieving them. Next, write down your goals on a piece of paper using red ink or marker. Be specific and concise with your intentions. As you write each goal, infuse it with your ambition and drive. Once you have written down your goals, hold the paper close to your heart while focusing on the flame of the candle.

Visualize the flame igniting within you, filling you with motivation and determination. Recite an affirmation such as "By the power of this Full Moon in Aries, I summon ambition and energy within me. I embrace my goals with passion and take bold action toward their manifestation." Fold the paper neatly and set it aflame, placing it into the cauldron to turn to ash around the burning candle. Let the candle burn completely or extinguish it and relite daily until completely spent.

New Moon in Libra

On October 21 at 8:25 a.m., we experience a New Moon in Libra. Known for its balance, harmony, and diplomacy, Libra encourages us to find equilibrium in our lives and relationships. The energy surrounding this Moon is focused on creating harmonious connections with others. It urges us to seek fairness and justice in our interactions, promoting open dialogue and understanding. It invites us to reflect on how we can bring more balance into our lives and address any imbalances or conflicts that may be present.

Symbolically, the New Moon in Libra represents a fresh start for partnerships and collaborations. It encourages us to examine the give-and-take dynamics within our relationships and make necessary adjustments for greater harmony. This is an opportune time to mend any strained connections or initiate new relationships based on mutual respect and understanding.

In terms of rituals or spells during this time, one can focus on enhancing their social justice efforts. This could involve engaging in acts of kindness or advocating for causes related to equality and fairness. Additionally, incorporating rituals that embrace the Venusian nature of Libra can be beneficial. Pampering oneself through self-care practices such as indulging in a luxurious bath, practicing mindfulness or meditation, or engaging in creative activities can help align with the nurturing energy of Venus. By leaning into its Venusian nature and prioritizing self-care while also addressing social justice issues, we can harness its transformative energy for personal growth and positive change.

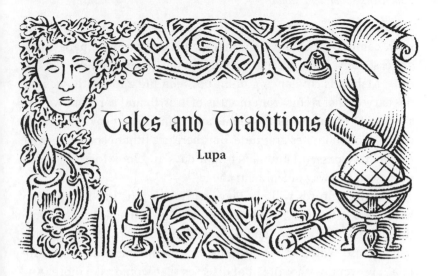

Tales and Traditions

Lupa

THE FALL EQUINOX SIGNALS a turn to cooler temperatures, shorter days, and the beginning of nature's retreat for the year. Deciduous plants reabsorb their chlorophyll, causing their leaves to turn bright shades of red, yellow, orange, and brown. Some animals prepare for the winter to come by hoarding as much food as they can, while others pack on every pound possible before heading to bed to sleep the cold weather away.

Those who farm or garden are pulling in the produce for use, storage, or sale, and preparing fields and beds for either winter planting or a fallow time. We, too, draw inward, spending more time indoors as temperatures drop, and perhaps contemplating changes in our lives as the seasons continue to turn 'round.

Turkey Vulture (*Cathartes aura*)

I've always lived where there were turkey vultures, but most of that time I only got to enjoy their magnificence during their breeding season. Once fall arrived, they would depart for southern wintering grounds, and I anxiously awaited the first turkey vulture of spring the way some keep their eyes peeled for robins.

For me, the turkey vulture is a reminder that all good things must come to an end. As summer wanes and birds prepare to migrate, so must I also accept that parts of my life may fall away in due time. Mabon is a balancing point between life and death; we reap the harvest that stems from months of growth and care, but we also say goodbye to many of the plants and animals that gave this abundance. Mabon invites gratitude, but there is a hint of sorrow as well, for we have passed Lammas's bright days and look forward to the shadowed gateway of Samhain ahead.

But the vultures will not leave without a gift. In the time they have been here, they have ever stood in liminal spaces. They soar through the air, only to land on branches, rooftops, or the ground itself. These skilled scavengers devour the remains of deceased animals, preventing the spread of diseases that would take more. And they disseminate the nutrients from those remains throughout the land, making them available to the living beings reliant on the food web again. Though they may disappear for a time, their effects resonate throughout their absence. In a way, they never really leave us entirely, and even as I wave goodbye to their broad, black wingspans in the fall, I eagerly anticipate their return, and am grateful for what they leave behind.

Pacific Aster (*Symphyotrichum chilense*)

By Mabon, almost all the native wildflowers have long since turned to seed; many plants are dying back for the year, losing their leaves, or otherwise preparing for winter dormancy. Most of the insect pollinators are waning as well, their numbers diminishing, as only some of the young and a few adults may sleep through the winter. But a few blooms remain as the warm months wind down, and among my favorites to welcome fall is the Pacific aster.

The dry grass in meadows here is dotted with patches of pale violet surrounding splashes of gold that reflect the season's softening sunlight. I share these lovely flowers with places ranging from southern California to the southern end of British Columbia, and all points in between along our coastline. Each flower is usually no more than an inch across, though the plant it grows on may tower above its neighbors at up to four feet in height. This makes it easier for the last remaining pollinators, whether they will migrate south or hole up here for the winter, or are among those simply enjoying one of the last meals of their lives before succumbing to fall's senescence.

To me, Pacific aster is a symbol that not everyone will be at the same stage of life in any given moment. I think about how my fellow humans often have different life schedules too. Yes, it's important when some of us are able to bring something to fruition after a long effort of cultivating and coaxing it along. But if you feel like you've fallen far behind everyone else—that's okay.

In the realm of humans, every time is a good time to start something new, even if that's only planning. Someone will always need to be inspired by another's efforts; there will always be a need for support and connection. You're also never too old to pick up a new endeavor, so rather than bemoaning time that has passed, capture the moment that is now. Amid the bounty of the harvest, some blooms are welcome, for they will be the harvest of the future.

Oyster Mushroom (*Pleurotus ostreatus*)

Of all the edible fall mushrooms, oysters are among my favorites. They're easy even for beginners to identify, making them a great teaching example. They are often found on dead or decaying hardwood trees such as alders and maples. And when they fruit, they fruit in abundance; one snag or log may have several pounds of these pale mushrooms sprouting from it. Plus, they even smell like black licorice, a delightful surprise!

As saprophytic fungi, oyster mycelium spends much of its time permeating dead wood, breaking it down into smaller components that then re-enter the food web to the benefit of all. So for most of the year, you might not even know it was there, though savvy mushroom hunters can guess which trees might produce a flush in fall. They go through their own harvesting activities unseen, and yet, they are among the most important beings in their ecosystem.

Yes, Mabon is a time to celebrate the food we have access to, whether through farming or foraging. But I think sometimes we get so focused on the edibility that we don't always appreciate the other things these species are up to when we aren't eating them. It was likely a fungus that first developed the ability to break down wood hundreds of millions of years ago in the Carboniferous period. Until that time, when early trees died, they simply sank into the surrounding bogs and eventually became fossil fuel deposits such as coal. So much carbon was locked into them with no beings to release it through decomposition that it caused a global cooling event. Only when the first wood-eating saprophyte appeared was the wealth of the trees released back into the food web.

So yes, enjoy your oyster mushrooms should you happen upon a harvest. But also think about what these fungi have accomplished long before we ever arrived on the scene, and how different our world would be without them.

Feasts and Treats

Dallas Jennifer Cobb

THE MIDDLE OF THE three harvest festivals, Mabon is a time for giving thanks for the harvest. It is also a time when people are aware of the shifting season, the change in weather, and the coming winter. As our minds turn to survival, activities like canning, preserving, and filling our root cellars are common practices.

Mabon takes its name from Mabon ap Modron, a mythological figure from ancient Wales whose name means "son of the mother." It is a time of deep transition and symbolically represented by Persephone and her mother, Demeter. Mabon is when Persephone took a journey from the abundant earth down to Hades. Her mother, who made all the plants grow and ripen, journeyed into grief, loss, and eventually despair. She forgot to make the plants grow and the sun shine.

Mabon is a great time to draw family, neighbours, and friends together to celebrate the seasonal abundance with a huge meal. Together, we celebrate the harvest, and we renew relationships that can help each of us survive the harsh winter ahead. Feasting on root vegetables and corn, we honour the gods and goddesses of the harvest.

Our Mabon feast is Jiggs Dinner featuring salt beef, with Zingy Cornbread to sop up the juices, followed by a Sweet Bread Pudding for dessert.

Jiggs Dinner

Jiggs dinner is a traditional Newfoundland Sunday dinner featuring salt beef, turnip, cabbage, potato, and carrots. Also called a "boiled dinner," Jiggs Dinner is traditionally cooked all in one pot, with the salt beef flavouring the water, which in turn flavours each of the vegetables. Small mesh cooking bags or cheese cloth are used to keep potatoes separate from carrots, turnip, and cabbage. As each vegetable is sufficiently cooked, it is pulled out of the pot and out of the mesh bag. It goes into a bowl and is mashed (potatoes and turnips) or buttered (carrots) before serving.

Newfoundland is the farthest eastern province of Canada, and as an island community in the North Atlantic Ocean, it is remote, rugged, and individualistic. The Newfoundland people have survived many harsh winters, sustained by their root vegetables stored in below-ground root cellars.

Infused with the rugged determination of the Newfoundland people, the magic of a big, shared Jiggs dinner is something we all need as we look ahead to the coming dark. Most Newfoundland families still make Jiggs dinner for Sunday night family dinner. Let us make it for the Mabon feast with a sweet bread pudding for dessert.

I like thinking of my neighbours and friends as extended family, because here in southern Ontario, the winter is harsh and cold, and we can use all the allies we can find. Sharing a "family" dinner is a way to cement those relationships.

Please note: Salt beef is available in a can in many North American grocery stores. Either look for it or substitute corn beef and cook the same way. Because the vegetables are all cooked in the same pot with the salt beef, this meal will not be suitable for vegans or vegetarians, unless you cook their vegetables separate from the beef.

Prep time: 15 minutes
Cooking time: 2 hours
Servings: 8

4 muslin or cotton bags to cook vegetable ingredients in (You can
   find these in most grocery stores, offered as "environmental vegetable bags.")
2 pounds salt beef
Water to mostly fill a large pot
1 turnip
6 large potatoes
6 carrots
1 green cabbage

Add your rinsed and drained salt beef to a large pot. Fill about
three quarters of the pot with water and bring to a boil on high. Once
it is boiling, turn the heat down to medium and cook for 2 hours.

While the beef is boiling, you have time to prepare the vegetables
needed, peeling turnip, potatoes, and carrots, and dicing them all.
Then cut the stem out of the cabbage and subdivide it into 6 wedges.

Place potatoes, cabbage, carrots, and turnips each in their own
separate cloth or muslin cooking bags and add them to the pot that
contains the salt beef.

While vegetables are cooking, prepare your cornmeal mix and
pop it in the oven.

In half an hour, check the potatoes. When they are tender, it is
time to remove each of the vegetables from their bags, place them
in big serving bowls, and get ready to eat.

Serve the Jiggs dinner with bread, dumplings, or Zingy Cornbread (see the recipe below) to be used to soak up all the juices.

Zingy Cornbread

While corn is harvested in the late summer and early autumn, dried
corn and cornmeal are easy to keep throughout the winter, and
wonderful for eating as part of the Mabon feast. This cornbread is

savoury with a bit of heat. It is ideal to eat with Jiggs dinner because you can sop up all the delicious juices with the cornbread.

If you prefer to make this cornbread into a dessert, skip the savoury flavours of onions, garlic, chives, and red pepper flakes, and serve the plain, warm cornbread with a drizzle of maple syrup or honey and butter.

Prep time: 5 minutes
Cooking time: 30 minutes
Servings: 8

1 tablespoon olive oil
1 small onion, chopped
1½ cups corn meal
½ cup oat flour (gluten free)
1 teaspoon salt
2 teaspoons baking powder
1 teaspoon honey
3 eggs whisked together, or an equal amount of flax egg for vegans
1½ cups buttermilk, or oat milk
1 cup sweet corn kernels, cut off of the cob or from a can if it is winter
¼ cup chopped chives
1 teaspoon red pepper flakes

Preheat your oven to 425°F.

Spread olive oil on a large cast-iron frying pan. Then turn a burner on to medium and heat the frying pan. Add chopped onion and sauté until the onion is translucent. Make sure the oil is covering all the inner surfaces of the cast-iron pan.

In a separate bowl, mix together the dry ingredients: corn meal, oat flour, salt, and baking powder. And in another bowl, whisk together the wet ingredients: honey, eggs, and buttermilk. Pour wet mix into dry mix and stir well.

Add the fresh corn kernels, chives, and pepper flakes and stir. Pour this mixture into the hot cast-iron pan with the onions already in it. Don't worry, the kernels will cook as the cornbread bakes. They make the bread moist and slightly chewy.

Put the pan in the oven and bake for 30 minutes until golden. You can prepare and bake this while your Jiggs dinner vegetables cook.

Remove from the oven and let sit for 5 minutes. Cut and serve with butter and Jiggs dinner.

Sweet Bread Pudding

Think of a long winter and the dwindling supplies of root vegetables. So many Newfoundland foods feature flour and eggs and are rooted in a practice of using every part. So it is no surprise that bread pudding is popular. Old, dry bread can be revitalized in this creamy, warm, and fragrant dessert.

Prepare your pudding while the cornbread is baking, and once the cornbread comes out of the oven, turn the temperature down to 350°F.

I like to prepare the Sweet Bread Pudding in advance, and as we sit down to dinner, I pop it in the oven. It will be ready in good time once the meal is finished. You will smell the delicious aroma wafting out of the oven when you open the door to check on your pudding.

Prep time: 15 minutes

Cooking time: 45 minutes

Servings: 8 huge servings, or 8 servings with lots of leftovers

6 cups old, dry bread chopped into one-inch cubes
2 tablespoons butter
2 cups milk
4 large eggs
⅔ cup sugar
1 teaspoon vanilla extract
1 teaspoon ground cinnamon
½ teaspoon ground cardamom
Optional: ½ cup currants or raisins

Preheat or turn down oven to 350°F. Cut the bread into 1-inch cubes. Place them in a buttered or oiled 8 × 8-inch baking pan. Sprinkle currants or raisins overtop if you want them. Melt butter, then pour it over, massaging it into the bread.

In a separate bowl, vigorously combine the milk, eggs, sugar, vanilla, cinnamon, and cardamom. Pour the liquid over the dry bread, making sure all the bread gets coated.

Bake for 45 minutes or until golden brown on the top.

Crafty Crafts

Elizabeth Barrette

WITH MABON COMES THE height of the harvest season. Summer gardens are winding down with winter squash and full-season corn like popcorn. In many areas, frost has already killed off tender crops like tomatoes. Fields of grain are being harvested. Winter storage varieties of apples and pears are starting to ripen. Leaves are beginning to turn colors. The weather cools and the fall rains come. Many species begin to migrate south to warmer wintering grounds. Others gorge on nuts and seeds to put on fat. Mabon themes reflect the autumn events and the bounty of harvest. Motifs such as autumn fruits and colorful leaves are popular.

Leaf Altar Cloth

This is a more permanent, grown-up version of the leaf-tracing placemat that many children enjoy. The beauty of it is that this approach creates an autumn altar cloth matched to the trees of your own locale.

Materials
Large leaves
Fabric chalk or washable marker

Background cloth or tablecloth
Leaf cloth (several colors)
Fabric glue, bonding film, sewing machine, or embroidery floss and
    embroidery needle
Scissors
Fabric pins
    Cost: $15–$20
    Time spent: 1–2 hours

Design Ideas

Autumn leaves feature in many Mabon decorations. For this project, choose large leaves with a relatively simple shape that you can trace easily. Trees like oak, maple, and sycamore work well. Complex leaves like ash or walnut are harder to work with.

Natural fibers such as cotton, linen, bamboo, or hemp typically work best for magical crafts. However, if you want something flashier, consider lamé or holographic fabric for a few of the leaves—gold or copper look great here. You need a solid background color, like brown linen or unbleached muslin, that will show off leaves of several contrasting colors such as red, orange, and yellow. Small patterns like polka dots, calico, or tie-dye are okay on the leaf cloth.

If you're sewing your altar cloth, get several colors of embroidery floss in autumn leaf colors. This is a good place to use variegated floss that changes colors along its length.

Assembly

First, gather large fallen leaves from your yard or neighborhood. About a dozen will work for most projects. Pick up as many different kinds as you can find that will be easy to trace. If making an altar cloth for your coven, invite other members to contribute leaves too.

For a small altar table, 1–2 yards of fabric may be enough backing to cover it properly. For a large table, it's easier just to measure the top so you can buy a tablecloth that fits it and put leaves on that.

Lay the leaves on the leaf fabric, using all the colors of fabric.
Trace around each leaf with fabric chalk or washable marker. Then
cut out the leaf shapes.

Flatten out the backing cloth. If it has raw edges, hem them with
fabric glue, bonding film, thread, or embroidery floss.

Lay the cut-out leaf shapes on the backing cloth in a design you
like. Pin them down.

Attach each leaf to the backing cloth. You can use fabric glue or
iron-on bonding film. Another way is to sew them on as appliqué
by going around the edge of each leaf with something like a blanket
stitch if working by hand, or on a sewing machine with zigzag or a
decorative stitch. Choose embroidery floss or thread that contrasts

with the leaf and background. If you want to get fancy, you can also embroider veins on the leaf shapes, using the fallen leaves as inspiration for the pattern.

Natural Birdfeeders

You can make your own birdfeeders from many different materials. Gathering local items from your yard means less to buy, which lightens the load on the earth. Feeding birds helps them survive in a world with less and less food and habitat for them. This is a good make-and-take craft for coven events.

Materials

Peanut butter and/or suet
Birdseed
Large fruit rinds (like orange, grapefruit, or pineapple)
Lengths of knotty branch and/or sturdy rough bark
Pine cones
Twine
Scissors
Large mixing bowl
Spoons
    Cost: $5–$10
    Time spent: 30 minutes

Design Ideas

Many birds such as woodpeckers and blue jays enjoy sticky, high-fat foods like peanut butter and suet. You can use either or both for making this craft. Suet gets softer and easier to work with when warm. Peanut butter works fine at room temperature.

Birdseed comes in many varieties. You can use an individual seed such as sunflower or cracked corn. A mixed bag of seeds also works well.

Collect natural items that have either a rough texture or hollows that you can stuff the food paste into. Pine cones, knotty branches, and fruit rinds make good choices. Cut branches 1–2 feet long. If you can find sturdy slabs of rough bark, you can also spread food on those.

Assembly

Begin by gathering things to hold the bird food, such as pine cones and knotty branches. Cut lengths of twine, then tie a piece of twine to each item so you can hang them in trees later. For fruit rinds, make a little net of twine to hold them, like a hanging planter.

Next, make the food paste. Put a cup or so of peanut butter or suet into a large mixing bowl. Add birdseed a little at a time, using a spoon to mix it in, until you have a thick paste. If you make different flavors—say, peanut butter with sunflower seeds and suet with cracked corn—then you may attract a wider variety of birds.

Pick up the natural items one at a time and use a spoon to spread food paste over the rough surface or press it into hollows. Usually you can get about half a cup of food paste onto each feeder.

After you finish filling the feeders, take them outside. Hang them in trees using the twine, anywhere you've seen birds gathering. Everything is biodegradable, so you can just refill them as long as they last, then toss them on the compost pile.

If you want to send these home with coven members, small feeders like pine cones or fruit rinds should fit inside a baggie. For larger items like a knotty branch, wrap them in aluminum foil or plastic wrap. Label with people's names if they're not going home immediately so everyone can keep track of theirs.

Mabon and Dice

Charlie Rainbow Wolf

CASTING LOTS HAS AN ancient history and is the forerunner for today's modern six-sided dice. Dice are an integral part of many games and have evolved to have additional faces and uses. They're tossed to determine how many moves to make, what score to take, or even how much money is to be won.

Divination with playing dice is easy to do, but like many things that are simple, there's a learning curve before becoming proficient. Three dice of three different colors are required. I'll use red, green, and white because these are what I have used in the past, but a quick search of a popular online retailer resulted in me finding sets of up to one hundred multicolored dice for under $10. It doesn't matter if the dice are different colors than I have illustrated, but once the colors have been assigned to the interpretations, stick with those choices.

Reading the Dice

The main part of divination with dice (called *astragalomancy*) is memorizing what the pips on the different dice mean—and they mean different things on the different colors. Each of these meanings tells part of a story, and they all have a purpose, and the divinatory art is piecing those meanings and purposes together to form a message. There will be three parts to the story: one from the red die, one from the green die, and one from the white die.

The Red Die Meanings

- Red 6, Mystery: This is a good symbol for omens and prophecies, but it often comes with a warning for caution or to be very observant, for things may not always be as they appear.
- Red 5, Determination: There's an energy of cleaning up with this story, of tenacity to see things through to the end, even though the task may not be a pleasant one.
- Red 4, Luck: This is always good luck. It's usually accompanied by happiness and success, but it is important to look at the stories on the other dice to see just how that luck is going to manifest.
- Red 3, Movement: This could be any kind of movement, from new ideas and moving from one situation to another, to physical movement such as some type of travel. Sometimes the red 3 highlights communication issues; look to the other stories to see just how to interpret this.
- Red 2, Rebirth: This is a major transformation, and often it is something that seems to happen out of nowhere. There could be upheaval associated with it, but it is something that has to occur so the next chapter can open.
- Red 1, Fate: I see the red 1 as the weaver of destiny. Weave good things, and good things will return. Weave illusions and dishonesty, and that is what will come back. We're all co-creators of our own destiny; look to the other stories to see what is being created.

The Green Die Meanings

- Green 6, Abundance: Abundance is great, but it's easy to get complacent when things are going well. This is a call to take notice of what is happening, to count blessings and be grateful, otherwise things could change quickly, and what was once abundant could become unattainable.

- Green 5, Celebration: This is not something that has been earned or worked for like a promotion or a retirement party. This is pure enjoyment, just fun and happiness, like a wedding or a baby shower. It does come with the caution not to overindulge though!

- Green 4, Opportunity: These opportunities are doors opening, chances for improvement, and what some might call "lucky breaks." If there's a problem to be solved when this story appears, the answer is close.

- Green 3, Initiative: *Initiative* (to me) is an interesting word, in that it can be inspiring or it can be disadvantageous. This story reveals that things could go up or down, depending on what initiative is taken and how things are handled.

- Green 2, Carelessness: Green 2 is the old proverb "act in haste, repent at leisure." Something is sloppy, unfinished, or badly thought out, and it is likely to have repercussions that may include people being misunderstood, frustrated, or angry.

- Green 1, Moderation: This is nearly the opposite of green 2; green 1 is taking things slowly, considering all angles of the situation and not making any life-changing decisions yet. Sometimes this can point to health matters that need attention too.

The White Die Meanings

- White 6, Choices: Sometimes the choices the white 6 indicates come thick and fast and have to be made quickly. It's not quite the sudden surprise of the red 2, but if the two stories appear together, then make sure to stay grounded in reality so the best way forward can be found.

- White 5, Family: This includes all aspects of family life, from relatives and in-laws, to the family home and its traditions, to the children and other people who dwell there, to those dear friends who are adopted family.

- White 4, Jeopardy: Not the nicest of stories but one that happens to many people all too frequently. Jealousy, arguments, deceit, and consequences of acting in the heat of the moment are all indicated by the white 4.

- White 3, Love: While this does include romance and passion, it also refers to compassion, understanding, and friendship. It is both the ego-centered love of wanting to be needed and cared for, and the universal love that embraces benevolence and grace.

- White 2, Fertility: This is another story that has two meanings. It's *fertility* in the true meaning of fruitfulness and reproduction, but it is also fertility regarding new plans and projects, new beginnings and ideas.

- White 1, Light: The light of this story shines to bring things out into the open. It is associated with purpose and drive, triumph and achievement, taking control and being successful.

Casting the Dice

Just like playing games with dice, all that is needed to cast them is to throw them onto the table. For a quick past, present, and future reading, just throw the dice one time and interpret the meanings of the pips on the different colors. I use the left or first dice for past, the second or center for present, and the last one on the right for the future, or potential outcome. The three dice could also represent opportunities, obstacles, and outcome or desires, assets, and direction—or you could come up with your own.

For a more involved reading, focus on the current concerns, then throw the dice once and make a note of the stories. This reveals information about the general situation. Throw them a second time and take notes; this casting reveals material things about what's going on, such as financial matters or issues related to work. Do this a third time and let this casting reflect relationship matters—and remember, *relationship* does not always have to mean romance.

Just for Fun

Remember the big "hopscotch" grid from the Lammas section? Toy shops and online retailers sell big foam dice in different colors. Try rolling the oversized dice, one at a time, and combining the meanings of the stories from the dice with the areas of the grid where they land. This has the potential to provide excellent divination readings—and be most enjoyable at the same time!

Reference

Line, David, and Julia Line. *Fortune-Telling By Dice: Uncovering the Future through the Ancient System of Casting Lots.* Aquarian Press, 1984.

Mabon Ritual

Nathan M. Hall

THIS RITUAL FOR MABON will tap into the themes classically associated with the fall season. These include harvesting the fruits of our year-long labors and sharing our abundance, as well as saving the seeds from this harvest to plant for next year. While we may pluck and glean the fruits of the Tree of Life, giving offerings of energy back into the tree is part of our responsibility to ensure that the cycle keeps moving forward. Before you move ahead with the ritual, take some space to meditate upon your last year. What were some of the goals you had? What came to fruition? Were there any surprises along the way, either in efforts that did not bear fruit or in unexpected bounty from a surprising place? Write down three to five of these things if you can, but at the least, be sure to include at least one thing that didn't come to pass and one that did.

Gathering Up the Fruits for the Harvest

In this ritual we will honor agricultural as well as metaphorical gathering in. The fruits of our year are coming together, and we can look back over the last year to take account of where we are and how far we've come. We'll acknowledge this in ritual and save the "seeds" from those "fruits" that we want to plant in the spring and encourage to grow in our lives.

You Will Need

An altar space, either your own permanent altar or an area temporarily set aside for your rite. This can include a table or bench covered in a cloth in colors appropriate for the season.

At the very least, you need to have one apple on hand. Other ripe fruit or nuts in your offering bowl are also appropriate. (If you've been hitting up thrift stores or garage sales lately, a wicker cornucopia is both cheesy and appropriate. Otherwise, don't worry; the bowl will do just fine.)

A tall candle, either a taper or a pillar, any color will do, but red, orange, dark green, or white will keep with the theme. If you have candles that you typically light for any gods and goddesses, you can bring those in too; we're sharing our bounty, after all!

A knife and cutting board or plate to cut the apple on.

A beverage (apple cider or wine are great choices) and some festive food for after the ritual. (If you're doing this ritual with friends, make sure to bring enough for everyone!)

A small pouch to collect the apple seeds in.

Your list of things that did and did not bear fruit in the past year.

Optional items: athame, wand, or offering bowl or cornucopia.

Get everything set up, with the knife and cutting board and your list up front and easily accessible. Take a ritual bath, or if you're with friends, you can use a cleansing spray such as Florida water.

Center and ground yourself by casting your energy deep into the roots of the earth, down to the very core, where you pull up warm earth energy and anchor it in your heart space. Now, send your energy branching out into the heavens, beyond our solar system into the celestial darkness, and pull down cold, stellar energy, down through your crown and into your heart space, where it mixes with the warm earth energy.

Take three breaths (each time, imagine pulling in some of the power and energy of the universe), and then send one final breath as an offering up to your godself, the part of you that is always connected with the divine.

Cast the circle in whatever way is comfortable for you. If you need inspiration, I sometimes like to combine calling in the elements as I cast the circle. Start in the north, point your finger or athame out, and recite the following as you pivot to your right, calling out each element as you face the appropriate direction, and end back in the north.

In the north and by the element of earth, I ground my circle.
In the east and by the element of air, I breathe life into my circle.
In the south and by the element of fire, I bring energy into my circle.
And to the west and by the element of water, I purify my circle.
The circle is now cast and [I/we] stand between the worlds.

Light the central candle on the altar and call upon the Goddess, she who is all, the universe in all of its unimaginable expansiveness. If you have other gods and goddesses that you regularly work with, you may call them in now as well. Thank them for their presence during your rite.

Recite the following:

[I/we] come in the name of the Great Goddess to turn the Wheel of the Year and celebrate the sabbat of Mabon, the second harvest. Throughout the course of the last year, [I/we] have sewn seeds in [my life/our lives] and seek to honor those things that bore fruit as well as those things that withered on the vine. To be alive is a holy opportunity to experience the joy of our successes and reflect upon and learn from things that did not come to be.

[I/we] offer these things to return to the cauldron of the Great Mother, that they may feed the tree and begin the cycle anew.

Read now from your list the thing(s) that did not bear fruit and release their energies into the flame of the central candle.

[I/we] offer these things that bore fruit to be celebrated by the Great Mother and retrieve their seeds in order to plant more successes.

Read from the list the thing(s) that did bear fruit and send their energies into the apple on the cutting board. Cut the apple in half— from its side, not top to bottom—so that the cut reveals a star pattern. Retrieve the seeds and place them into your pouch (and your friends' pouches if in a group).

[I/we] thank the Great Mother for the blessings [I've/we've] received this year. Please bless these seeds to grow into new bounty over the course of the next. Blessed be.

Breathe that energy into the pouch over the seeds and seal them up. Keep it somewhere safe, and when you begin a new task or job in the coming year, place it on your altar to seed it with the energy from this ritual.

Now it's time to close out the ritual. Recite the following:

[I/we] give thanks to the Great Goddess for the blessings and bounties on this Mabon day, and may [I/we] continue to receive them throughout the year ahead. Blessed be.

Thank any other gods and goddesses that you called into the rite, and close out the circle, going from north to west to south to east.

I thank and release north and the element of earth.
I thank and release west and the element of water.
I thank and release south and the element of fire.
I thank and release east and the element of air.
The circle is gathered in, and we release the energies of our Mabon celebration to the cosmos. So mote it be.

Enjoy some food and drink! Blessed Mabon!

Notes